THE
SIBERIANS

FARLEY MOWAT

AUTHOR OF NEVER CRY WOLF

PENGUIN BOOKS

THE SIBERIANS

Farley Mowat was born in Belleville, Ontario, in 1921. His early interest in nature was maintained by travels through the Canadian plains and mountains in his parents' trailer—and by a collection of household pets that included crows, magpies, gophers, and owls. In 1938, he made his first "scientific" expedition, spending a month at Kazabazua in search of birds and mammals to convert to museum specimens. During World War II, Mowat commanded a platoon in the invasion of Sicily and later was instrumental in the surrender of the German forces in Holland. A postwar canoe trip from Nueltin to Brochet, Manitoba, drew his attention to the plight of the Eskimos and Indians, and led him to write the highly successful and controversial *People of the Deer*, which was published in the spring of 1952. Today, nineteen books by Farley Mowat have appeared in more than forty editions in countries as far apart as Japan and Norway. As for the future, he says, "Well, I'll keep on writing, and traveling, and sniffing out interesting things to do."

FARLEY MOWAT

THE
SIBERIANS

Penguin Books Inc
Baltimore · Maryland

Penguin Books Inc
7110 Ambassador Road
Baltimore, Maryland 21207, U.S.A.

First published by Little, Brown and Company 1970
Published in Penguin Books 1972

Printed in the United States of America
by Kingsport Press, Inc., Kingsport, Tennessee 37662

PREFACE

I was thirteen years old when I made my first visit to the arctic. Ever since then the northern regions of the world and the people who inhabit them have fascinated me. Over the years I have visited most parts of the Canadian arctic; and I have read extensively about, or traveled in, other northern regions but, until 1966, I knew almost nothing about the realities of the Soviet North. This was not because of any lack of interest on my part; it was because of the almost incredible paucity of information in the West about the "other half of the arctic world." Most English language sources have painted, and continue to paint, the Soviet arctic and subarctic as a wilderness of trackless forests and snow-covered tundra inhabited mainly by ravening wolves and doomed political prisoners. Even professional northern experts in Canada and the United States seem to have surprisingly little interest in, or knowledge of, the Russian North except insofar as they profess to be concerned about it as a possible springboard for a Red invasion of North America.

By 1965 the Soviets had published several of my northern books in translation and as a result I had been in correspondence with a number of Russian writers. One of these was Yuri Rytkheu, himself an arctic native, born and bred. In the autumn of 1966 he suggested that I visit him. As it happened I had spent that summer making a comprehensive tour of the Canadian arctic, gathering material for yet another northern book.* The idea of comparing what I had seen in northern Canada with what I might see in the Soviet Union was irresistible. Accordingly I arranged to sail to Leningrad, accompanied by my wife, Claire.

My first visit to the USSR turned out to be far more extensive than I had anticipated. The most important aspect of it was a fifteen-thousand-mile peregrination through Siberia, at the end of which I felt I had acquired some firsthand knowledge of what was taking place in that huge and, for Westerners, mysterious region. The idea of writing a book designed to dispel some of our misconceptions about Siberia naturally occurred to me on my return to Canada, but I did not feel I knew enough, as yet, to warrant such a book. A second trip seemed to be called for, but I was not able to find the time until the autumn of 1969, when, accompanied by photographer John deVisser, I returned to the Soviet Union. Yuri Rytkheu met us and we three traveled together for some fourteen thousand miles from the Ural Mountains to the Sea of Okhotsk, from the Mongolian border to the Arctic Ocean. This book is the outcome of these two journeys.

A word about the problems of collecting information in the Soviet Union. I speak no Russian and made no real attempt to learn the language. In my experience it is a mistake to speak a foreign language badly. Local people tend to assume you understand it much better than you do and will use their own tongue in conversation with you. How-

* *Canada North,* Atlantic–Little, Brown, Boston, 1968.

ever, if they realize that you are a linguistic dub, they will often make the effort to communicate in *your* language. To a surprising degree the people I met in Russia were able to do just this. Most of my major informants spoke reasonably good English or French. Those who did not conversed with me through Yuri or through interpreters. To obviate errors as much as possible, I made use of a portable tape recorder. On my first journey both Claire and my interpreter took comprehensive notes, so I had three independent sets of notes to work from. During my second journey Yuri acted as a check on the interpreters to ensure that I missed nothing of importance.

Statistics are always a problem. To some extent they have to be accepted at face value, but whenever it was possible to check them through other sources I took care to do so. The statistics I have used here appeared, on the basis of what I saw with my own eyes, to be believable. The population figures I have used are not official because the last Siberian census was in 1964 and was an interim one. The figures I have used — given in round numbers — are the informed estimates of the appropriate local officials.

A word about money comparisons. The ruble had an official exchange value of $1.10 during both my visits. However, a socialist country provides so many economic side benefits that to compare directly, for example, the ruble income of a Soviet truck driver with the dollar income of his North American counterpart would be misleading. In terms of the benefits a Russian worker receives over and above his salary, and the relatively small deductions to which he is subject for taxes and social services, his wages have a real value on the order of two to three times their apparent one. This is a point usually ignored by Western writers.

It is our common practice to use the word "Russia" as a

generic term to embrace the whole of the USSR; and to identify the citizens of that entire region as "Russians." The fact is that there are fifteen distinct Soviet Socialist Republics in the Union, and the "Russian" one — the Russian Soviet Federated Socialist Republic — itself contains sixteen Autonomous Soviet Socialist Republics, and five Autonomous Regions and ten National Districts, most of which are not ethnically Russian. Nevertheless, for the sake of simplicity, I have employed "Russia" and "Russians" in their sloppy but widely accepted Western usage.

In dealing with the literal translation and spelling of Russian words I have been somewhat arbitrary since there is no universally accepted standard. However, Russian friends assure me that my translations are quite comprehensible.

It is obvious that I could not have assembled the information in this book, or indeed made the journeys at all, without a great deal of cooperation from organizations and individuals in the Soviet Union. They are all mentioned in the book, so there is no need to list them here. I extend my heartfelt thanks to all of them.

Port Hope, Ontario.
June 1970

CONTENTS

I
MOSCOW

When Claire and I arrived in Leningrad in the autumn of 1966 aboard the *Alexander Pushkin*, we were met by Yuri Rytkheu. Yura (the affectionate form of Yuri) was then thirty-five years of age. He was a Chukchee — a member of a native people living in the extreme northeastern corner of Asia almost within sight of Alaska. Born in a *yaranga* — a sod shanty roofed with walrus hide — Yura grew up in a primitive coastal village where he attended the first school to be built in Chukotka. He did so well that he was chosen to go on to a higher education, which in his case meant Leningrad University. Even before graduation he had begun to write, first in his own language and then in Russian. When I met him he was already the author of twelve novels.

Erect, a trifle portly, with wide, mobile lips and a pair of horn-rimmed glasses which glittered inscrutably from an impassive face, he had the natural dignity and presence of an Asiatic princeling. But under his mask was a droll sense of humor, a questioning mind, and a complex blend of native Asian and acquired European characteristics.

Yura introduced me to the foremost Northern experts in Leningrad — men and women who were tremendous enthusiasts and who were almost embarrassingly anxious to tell me about their work. Later we went to Moscow and I was again introduced to many people involved in the development of the Soviet North. What all these people had to tell me was fascinating, but after a while I began to grow a little restive.

I confided the reasons for my distress to Yura. "This is all very interesting, but what I'd really like is to see for myself what is happening in your North."

"Where you want to go?" asked Yura.

That was a stopper. I knew so little of the Soviet arctic that I could not fasten on a single name.

"Oh," I said airily, "Northeast Siberia, I suppose. It's the closest to Canada."

Yura merely nodded. Next morning he arrived at our room in the Hotel Pekin to tell Claire and me we had permission to go anywhere in Siberia — as long as we could pay our way.

Concealing my incredulity, I accompanied him to the headquarters of the Union of Soviet Writers where, over cognac and cakes, the permission was confirmed by the Director of the Foreign Section. Furthermore, the Director instructed his assistant, Freda Lurie, to arrange with the local branches of the Writers Union in those areas we might visit to provide us with whatever assistance we should need.

It all seemed suspiciously easy. I had so often heard that, as far as foreigners were concerned, only Communist Party members or trusted fellow travelers were given any real freedom of movement in the USSR that I had the horrid feeling somebody had made a mistake about my status. The prospect that the mistake might be discovered while Claire and I were in the depths of Siberia was unnerving. Somewhat awkwardly I tried to explain my apprehensions to the Director.

He was amused. "It is true we do not open up our country to all foreign visitors. This is because so many only come to look for ways to make bad propaganda about us. Nevertheless, we Russians are naturally hospitable, and to any person of goodwill who is not a victim of too many misconceptions about us, we are happy to extend the best welcome of our people. That you are not a Communist is no difficulty. We believe you will be fair and therefore do not hesitate to let you go where you wish —" he hesitated for a moment, then smiled and continued — "anywhere within reason, of course. And I am sure you are a reasonable man."

The plan he proposed was that Claire and I and Yura would fly first to Yakutsk, capital of the Yakut Autonomous Soviet Socialist Republic in northeastern Siberia, and would make that city our operational base. The details of our further travels could be decided on the spot, in consultation with the local experts. Was this agreeable?

"Yakutsk," I said bluffing bravely, "is where I've always wanted to go."

"Then," said the Director, draining his glass, "I suggest you contact Aeroflot and get your tickets. Come and tell me about the trip when you get back."

The lady clerk at the Aeroflot booking office was discouraging. "Yakutsk? I don't advise it. Really, nobody goes there. And at the beginning of winter, too! Wouldn't you rather visit the Black Sea?"

Finding us adamant she gave us our tickets, shaking her head dubiously as she did so. When I paid for them I got a shock. The fare for the round trip of 7,600 miles was 132 rubles — approximately $145!

"At that price," said Claire pessimistically, "they'll probably just give us each a pair of wings . . . or perhaps a secondhand broomstick."

Although we were content to undertake the trip with only Yura as a companion, he demurred. Yura had studied English for several years but had not had much practice in speaking it until we arrived, and he was not happy at the prospect of serving as our interpreter. I think his pride was also involved. After all, he was a famous writer, and our friend — not our servant. He suggested we should hire a professional interpreter. We called the ever-helpful Freda Lurie and she recommended a young man named Nikolai Kosolopov. Kola, as we soon came to call him, was twenty-three years old and a student of political economy at Moscow University. He was small, taut, tidy, and quick as a bird. The son of an engineer father and an engineer mother, he had eschewed that profession himself but had married an engineer, possibly to keep the family tradition alive. Skeptical, but not cynical, he had a flashing sense of humor and an encyclopedic mind combined with an insatiable curiosity. He had one other important qualification: during the previous two summers he had worked as an Intourist guide, so he knew all the ropes. The prospect of absenting himself from his classrooms in favor of a tour of Siberia delighted him. We were equally delighted to have him with us.

That evening, in the ornately decorated dining room of the Hotel Pekin, we held a meeting of the First Chukchee-Canadian-Russian Siberian Expedition. Yura's suggestion that the rest of us pledge fealty and obedience to him by inscribing our names in blood on the back of the restaurant's twenty-five-page menu was unanimously opposed.

I had hoped we could get clear of Moscow in a day or two but this proved impossible. Nothing — but nothing — can be done on the spur of the moment in Moscow. Everything must follow a rigidly preordained path. Being used to it, the Muscovites don't seem to mind, but I found it monumentally frustrating to have to spend days chasing petty bureaucrats all over the city in order to conclude simple formalities. Claire nearly went out of her mind trying to assemble a wardrobe suitable to the Siberian climate. Kola was infinitely helpful, but with the best of intentions and the maximum of effort it took the two of them several days to track down the essentials Claire needed.

Although we were delayed in getting to the North we had the compensation of having the North come to us. At ten o'clock one Saturday morning Yura phoned our room with the ominous message, carefully enunciated: "They . . . are coming . . . now . . . for . . . you!"

"They" turned out to be not the secret police but a posse of Yura's Northern cronies. To the distress of Claire's stomach, they insisted on ordering breakfast in our room — breakfast which consisted of steamed garlic sausages, salami, fried smoked fish, cognac, and champagne. We now discovered that the hotel had been invaded by scores of Northerners, mostly from Siberia, who were in town attending some sort of planning conference. I concluded it was not going to be a quiet weekend. Northerners are essentially the same the world over, and when they hit the big cities they do not spend much time resting.

The Northern crowd in the Pekin was typical. The only

time they simmered down was for a few hours on Saturday afternoon when they crowded around TV sets to watch a football game. After the game we were hauled off to attend a party in the suite of another Yura — an enormous Tatar who, Yuri Rytkheu told us, was a Big Chief on the northern Pacific coast of Siberia. The other guests were a weird mélange of nationalities and professions. There was an Armenian geologist named Edvard who was the discoverer of the Kamchatka goldfields; a magnificently bosomed Hungarian lady who was, aptly enough, the director of nursery schools in Krasnoyarsk; two geophysicists who had just finished a three-year stint in the Kolyma Mountains and were now beginning six months' leave; an Evenki reindeer breeder (the Evenki are a native race from northeastern Siberia); a long, lean, and bespectacled young poet named Gleb; a blond editress of children's books; one Chukchee author (Yura); two befuddled Canadians; and a bevy of attractive ladies who may or may not have been party girls — in the nonpolitical sense of the word. Since everybody seemed to be able to speak at least three languages, the place was Babel. It did not seem to matter. A big radio was carted in and set playing full blast and those who could find room began to dance.

Relays of waitresses appeared laden with trays of food and drink, and when the table would hold no more they spread their largesse on the beds. The provisions seemed to be mainly raw eggs, raw tomatoes, Ukrainian baked chicken legs, and enough vodka, cognac, and champagne to sink the place. The raw eggs were eaten by sucking them, and they were not at all bad if followed immediately by a dollop of vodka which doubtless cooked them before they reached bottom.

The reindeer breeder spoke French and the Hungarian

lady spoke French and English so we three had a conversation. I learned quite a lot about reindeer and would have learned more except that the lady's dress was so décolleté that every time she turned toward the reindeer man he lapsed into passionate Evenki which *none* of us could understand. Edvard, the Armenian, had taken a fancy to Claire and she was learning a great deal about Armenians.

It was a good party. I have enjoyed many like it in the Canadian North, although this one had a notable distinction; these people never did get out of hand. When the singing began (and you have to hear Russians singing at a party to believe it) Yura (Tatar) went down the hall both ways from the suite, checking with the neighbors to see if they were being disturbed by the noise. Apparently nobody was. In fact most of them came back with Yura and joined the party. But at 1 A.M., apparently by common consent, everyone packed it in and we all went off to bed.

It may be thought that we saw little of the tourist attractions of Moscow. This is true, although it was not for want of trying. On one occasion we set out to visit the famous Moscow Exhibition Park. After an hour's drive we arrived there to find the main gates open, the ticket sellers happy to accept our money, but every single one of the pavilions locked up tight. On another occasion I tried to visit the Military Museum and had the same experience, even though I had carefully checked the hours when it was supposed to be open. There is a special kind of independent arbitrariness in the way public institutions are run in Moscow, and this includes restaurants and stores. They seem to close when, and for as long as, the whim of the moment dictates. This lends a piquant element of uncertainty to Moscow life. One is never sure how any expedition will turn out; and this could hardly be better illustrated than by the Franko affair.

It began in the dining room of the Writers Club, one of the most sumptuous establishments in Moscow and formerly the headquarters of the Masonic movement, and a favorite haunt of Leo Tolstoy. Claire and I were there one evening in company with Laura Kuskov, a petite blond translator. We were relaxing after a five-course meal and desultorily discussing life and letters with an admiral of the Soviet navy who was also a much-published author, when a brisk young man named Sasha dashed up to our table. Sasha was a secretary with the Foreign Department of the Writers Union. He thrust three tickets into my hand.

"Great surprise," he cried. "Invitations to celebration of most famous Ukraine poet. Special good seats for you to see!" Whereupon he turned and dashed away as if, just possibly, he wanted to be sure we had no chance to refuse.

"Where is it?" Laura called after him.

"Is here . . . at eight o'clock!" Sasha replied and vanished.

We assumed he meant the theater on the second floor of the Club, so we sipped our cognac and continued chatting with the admiral, who was greatly interested in the kilt I was wearing. He seemed a little dubious about its practicability in Siberia, whither we had told him we were going.

A few minutes before eight, we ambled upstairs to the theater and presented our tickets. The lady doorkeeper seemed puzzled. "Tonight is here scientific films . . . you are welcome, of course, but here is no poet celebration."

Laura snatched the tickets and scrutinized them. "Oh God!" she cried. "It's at Tchaikovsky Theater! That *Sasha!*"

Happily there was a taxi outside and under Laura's

goading the driver made speed. A few minutes later he slued to a stop and Claire and I were about to bundle out when Laura leaned over, clouted the driver on the shoulder, and screamed: "No! No! You idiot! This is Tchaikovsky *Hall!*"

The driver took off before I could even slam the door, and at exactly 8 P.M. delivered us to the ornate portico of the Tchaikovsky Theater.

Now although it may be socially acceptable for North American theatergoers to arrive late at a performance, in the Soviet Union such an action constitutes the worst kind of gaffe. Laura was in a state bordering on panic as she whipped us into the inner corridor, waving our tickets like flags in front of every usher she saw, and running us along like driven sheep in the general direction they indicated. Nobody looked closely at the tickets.

At one minute past the hour we scurried into a huge room from which a single set of double doors led toward a glare of lights. The backs of a group of people almost filled the wide doorway. We dashed up behind them, followed them through . . . and found ourselves on the stage of an immense auditorium in company with about fifty soberly dressed, distinguished-looking men and women.

Five tiers of chairs had been arranged on the stage behind a long, baize-covered table bristling with microphones. The chairs were filling fast. By the time we reached them (carried along by sheer momentum) there were only a few still unoccupied — directly behind the long table and close beside a sort of podium or lectern. At this point I hesitated, contemplating flight, but Claire nudged me cruelly. "Sit down for heaven's sake! The whole place is staring at you!"

It was true enough. Fifty solemn faces on the platform were turned our way with expressions of polite incredulity. Beyond the footlights we could see a wash of faces whose owners also seemed much interested in the spectacle of three brightly attired ladies — one of whom sported a large red beard — milling about in a confused way at front stage right.

We sat down and tried to disappear. It was difficult. Spotlights were trained onstage to provide illumination for several television and motion picture cameras. Still photographers added their own illumination, producing a recurring flicker of flashbulbs.

A robust, black-suited gentleman on our left, who turned out to be a high-ranking member of the Politburo, got to his feet and announced that the evening's entertainment was to be in honor of the famous Ukrainian poet Ivan Franko, who, though dead these many years, was loved and honored throughout the Soviet Union. Many famous guests, the chairman told us, were present onstage this night to do Franko honor. He proceeded to name the guests and each stood up and made a little bow. They included the cream of the Moscow literary élite, not to mention a score of major political figures. The audience, many members of which had equipped themselves with opera glasses (these can be rented in any theater in Moscow) closely examined each famous figure. Having made all the introductions on his list, the chairman seemed to realize that something had been left out. He cast a perplexed glance at us and the opera glasses all swung our way — but inspiration failed the chairman. He shook his head in a baffled manner and turned back to the program.

Speakers and singers and reciters of poetry now came forward one by one to the podium. Since I sat on the outside chair beside the podium I was not screened by the table, and the TV cameras had an unobstructed view of me. Claire drew my attention to this fact with a murderous, "Cross your legs! *And keep them crossed!*"

Some of the speakers spoke in Russian, and Laura, slowly recovering from acute paralysis, gamely translated for us. However, many more spoke in Ukrainian and this was outside Laura's province. Finally she turned to a dignified lady sitting on her left and politely asked if the stranger would mind translating from Ukrainian. The lady seemed startled, but before she could reply she herself was called on for a speech — after all, she *was* the Minister of Culture for the Ukrainian Soviet Socialist Republic.

Since there was nothing much else to do except consider what fate I would visit on Sasha when I caught him, I began to ponder the implications of this celebration. For centuries Ukrainians and Russians have lived uneasily as neighbors, and often there has been violence between them. Both are intensely nationalistic peoples. Each race has stubbornly defended its own culture and language against encroachments by the other. The situation has some similarities with the one which still exists between the French and English in Canada. Yet here was a Ukrainian national (and very nationalistic) poet being honored, not only in Moscow but simultaneously throughout the Soviet Union, with all the pomp and ceremony the State could muster. I have no way of knowing if Franko was a good enough poet to warrant this attention. However, I *do* know that the honor being paid to him, and through him to all Ukrainians, was a clever piece of practical politics. How much, I thought to myself, could be done to heal the spreading rift between Quebec and the rest of Canada if we had the intelligence and the will to make similar gestures.

I was still musing when intermission arrived — an hour and a half later. We were the last to leave the platform but we did not linger in the VIP waiting room. With averted eyes we scurried for the exit.

We went back to the hotel, and as we sipped our nightcaps we considered the nature of the problem we had presented to the audience at the theater, to the television watchers, and to the cinemagoers in the Ukraine and elsewhere who would never have any explanation for the abrupt materialization and equally abrupt disappearance of those three strange ladies.

2
AIRBORNE

A disquieting episode preceded our departure from Moscow.

Claire and I had gone to bed early, but shortly after midnight we were awakened by a gut-shaking rumble which seemed to permeate the entire building, setting the dishes on our table tinkling nervously.

I went to the window. Moscow normally goes to sleep at midnight and the broad, dimly lit street five stories below was empty of life. Nevertheless the air throbbed with a harsh, metallic thunder. The sound grew closer until a massive column of tanks loomed into view at the far end of the street.

These squat behemoths were the precursors to a truly Orwellian spectacle. For three hours an unrelenting river of steel thundered through the black October night. The buildings on both sides of the street shuddered to that passing-on, but did so eyelessly. Not a single lighted window broke the obscure façade.

The tanks were followed by echelons of armored carriers,

15

self-propelled guns, atomic cannon, and an array of tank-towed missiles which looked particularly menacing because each was wrapped in a dark canvas shroud.

Although I knew this chilling display of weaponry could only be a rehearsal for the military parade which is a feature of the annual celebration of the Great October Revolution, the effect was to make me feel naked and alone in a potentially lethal and hostile world.

Claire, who had joined me at the window, was less impressed. She soon became bored by this display of male bellicosity.

"From up here," she said, stifling a yawn, "they look like a lot of children's Dinky Toys. Come back to bed!"

I slept uneasily for the remainder of the night, my imagination haunted by all the propaganda I had ever read, or heard, about the Communist hammer, poised high to crush the life out of the Western world.

I was still bleary-eyed next morning when we boarded a big black Chaika limousine for the trip to Domodedovo airport. Domodedovo lies sixty kilometers distant and the route to it follows a long segment of the circular bypass highway which is supposed to be Moscow's ultimate boundary — a ring of concrete intended to contain the burgeoning city and prevent it from spilling out over the surrounding countryside.

There was a heavy snowstorm and the road was crowded with trucks carrying concrete sections for the prefabricated apartment buildings which were springing up everywhere. We drove for miles and miles past rows of apartments, built and building. In some areas they were sprouting in the midst of age-old growths of log houses which must have looked the same when Napoleon came among them. Tiny, and ornately decorated, the log houses were Old Russia, and they were doomed. Their passing does not depress the Muscovites, particularly those who grew up in such homes without water or plumbing and often enough with three or four families squeezed into as many rooms. What the average Muscovite seems to want — and the quicker the better — is a brand-new apartment of his own; and he is not apt to be overly critical if the walls are so thin he can hear his neighbor breathing.

Against all odds of weather and traffic we reached the airport on time — one full hour before *scheduled* departure, which is not to be confused with *actual* departure time. Aeroflot treats its schedules with a casual disdain which can be a trial to the keyed-up nerves of Westerners.

Russians have a saying (they have one for every eventuality) which sums up their attitude towards Aeroflot's cavalier disregard for schedules. "You should not complain if the plane leaves late," Kola told me solemnly. "Be grateful that none have ever been known to leave ahead of time."

Russian tolerance for such delays is at least partly due to the knowledge that Aeroflot's safety record is unmatched. Generally speaking Soviet civilian aircraft will not take off if there is the slightest doubt about the weather, or about any other factor bearing on safety.

However, the cautious policies of Aeroflot are not universally observed. Claire and I once shared a three-seat section on a flight from Moscow to Tbilisi, capital of the Georgian Republic, with a Moscow physicist who, from the moment we boarded the plane, was in an unabashed state of funk. We asked him why he seemed so unhappy.

"Georgian pilots . . . and watermelons!"

Pressed to explain, he described a trip he had made a year earlier.

"We boarded our plane at Tbilisi airport and then were

kept waiting an hour in the broiling heat while the crew personally put aboard an entire truckload of watermelons Since there wasn't room in the cargo compartment they just stacked them in the center aisle, five or six deep. When we got into the air and hit some turbulence, the cursed melons were the only things aboard that had room to move and they rolled under seats and even burst open the door into the pilot's cabin. We human passengers were stuck where we were. No chance to reach the toilet. I had to sit with my knees under my chin most of the way to keep from getting my feet squashed.

"I'm sure we didn't actually go *over* the Caucasus Mountains. We were too heavy to get enough altitude. We must have flown between them, but it was such thick cloud I can't say for sure. Anyway we did get to Moscow and then we had to sit in the plane for another hour until a truck appeared and the crew got the melons off the plane."

"What happened to the melons?"

"Oh, the crew doubtless sold them for twenty times what they cost. Good businessmen, the Georgians, only the government really shouldn't let them play about with airplanes."

Domodedovo airport was swarming with the most fantastic mixture of people. They seemed to include representatives, often in native dress, of every known race, together with some of totally unknown origin. There are more than ninety ethnic groups in the USSR and the majority live south or east of the Ural Mountains. Domodedovo is their airport, serving Siberia and the Far East, but it also serves most of non-Soviet Asia, and Asia has taken to the air with passion and abandon. For almost the only time I was in the Soviet Union, I was able to wander about almost unnoticed, despite being kilted, bearded and draped in an Eskimo

18

parka. By the standards of Domodedovo my garb and my appearance were relatively square.

Our flight departed only thirty minutes late, which seemed to surprise Kola and Yura. After we had settled ourselves, and endured the takeoff, I asked Yura to tell me something about the TU–104 jet in which we were flying. He was unhelpful.

"Airplanes I do not like! Dog team is better."

"We'll ask the pilot," Kola interjected, and without more ado shepherded Claire and me forward to the cockpit, apparently treating it as the God-given right of every Soviet citizen to visit that sanctum if and when he chose.

The captain, a fatherly looking fellow, explained his plane with gusto. It was a civilian modification of a bomber type, he told me. Then, with a grin, "In the United States they call it Badger bomber and they worry because we have so many. Don't tell them most of our 104s carry passengers instead of bombs. Is big military secret!"

When we returned to our seats, the copilot, a handsome young chap from Kiev, came along with us. He was infatuated with Northern aviation, having spent several years with the polar division of Aeroflot. His Northern flying had been mostly over the Chukotka Peninsula (Chukotka and Alaska are only fifty-six miles apart) and he amused us with an account of how American radio stations sometimes sought to seduce Soviet fliers into defecting across the intervening Bering Strait.

"They have one fellow who speaks good Russian, and he calls us up on our working frequency and tells us we are foolish to live in slavery when all we have to do is bear west for fifteen minutes to reach a free country.

"One time my captain told him: 'Yes, you are right, okay, we are coming right away.' He got very excited and wanted

to know how many of us would come. We told him not many
. . . maybe four squadrons of MIG-21s. He lost his temper
at that and told us, anyway, we were too stupid to be free!"

At this juncture the copilot, who had been eyeing Claire
in a frankly admiring manner, bent smoothly toward her
and slipped his arm around her shoulders.

"Look down!" he told her. "The Ural Mountains! Soon
we leave Europe behind. Then is *Sibir* — the name means
the Sleeping Land — but it is not sleeping now. It is the
New Land of the Soviet people, wide awake at last!"

Pilots are the same the world over. They are not to be
trusted with pretty girls. Although I was very curious to
see the legendary Urals, the porthole was completely
blocked by two blond heads. Kola leaned across the aisle.

"Never mind, Farley," he said sweetly, "come and look
out my side. The view is just as good."

Actually the view was terrible. Seen from a height of five
kilometers, through a filter of thin cloud, the Urals appeared only dimly as an ill-defined pattern of gray rock,
darkened by the forests clinging to the slopes.

Although not physically as impressive as most of the
world's great mountain ranges, the Urals have nevertheless
loomed surpassingly large in human history. In ancient
times they were believed to be the eastern limit of the habitable world, if not of the world itself. The long, sinuous
sweep of the Urals had a similar quality to that of the bleak,
gray sea horizon of the Atlantic Ocean. Beyond both lay a
void in human knowledge and for an almost equal length of
time both served as barriers blocking the spread of European man and denying him access to the greater world
beyond.

Lev Belikov, a Leningrad historian, has his own name
for the Urals. He calls them the Great Wall of Europe.

Immediately east of that wall lies a gigantic basin filled with bogs and so thickly forest-grown that the entire region used to be considered impenetrable except along the tortuous river routes. To the north the wall is anchored in islands far out in the Arctic Ocean in a realm of perpetual ice. To the south it is bedded in the arid steppes, beyond which lie the deserts of Kazakhstan. From its glacier-weighted northern tip in Novaya Zemlya, the Great Wall runs almost due south for two thousand miles. So effectively did it divide two worlds that it became permanently imbedded in human thought as the line of demarcation between two continents, Europe and Asia.

It was not until almost the end of the sixteenth century that the Great Wall was effectively breached by the social explosion which dispersed the men of Europe on a rampage of pillage that eventually embraced most of the world.

Even after it was cracked, the wall remained large in men's minds. During the seventeenth century it was the line of departure from which traders, colonizers and outlaws moved into the vast wilderness stretching eastward to the Pacific coast.

During the eighteenth and nineteenth centuries it took on a new and sinister connotation. It became a prison wall. Countless thousands of men and women were exiled beyond its gates to the depths of Siberia, most of them never to return again.

"We must be about over Sverdlovsk now," Kola said. "The gateway to Siberia. From here we fly along the line of the Trans-Siberian Railway. Thank your stars we're not on it. Six thousand miles and seven days from Moscow to Vladivostok! I did it once with a group of French industrialists and nearly went mad from boredom. So did they, only they were too polite to say so. It runs pretty well along the southern boundary of the USSR, too close by far, the way the Chinese are acting.

"Between Sverdlovsk and the halfway mark at Irkutsk, there's a string of big cities four or five hundred miles apart. Most of them began in the seventeenth century as forts, trading stations and administrative centers, and until the 1930s they were backwoods towns with wooden buildings and mud streets. Most of Siberia was one big backwater in those days. Then in the mid 1930s it began to be obvious what Hitler had in mind, and our leaders could see there was a good chance much of European Russia might be overrun. If that happened the Urals were going to serve as our last line of defense.

"The government began moving whole factory towns — machines and people — from Western Russia across the Urals. By the time the war ended, provincial places like Sverdlovsk and Omsk had turned into industrial cities, and after the war they kept on growing, faster and faster. Siberia came awake with a jump! Within fifteen years the whole western region of the Trans-Sib, as far east as Irkutsk, had jumped into modern times. Sverdlovsk, Omsk, Novosibirsk, Krasnoyarsk, Bratsk, Irkutsk, the flame of a new industrial society set each one of them alight in turn. They've got almost four million people between them now, and they'll have double that by 1975. . . ."

Kola was so carried away he did not notice he had lost me. I was preoccupied with observing another kind of Russian enthusiasm, which the copilot was demonstrating. I was by no means discontented when he glanced at his watch, removed his arm from Claire's shoulders and, with manifest reluctance, returned to the cockpit. Muttering an apology to Kola I slipped back into my own seat, firmly resolved to remain there until the flight was over.

The cloud deck below us became impenetrable, and I fidgeted with impatience at being denied an aerial glimpse of this unknown land. Yura distracted me by telling me the story of Sorokin, the Mad Poet of Omsk, the Siberian city which was to be our first stop.

Sorokin was a Siberian, born about the turn of the century of a Buryat mother and a Russian father. At the time of the Revolution he was one of the more eccentric characters in the Tsar's realms. He also seems to have been something of an early hippie. He dressed in ornate robes in the Manchu style, let his hair grow to his shoulders, sported a divided beard which he sometimes dyed orange, and was a perpetual burr under the saddle of the establishment of his time.

His reaction to the Bolshevik Revolt was to start a revolution of his own. He declared himself king of the mid-Siberian town of Ulan-Ude and set up a farcical state which was intended to ridicule not only the Tsarist regime but that of the Bolsheviki as well. He printed his own funny-money and was so well regarded by the peasantry that they accepted it and gave him what food and shelter he needed in exchange.

While the Civil War raged back and forth across Siberia, Sorokin wrote a savagely antimilitarist novel and mailed handwritten copies to kings and queens and other heads of state around the world. Only one recipient acknowledged the gift. The King of Siam wrote to thank the author but also to apologize because, not knowing any Russian, he had been unable to read the book.

When Admiral Kolchak's White Guards temporarily chased the Bolsheviki out of Omsk, Sorokin was hard on the Admiral's heels. In the dead of night he went around the town pulling down the Admiral's proclamations and pasting up his own, announcing that the *real* King of Siberia would appear in the city in solemn procession at noon the following day.

Promptly at twelve o'clock Sorokin did appear . . . clad in a mock king's robe and riding an elderly camel. His saddlebags were crammed with manuscripts of his own epic verse which he proceeded to sell to the cheering populace, one page at a time.

The import of the verse was bitingly satiric condemnation of *all* military men, and an invitation to the people to reject militarism in any form.

Anton Sorokin continued to make mock of militarism until he died in 1924. He was officially forgotten until many years after his death, when certain stolid bureaucrats were persuaded to believe that Sorokin had been, in all seriousness, Siberia's great national poet. A statue to him was erected in Moscow and there it still stands, a subject of some secret mirth to those who know the tale.

The seat belt lights went on and we began to descend through the overcast. The plane broke clear, and we seemed to be flying through a rain scud over the Saskatchewan prairies where I spent my boyhood. There were the familiar fields, as black as death with autumn plow, or pallid yellow with old wheat stubble. And there, surely, was the Saskatchewan River, muddy and broad and meandering between poplar-grown banks toward an incredibly distant horizon. Under the port wing appeared a modern city which might have been a ringer for Saskatoon, except that it was about ten times too big.

The sense of recognition was so strong that it was not until we had landed and taxied through seemingly endless coveys of unfamiliar aircraft that the illusion faded and

Saskatoon became Omsk, sprawled on the fertile black prairies of southwestern Siberia.

Our stewardess informed us we would be on the ground "for some time" and promptly departed on business of her own. We passengers followed the lead of the captain and straggled across a mile of tarmac to a log shanty grossly overheated by a wood stove and filled to the doors with travelers. This, it developed, was the airport buffet, and if it seemed somewhat physically inadequate for a booming industrial and agricultural city of nearly a million people, it made up for it by the quality of the hospitality it dispensed. We shoved our way to the bar and bought slices of thick black bread liberally spread with clotted cream and caviar. Washed down with tumblers full of red Georgian wine and eaten in an atmosphere of cheerful camaraderie, it was a meal to remember.

Our captain slipped away to return shortly in command of a little tractor pulling a train of open cars behind it. Throwing open the buffet door he shouted an invitation to all and sundry to join him for a ride back to the plane.

Having now left Moscow far behind, we had also left any pretense at normal airport procedures. When the little train trundled up to our aircraft, people swarmed aboard without any pause for examination of boarding passes. The one concession to the organizational approach was when our stewardess belatedly arrived, red faced and puffing, and announced:

"Comrades! This plane is going to Irkutsk. Anyone *not* going there had better get off now."

3
IRKUTSK

From the Urals to Novosibirsk we flew a thousand miles across the famous steppes. However, these fat, grain-growing lands form only a relatively narrow strip along the southern edge of the West Siberian Plain, which for the most part is a sodden morass of swamps, muskeg and virtually impenetrable forests reaching far north of the arctic circle to fade at last into the treeless and frozen tundra of the polar coast.

Under this gigantic Northern jungle the Soviets have found a reservoir of oil and natural gas so vast that, by 1969, when less than half of the potential region had been tested, the proved reserves reportedly equaled those of North America.

As I looked northward from our high-flying aircraft over an apparently limitless expanse of blue-green forest, I saw only the Siberia of legend — an inscrutable and timeless world where human life is restricted to an attenuated fringe along the muddy banks of slow-flowing rivers meandering through dark forests to join that northern Amazon, the heavy-bellied Ob.

Some time after I had that first compelling view of it, I saw the West Siberian Plain again, this time represented on a map at Novosibirsk. True to Soviet doctrine for the development of distant regions, the map was not an illustration of how oil and gas would be extracted and then transported out of the wilderness — it was instead a design to demonstrate how an almost uninhabitable region would be developed and made habitable. On a swampy enclave of several hundred thousand square miles of taiga,* which in 1966 contained only a handful of small villages inhabited by timber cutters and trappers, the map boldly showed the location of three as yet unborn cities, each with a population of up to fifty thousand people, centered upon a vast complex of petrochemical industries.

Had I looked at that map prior to my visits to Siberia I would have been openly skeptical; but those three cities probably will be in existence and the petrochemical plants built and in operation before 1975. This conclusion, which results from my observations of many "impossible" developments throughout Siberia, does not give me any personal pleasure. On the contrary I would be much happier to see the mighty basin of the Ob remain inviolate as one unspoiled fragment in a world defiled. I implied as much in conversations with the young scientists of Novosibirsk who were so proudly explaining the future to me, and they were horrified.

"But," answered one of them as politely as he could, "surely you agree it is man's duty to develop the physical

* The generic Russian term for Northern forests.

world. There can be no higher achievement for modern man than that!"

His comrades nodded their heads and I realized they were as one with their peers the wide world over.

On this first visit Novosibirsk passed far below and the sprawling plains were left behind. Ahead of us old mountains swelled under a forest shroud. They grew higher and bolder as we passed south of Krasnoyarsk and over the upper reaches of the river Yenisei. The evening sky had become miraculously clear and a wall of towering cloud on the southern horizon resolved itself into a line of snow-capped peaks. These were the palisades of the Sayan Range, and as we drew closer we could look beyond them into the great mountain massif of Outer Mongolia. It was a spectacle which would have pleased me more had I not been distracted by what appeared to be the outpourings of a volcano amongst the hills ahead — a volcano of factory chimneys whose smoke cast a shadow for at least fifty miles up the wide valley of the Angara River.

Kola also viewed this banner of progress with a jaundiced eye.

"The new satellite industrial cities of Irkutsk," he explained. "In old times people called Irkutsk the navel of Siberia. Maybe now they had better refer to it as a different orifice."

Dusk and our plane settled together on the Irkutsk airfield and we were met at the foot of the boarding ramp by a tall, urbane man with dark, vital eyes. Mark Sergei, a renowned Siberian poet and writer of children's books, was an old comrade of Yura's. He was also secretary of the Irkutsk Writers Union, and our host. When he had settled us in our room in the Hotel Siberia he took us to the dining hall for a "little snack," which translated itself into a five-course meal featuring fish soup and reindeer stroganoff. Mark took his hostly duties seriously. After we had stuffed he gave further evidence of this.

"I don't know what you would like to see most, but the Writers Union has made some small advance arrangements, subject to your approval. First we might visit the great hydroelectric plant at Krasnoyarsk — it is only five hundred miles to the northwest. Then we could go to the gold-fields at Bodaibo in the mountains five hundred miles to the northeast. After that, perhaps a short trip southward to Mongolia; then a visit to our sacred lake, Baikal, and to the Buryat people at Ulan-Ude. In Irkutsk itself we hope you will be the guests of the city at the celebration of the Great October Revolution and after that. . . ."

I caught Yura's eye and he gently interrupted Mark's outline for an epic odyssey, explaining that, alas, the North was calling and we must go to Yakutia before the winter began in earnest.

At breakfast next morning Mark introduced us to our first Yakut, Nadia Komarova, a beautiful twenty-year-old with raven hair, glowing olive skin, full red lips and snapping black eyes.

Nadia was a student at the Irkutsk Institute for Foreign Languages, majoring in English and Spanish, en route to her degree as a high school teacher. When she apologized because her command of *French* was not very good, I asked a question that had been bothering me. During our short time in the USSR we had met an uncommon number of people who spoke English, and an equally large number who spoke some other European language. Was this coincidence?

"Not at all," Kola explained. "Russian people are very sensitive about the problems of communicating in strange languages. They have to be. There are ninety-three *official* languages in the Union. Apart from those who are born to the Russian tongue, most people still speak their own ethnic language, plus Russian, which serves as the common language. People with a higher education, and that now includes almost all our young people, learn a third language as a matter of course. The preference is for English, French, German or Spanish, in that order."

Nadia was not only an intellectual surprise but a sartorial one too. She looked, as Claire rather wonderingly remarked, more chic than most college students in Canada; complete with eye-shadow (which stressed her oriental cast), a teased hairdo, a formfitting black dress and high-heeled shoes. She was by no means unique. With their multiracial background and their flair for dress, the girls of Irkutsk have to be as eye-appealing as any in the world. When I revisited the city with John DeVisser, he shot so many pictures of the pretties that I felt constrained to caution him against using up too much of his film.

"Mind your own business!" he replied shortly. "I'm going to do a *special* book . . . Birds of Irkutsk."

While we men discussed the day's plans, Nadia and Claire were deeply engaged in a conversation of their own. And when we announced that we would begin the day with a visit to the Angarsk Power Plant, we found ourselves facing a revolt.

Claire is an ikon addict and she had confided her passion to Nadia.

"Power plants is nice," said Nadia, "but is not fair. It makes bad impression for visitors, because always you doing what men want to do, and here in Soviet Union women are your equals. So please, will we not go to some churches now and look at ikons!"

It was not a question. It was a statement of intent.

Smiling sardonically Mark capitulated and drove us across town to the oldest Russian Orthodox church in the vicinity. It was a chilly morning, hazy and windless. We crossed the Angara River, glittering with moving crystals of shell ice. The church stood behind ancient walls a mile or two from town and beyond it farm lands rolled gently to an encircling rim of distant forests.

The church (a nunnery once) was crowned by bulbous towers inhabited by what seemed like a million pigeons, wheeling and spiraling like living smoke. The tree-filled grounds and the old stone buildings had an air of gentle decrepitude about them.

Irkutsk, Mark told us, was one of the earliest bastions of the Russian Empire in the East. It was founded by a band of marauding Cossacks who reached the region in 1634 and chose this spot to build a wooden fort as a base from which to harry the native Buryat people. The fort developed into a great trading center. In the nineteenth century, it became the final staging point for anti-Tsarists exiled to the salt mines and oblivion. From Irkutsk, many of the great overland and overseas expeditions to the Far East and beyond set out. Mark showed us an unpretentious memorial to Alexei Chirikov who, in 1741, sailed with Vitus Bering to become the first known Europeans to reach the shores of Alaska.

Even more impressive were the little stones, half buried under fallen leaves, marking the graves of the wives and children of the ill-fated Decembrist Revolutionaries of 1825 who were among the first to revolt against Tsarist rule. Wives and children voluntarily followed their men into Siberian exile along the incredibly arduous road leading to Irkutsk. They walked almost all the way, taking more than a year to complete the journey. Exhausted, sick, and starving, most of those who reached Irkutsk perished and were buried there.

Their graves were marked by very modest stones, but in the side yard, close to the gray wall of the church, was one grave marked by an enormous granite boulder which must have weighed a good forty tons. It belonged to a fabulously rich man who accumulated most of his wealth from the use of slave labor in the salt mines. Before his death he tried to insure a kind of immortality by having this gigantic rock rolled into the churchyard to mark where his remains would lie. He had a solid bronze plug poured into a hole drilled into the rock upon which was inscribed his name and fame. During the Bolshevik Revolution, when the Reds were fighting desperately for survival against the Whites, metal became so scarce that a local gunsmith chiseled out the bronze. Now only the nameless stone remains.

We went into the church where, although this was a weekday, a special mass was being sung. The service was being conducted with the full pomp and panoply of Orthodox ritual. A hidden choir sang a lugubrious chant and the air was thick with incense. We caught glimpses of the high priest wearing a towering pearl-encrusted hat, and all but hidden from the worshippers in the dark depth of an inner sanctuary.

There were ikons — hundreds of them of every age and degree of decay — glittering dully with gold and jewels. Alas, they were not for Claire. A venerable gentleman with a long, discolored beard shuffled up to us and in no uncertain tone informed Mark there was a service in progress and tourists were not welcome. Whereupon four members of the Soviet New Order and two embarrassed Canadians withdrew as unobtrusively as possible.

Crouched on the stone steps outside the door was the one and only beggar we ever saw in Russia. He was a bent, unkempt and dirty old man but not, apparently, crippled. When I asked about him, Mark replied, "Well, like everyone else his age he draws a full State pension. Perhaps he enjoys the role he plays. . . ."

As we left the churchyard the glaucous gold October sun broke through the haze and the old city of Irkutsk lying across the river from us became radiant and lovely.

Rather hesitantly, Mark asked if we still wanted to visit the power plant. Discovering that none of us really had any great hankering to see it, he was not-so-secretly relieved. Being a writer himself, he knew the inutility of such expeditions to anyone except industrialists, engineers and people of that ilk. He understood that the spectacle of thousands of men and women swarming over a concrete mountain in order to produce millions of kilowatts of invisible electricity would add little to our understanding of the Russian people.

"Well," he said. "Why don't I show you my Irkutsk instead?"

So we drove to a great stone-paved esplanade on the banks of the Angara at midcity. This broad wall, guarding the banks against spring floods, was dotted with men and women promenading in the pale, autumnal sunshine. The half-mile-wide river flowed strong and steady below us from its source at Lake Baikal toward its union with the Yenisei, and thence onward to the Arctic Ocean. On its congealing surface were dozens of tiny rowboats manned by fishermen who, unperturbed by the skim of ice, concentrated soberly on their rods and lines. They were engaging in one of the two great outdoor pastimes of all Russians. The season was a trifle late for the other: the passionate pursuit of wild mushrooms.

We left the car and walked through a park where platoons of well-dressed men were rehearsing for their part in the coming parade to celebrate the day of the Revolution. The quietness was startling. There was none of the pulsating roar that rises from a city of half a million people in the West, and yet the broad, tree-lined avenues seemed to carry a steady stream of cars and trucks.

"It is so quiet because Irkutsk is still a wooden city," Mark explained. "In the forest the trees absorb sound like a sponge and it is the same with the log houses of Irkutsk."

These wooden houses were all about us; long streets of them, even near the center of the city. They were beautifully constructed of squared logs, and many stood three stories high. Each was a work of loving labor and of art, decorated around doors and windows and under the eaves with scrolls and fretwork, sculptured shutters and complicated carved porticos painted in blues and greens to form intricate patterns against the chocolate brown of the ancient logs.

Here and there were gaps where these buildings out of another time had given way to the stark concrete constructions of the new age.

"The shape of things to come," I mused, half to myself, "when this city becomes as faceless as all cities, and thunders and reverberates to the sound of the machine, and knows no more quietness."

Mark stopped and looked intently at me for a moment. Then this New Man of a New Age said a heartening thing.

"We will not *let* that happen. There has been too much lost already in our land — by war and by senseless change. Change must come; but it cannot be allowed to obliterate the past. We have many destroyers among our planners — too many of them. But here in Irkutsk, as elsewhere, we are forcing them to be careful. Whole streets of these old houses

34

will be preserved, not as museums, but as living homes. Man is a living thing, and man has roots. Any fool knows that without roots all things die, and we are not going to go that way. Just last year we persuaded the administration to give us hundreds of pounds of real gold leaf so we could regild the domes of every church in Irkutsk. It was not religious zeal made us do that. It was our certainty that the old things belong to life as surely as the new — and must be cared for tenderly."

"But surely," I demurred, thinking of the tremendous concrete waste I had seen on the outskirts of Moscow, "people who think the way you do must be very much in the minority."

"Not so much. And we have the young people behind us now — we writers and painters. They believe we are right because they feel it in their bones. Each year there are more of us and we are already strong enough to stop the worst of the destruction. Don't misunderstand. We are not trying to stand in the way of changing times. We only mean to be sure change does not become a universal blight."

Thinking about my own country, I was skeptical of Mark's certainty, but I kept my doubts to myself. Later I concluded that he had not overstated the position. Wherever I journeyed I met more men and women who shared Mark's convictions than opposed them. On every human level I heard the echo of Mark's words. I came away convinced that whatever else may happen in the Soviet Union, the past will remain alive and vital and will continue to nurture man and to be nurtured by him.

One evening Mark offered us a choice of entertainment: a performance of the State Symphony Orchestra, a Chekhov play at the State Theater, a Verdi opera, or a performance by a troup of Koryak folk singers and dancers (the

Koryaks are the native peoples of the northern Kamchatka Peninsula on the Pacific coast). He apologized because there was no ballet scheduled that evening.

Claire elected to attend the symphony to satisfy her curiosity about the quality of music available in this provincial city some twenty-six hundred miles distant from Moscow. What she got was a set of five modern pieces by a group of five Leningrad composers all of whom were present in the flesh to conduct their own compositions. She reported that the theater was packed and that Russian modern music left her just as cold as does its counterpart in North America.

I forewent the bright lights in favor of an evening spent talking with a small group of Mark's friends.

It was mostly a writers' evening. I was thoroughly quizzed on the status of writers in my own country and in turn heard some revealing things about the other side. Mark presented me with a number of his books. The children's books were particularly impressive to look at, even if I couldn't read them. On the whole, books for adults in the USSR (unless they are art books) are poorly designed and rather shabbily manufactured. I remarked on this but Yura pointed out that in Russia adult books are sold for their content — not their appearance. They are intended to be read, not used as table ornaments or as status symbols. Furthermore, they are sold at a price everyone can afford. For instance an average length novel in hard covers sells for about eighty cents.

Children's books are different. Visual appeal is considered vital for children and the publishers go full out to achieve it. The best artists are hired to do the illustrations, which are always extensive and frequently superb. Production and design are comparable to ours but, because of the mammoth size of the printings, prices are kept to a tithe of what we must pay. Initial printings of Mark's children's books run from half to three-quarters of a million copies.

The shoptalk was interrupted by the arrival of a dapper, dark-complexioned young man named Yakob, bearing gifts — two bottles of Armenian cognac. Yakob was a Buryat, a member of the original cattle-breeding tribe who owned this region before the Russians came. He was also a town planner with a degree from Moscow University and, like all planners, was a rabid enthusiast.

He adroitly turned the conversation to his chosen field. Some years ago the state planning bodies realized that the twentieth century trend toward agglomeration (whereby the population tends to drift from the periphery of a country into a few mushrooming urban centers) had to be brought under control before it was too late — as it was almost too late for places like Moscow and Kiev. A first principle was established that the population growth of the most threatened cities would have to be arrested arbitrarily. The method chosen was to place stiff controls on the availability of housing — easily done since almost all the living space in the big cities is owned directly or indirectly by the State. Nobody who was not already a resident in Kiev, Leningrad or Moscow could obtain housing in those cities without a special permit, and permits were hard to come by. A would-be immigrant had to demonstrate that the city could not do without *him* — not vice versa.

This policy has been condemned by critics of the USSR as proof that Russia is a police state, since it obviously restricts the free movement of the individual. However, I met few Russians who looked upon it as a tyrannical interference with their liberty. Most of them saw the point and recognized it as the only immediately practical method of keeping the growth of the metropolitan monsters in check.

As Mark pointed out, it is not an *absolute* restriction. Those who yearn for big city life can earn a domicile permit by attaining such excellence in their jobs or professions that the city requires their services. Yura noted an interesting side effect. Hundreds of thousands of students go to study in Leningrad, Kiev and Moscow from all over the USSR. Since only a few are permitted to remain after graduation, the balance must return whence they came or otherwise disperse throughout the country where they are most needed. This is at least a partial explanation of why cultural, medical, teaching and technical services outside the big cities of Russia are of such high standard.

Now things have moved a step farther. A planned process for easing the pressures inside the big cities is taking place through the decentralization of industry. It consists of shifting heavy, noisy industries (and those which produce noxious by-products) far away from the parent cities, which then become more habitable. Those who work in the dispossessed industries follow them to greener pastures — *literally* greener pastures. All new industries, as well as the old ones which are being relocated, are established in satellite towns separated one from the other, and from the metropolises, by many miles of agricultural lands or forest belts. Furthermore, each new satellite town has a planned upper limit to *its* population. When that limit is reached the satellite must begin budding-off to spawn new and more distant satellites.

"We believe in the dispersion principle as opposed to the concentration principle," Yakob said vehemently. "Just see what we are doing here in Irkutsk. . . ."

He outlined the master plan which now guides the destiny of the Irkutsk district. The original city is to be maintained, improved, and to a degree modernized (a phrase which made Mark wince) as the cultural, administrative, communications and education center for the entire Irkutsk province, an area of about the size of France. It is to be the center of concentric rings of satellite industrial centers, which will be separated from each other by wide stretches of taiga given over to reindeer and cattle raising and other agricultural pursuits. Irkutsk and the satellites will be linked to each other by rapid transit systems — air-bus shuttles, road-bus service (both of these are already functioning) and high-speed electric trains, probably of the monorail variety.

Three satellite cities already exist. Two of them are brand-new, and one, based on an old coal mining center, has been completely rebuilt. This is Cheremkhovo, ninety miles away to the northwest. Much closer are Shelekhov and Angarsk, neither of which existed prior to 1956. Shelekhov now has fifty thousand people living in a model town two miles distant from the aluminum smelting plant which is its *raison d'être*. It can absorb another fifty thousand people in secondary manufacturing before it reaches its planned upper limit. Angarsk is the "power city" based on the Angara hydroelectric power station; it will develop as a "power intensive" manufacturing city until it is about the size of Shelekhov.

Because they are carefully planned, and don't just grow like Topsy, the satellites are far more spacious and comfortable places in which to live than are the old-fashioned industrial cities. There is no problem persuading people to move to the satellites since, in so doing, they obtain better housing, better living and working conditions, and yet do not lose touch with the mother city and its amenities.

When I suggested that perhaps this decentralization program might have a military purpose in this atomic age, Yakob scoffed.

"We do all this because it makes better living conditions for human beings. It is expensive. It uses up time and materials and energy that could be spent increasing productivity in existing plants. But it is worth it. We are making sure the next generation won't have to live in swarming dunghills. Perhaps you have to be Russian to understand this; perhaps you have to have a history of hundreds of years when people were crowded into real pigpen slums. But if you have read Dostoevski, you will know why it is we want to be free forever from that sort of threat."

4
BAIKAL

Nearly thirty million years ago a cataclysmic event took place in the middle of Asia. The continent split latitudinally into two parts, and the northern and southern halves ground against one another like two titanic pans of ice. Along the line of pressure the earth's crust broke and crumbled and the debris piled up to form the highest and most extensive mountain regions on earth.

Eventually the pressure eased. The two vast land masses resolidified as one but, before doing so, they rebounded slightly, opening a fissure thirty to forty miles in width, more than a thousand miles long, and as much as three miles deep. Because the earth's crust was exceptionally thick in this region, the gaping wound did not fill from the bottom with molten magma. Instead it began to fill with runoff water from the surrounding mountains. So immense was its capacity that it took many thousands of years before it filled to the rim and the overflow began to run out of its western end to form the river Angara.

This was the beginning of Lake Baikal. The passage of eons has made great changes in this, the earth's most ancient lake. Erosion of the mountains which enclose it and the accumulation of the dead husks of astronomical numbers of aquatic animals has gradually filled the fissure with sediment, reducing Baikal's length to about four hundred miles. Still it remains the deepest of all lakes, well over a mile deep in places. It contains about a fifth of all the free fresh water in the world (almost as much as the basins of all five of the Great Lakes of North America). Although much reduced from their original Olympian heights, the surrounding mountains still tower high above this ancient inland sea. Earthquakes still shake the region but, by comparison, they are only tiny residual shivers of the convulsion which gave birth to the Baikal fissure.

The lake's fantastically clear waters shelter a community of living things that have evolved in their own way through millions of years. More than a thousand species of plants and animals living in Baikal are found nowhere else. Hidden in the mountain heart of Asia, Baikal successfully protected and nurtured a unique community of life through an immense span of time.

And then came man. At first he did no harm. Evenki hunters were the last in the aboriginal line to occupy its shores. They and the Buryats to the south believed the lake was sacred. They peopled it with spirits and for the most part stayed off its treacherous waters, which can roar in oceanic fury under the lash of sudden, blasting winds of hurricane velocity.

About 1634 marauding Cossack bands became the first Westerners to see the lake. In its surrounding forests they found great numbers of a singularly beautiful member of the weasel family, the Barguzin sable.

Lust for sable pelts had been directly responsible for the first breaching of the Ural wall when, in 1581, Russia's most powerful merchant family, the Stroganovs, sent a ragtag army of Cossack mercenaries through the Perm Gates in search of sable — a search which led to the conquest of a new world.

Captained by a free-booter named Yermak, the Cossacks first destroyed the small Mohammedan Khanate of Kutchum, just east of the Urals, which was the only human society in Siberia capable of more than token resistance to the invaders from the West. Impelled by the same rapaciousness which motivated the Spanish conquistadors in South and Central America, and the Dutch, French and English in North America, small bands of Cossacks then swept eastward across Siberia, each band striving to outpace all others and be first into the territory of some undiscovered tribe which could be brutalized into paying tribute in "soft gold" — furs — but, above all, in sable furs. What the beaver was to the Mountain Men — those ill-famed buccaneers of the American west — sable was to the Cossacks. In just under fifty years they crossed the whole of Siberia and reached the Pacific.

The Cossacks, and those who followed, were one with their European compatriots who were then busily swarming into Africa, the Americas and the Pacific in search of loot. They were men who had abrogated one of the basic principles of life: that each living thing shall only take from the world around it what it actually requires to secure its own survival. The new kind of man — a mutant if ever there was one — took everything he could grasp, and then reached out for more. When the soft gold of the Barguzin sable and of the other land fur-bearers around Baikal had been almost exhausted, the invaders turned to the lake itself.

At least a million years ago one small group of mammals had given up the hard-won terrestrial way of life and returned to the salt seas from which all life originated. The sea was kind to these backsliders and they ultimately diversified into the many members of the seal family. Most of them chose to live in the open oceans where the greatest numbers of their kind still remain.

However, some hundreds of thousand of years ago, a few of the early seals entered the arctic estuary of one of the great Siberian rivers, the Yenisei, and worked their way south into the very heart of the Asian land mass to Baikal.

Here they found themselves in an inland sea where conditions were not so different from those in the greater sea — two thousand miles away to the north. The water was fresh instead of salt, but that was not material. Fish were abundant. Because of its great depth and the presence of convection currents of oceanic character, the ice formed late in the winter and there were always areas near the river mouths where it remained thin enough so that air-breathing mammals could keep holes open. In other areas of Baikal the mountain winds built up atop the ice heavy blankets of snow wherein the female seals could build snug caves in which to bear their pups.

When natural man arrived upon the scene he killed occasional seals, but his predations were so minor that they made no impression on a herd which, it is estimated, must have numbered several hundred thousand individuals.

When the European conquerors turned their attention away from the forests where life was growing silent, and looked upon the sacred lake, they must have been incredulous at the amount of life it contained. Here was a killing ground worthy of their mettle. But that world of water was so vast (some sixteen thousand cubic *miles* of water) that the rape took some time to complete. By the early years of the twentieth century there had been solid victories. The giant Baikal sturgeon was virtually extinct. The apparently inexhaustible schools of fine-flavored whitefish called *omul* were fading fast. A number of other fishes were becoming scarce. And the seals were almost gone; no more than four or five thousand of them still survived.

The battle to destroy the living world of Baikal was being won. Fishermen and seal hunters were receiving indirect assistance in their work of destruction from landsmen. In the mountain valleys drained by Baikal's three hundred sixty inflowing streams and rivers, the forests where the sables were hardly more than a memory were themselves being razed. Siberian cedars, high-towering patriarchs, many of them more than a thousand years old, all but disappeared. Larch, and the lesser species, took their turn. The logs were floated down the once crystal rivers, gradually coating the stream beds with thick layers of bark until many of the lake fishes that used the rivers as nurseries could no longer find suitable spawning grounds. Tannic acid and other decomposition products from sunken logs and bark began contaminating the waters of the lake itself.

Then, in 1962, the economic planners in Moscow decided to build a gigantic cellulose and wood-chemical combine on the south shore of Lake Baikal. Even by Soviet standards the plans were grandiose. There were to be five plants with their associated towns in the combine. Secure in the conviction that the true good is to be found in more production, the planners turned their blueprints over to the builders, and in 1963 work on the first two plants began.

At this juncture something truly remarkable occurred. In

the Soviet Union, that closed society where, so we are told, the voice of the individual is never heard, there arose a thunder of protests from individuals in every part of the land. The editors of the monolithic all-Union papers, *Pravda* and *Izvestia*, having proudly announced the birth of the gigantic new production complex at Baikal, found themselves inundated by letters of outrage. As the two plants neared completion the intensity of the storm strengthened.

An elderly, much respected Moscow writer described to me what followed:

"The word Baikal became a rallying cry even to people who knew very little about it except its name. They were acute enough to see that finally the high priests of progress-through-production had to be brought to their senses. The threat to Baikal made people understand that unless this was done the new world we were building would be no better than a ruined wasteland fit for machines, but not for human beings. Hundreds and thousands of professional writers, poets, artists and scientists took it on themselves to make Baikal the symbolic warning. They were joined by masses of workers and by revered members of the Academy of Science, and even by some State officials. Every magazine and newspaper heard the voice of what was a true mass movement of the people.

"For a while the authorities who had designed the cellulose combine tried to drown out the protests. There were long articles lashing out at reactionary sentimentalists who tried to stop the glorious march of our Revolution. There were some threats, and some of the more prominent of Baikal's defenders were told they would get into trouble if they did not keep quiet. They refused to be quiet. The fuss kept getting worse. The plants were completed and began operations. They began pouring their poisons into the sa-

cred sea. Within three months there were reports of fish
dying in Baikal and even of people getting sick from eating
fish caught in the Angara. The fight of the people to save
the lake became more furious and then, quite suddenly, the
authorities gave in. The plants were closed."

I visited Baikal several times and on one occasion sat in a
little café on the shore of the lake, watching its waters rage
in the grip of a roaring October storm. Boris Arimov, an
Irkutsk poet who spent seven years fighting for Baikal, sat
with me and told me more of the story.

"When they closed the plants we suspected it was only
for long enough to let things cool down. So, we did not let
things cool down. We kept the fire going and gave it more
fuel. Now we demanded that fishing be banned until the
stocks returned to normal. No more slaughter of the seals,
we said. We said that all lumbering must be stopped on the
Baikal watersheds. We demanded that this treasure — one
of the world's great treasures — be cleansed until it was
again as beautiful as it had been before men began to dese-
crate it. All over the Soviet Union the friends of Baikal
fought on.

"Some people thought we could not win. We knew we
could. Things are not the same in our country as they were
some years ago, and not the same as most foreigners seem
to think. Lenin said the will of the people must be supreme
. . . we *were* the people. In Moscow they listened, and at
last they bowed to the people."

The battle to save Baikal brought, at its conclusion, one
of the most significant human successes in recent times. It
was a major victory of reason combined with deep instinctive feeling, over the senseless and suicidal passion of modern men to exploit the world around them into ultimate
destruction.

To my Western mind the scope of the victory seemed staggering. In 1967 the Presidium of the Supreme Soviet of the USSR voted to make the entire Baikal region — the lake and thousands of square miles of surrounding territory — into a national park. All fishing along the north half of the lake was prohibited for five years and along the south side for seven years. Sport fishing only will be permitted after that. Lumbering operations on all watersheds flowing into the lake have been halted for good. Extensive reclamation projects are under way to restore tributary streams and riverbeds to their pristine condition. A series of new fish hatcheries are being built. All forms of wildlife ranging from wolves to wild flowers are now under complete protection. By the end of 1969 the seal population had increased to forty-five thousand animals, and even the very rare Barguzin sable was staging a remarkable comeback. The sacred sea has again become a sacred sea in truth.

I asked Boris about the fate of the multimillion-ruble cellulose plants and their adjacent towns.

"It was unnecessary to abandon them entirely," he said, with the magnanimity of a successful warrior. "So we were content to have the two factories closed until a complete filtration system was built which guaranteed no effluent of any kind would ever enter Baikal. They will continue to work, but they will be fed with wood from other districts to the south of the park regions. They can now do no more harm. Of course, the plans for the three other plants were canceled."

One day I visited the Baikal Limnological Institute where more than a hundred scientists were doing research on the infinitely varied problems connected with preserving freshwater lakes. The men and women of the Institute were foremost in the fight to preserve Baikal, and their satisfaction in the victory knows no bounds.

"We have done more than save Baikal," a woman zoologist told me. "The fight woke up the whole of the Soviet Union to one of the grave dangers threatening mankind. We will not go to sleep again. Our leaders now understand how great the danger is and they are really listening hard to those who can tell them how to control and stop the damage done by a thoughtless modern industrial society. What happened here at Baikal will help set the pattern for the future development of our country."

Whether or not she was overly optimistic I cannot say. I do know that some strange things have happened since the Battle of Baikal was won. I was involved, unwittingly, in one such incident.

In May of 1969, Mir Publishing House in Moscow published a translation of a book of mine called *Never Cry Wolf*.

This book was originally published in 1964 in Canada and the United States; it was an attempt to dispel the many myths about the destructive nature of the wolf, and to demonstrate that the wolf was a vital element in the balance of nature and, as such, merited protection from those who would exterminate it. More than three hundred thousand copies were printed in various editions in North America; but, as of 1970, the North American wolf was still being hunted toward imminent extinction, often by government hunters, and almost everywhere with the assistance of government bounties.

Mir published the book with a rather odd translation of the original title. They called it, *Wolves! Please Don't Cry!* A few weeks after publication a battle began between proponents of the wolf and those who felt he ought to be eliminated. The battle was of surprisingly short duration. In August the Soviet Government published an edict declaring that the wolf was to be regarded henceforth as a "threatened species," and placed it under State protection. The USSR thus became the first nation in the world to extend protection to the wolf. It would seem that the mistranslation of my original title was not unjustifiable.

On the morning of my first visit to Baikal it was bitterly cold and snowing. Mark drove Claire and me to the lake along the banks of the Angara, which has been dammed near Irkutsk to produce a man-made addition to the lake extending for some fifty miles toward Irkutsk.

This new lake is much favored as a recreation area by Irkutskians, many of whom have built their *dachas* along its shores. Dachas are the equivalent of North American summer cottages, but with an essential difference. Great numbers of Russians seem to feel the atavistic need to get back to nature, and this means as far back as possible. Consequently, the cottages they build are small and primitive, although often delightfully designed and decorated in "woodland peasant" style.

At first I was not convinced that the simplicity of the dachas was so much intentional as it was a product of a not-so-affluent society. Once, while visiting Yura Rytkheu's dacha near Leningrad I made a rather snide suggestion to this point, to which he replied: "Farley, you think I am a poor man? Ha! I make more money than President of USSR. If I want, I have electric lights and television here. Have everything. But why I want to do that, eh? Why anybody want to take city with him on his back when he go live with nature?"

Discreetly I dropped the subject, but several months later when Yura came to visit Canada as my guest, friends

took us for a weekend to their cottage at one of the summer
colonies near Lake Muskoka. Yura examined the place with
great interest, noting the electric dishwasher, power lawn
mower, color television and other essential elements of
North American cottage life, and he remembered his earlier
conversation with me at *his* dacha. Innocently he addressed
our host: "You are lucky man! Have *two* city houses! But
now, please, show me your dacha, your hiding place where
you go to get *away* from city life."

The Russian compulsion to have one's feet in the earth is
so great that there are large areas near all Soviet cities
reserved for "summer farmers." Anyone who so desires can
obtain use of a plot of land whereon he can build a cabin
and have a patch of soil to till. As early in the spring as
possible hundreds of thousands of apartment dwellers move
to the little cabins, and there they stay all through the
summer, and late into the autumn. Working members of the
family commute back and forth to their city jobs. On holidays or in the evenings they till their gardens, sit in the
long light of the setting sun, fish in the river or talk to the
neighbors. They are deliberately recreating the essence of
the ancient way of life, and spiritually and physically they
are the better for it.

Most dachas, incidentally, are privately owned. They can
be sold or passed on through inheritance. However the land
itself, as with all land in the USSR, belongs to the people
(which is to say, to the State). It can be used in perpetuity
by individuals or families but cannot be bought or sold.
Real estate manipulators and speculators have a thin time
of it in the Soviet Union.

Most of the road to Baikal leads through rolling taiga
(*tame* taiga Mark called it, in contrast to the wilderness
beyond) which seemed intensely familiar in its crowding

stands of spruce and birch, even to a red fox who sat on a snowdrift by the roadside and watched us pass with only moderate curiosity. Near the end of the Angara valley we began seeing the villages of lumbermen, boat builders and fishermen. Built entirely of logs, the houses were nevertheless very individualistic because of the work done by the owners in decorating gables and eaves and window frames with the same sort of ornate fretwork and carvings which distinguish the houses of Irkutsk.

"The men spend long hours at it during the winter evenings," Mark explained. "It is true folk art and very serious business. Every Siberian wants to be a little different from everyone else. The first Russians to settle in Siberia were men and women who had been serfs in Europe and could not stand that life. Although they were oppressed by the Tsar's rule even here, they never became serfs again. If the authorities drove them too hard they simply packed up their belongings and disappeared into the wild taiga to find places nobody even knew about. Siberians have a different spirit from European Russians. They prize their individuality very much and will fight hard to keep it. This is one of the reasons so many of them died in the Great Patriotic War against the fascists. They were among the best fighters Russia had."

The weather began to warm a little as we reached the outlet of Baikal, but in the distance dark clouds still massed over a phalanx of snow-clad mountains which crowded right to the edge of the inland sea, lifting peaks three thousand feet above its steel-blue surface. It was a truly magnificent spectacle, and it was not hard to understand why the friends of Baikal fought so hard for its preservation.

The road only managed to struggle a few kilometers along the northern shore before the cliffs brought it to a halt at a little village crouched in a steep alpine valley which seemed uninhabited except for a score or so of very friendly dogs that swarmed out to give us greetings. One of a succession of storms being spawned in the southern mountains swept viciously across the lake, raising great breakers that came crashing against the cliffs. We drove up a narrow, paved, switchback road away from the shore and eventually reached a lookout a thousand feet above the lake. At this altitude a snow-laden wind encompassed us, coating the larches with wet snow and obscuring the view except for brief, mysterious glimpses of the mouth of the Angara and the cliffs beyond it.

"I'm sorry about the weather," Mark apologized as we crowded back into the warmth of the car. "But I wanted you to visit Eisenhower's Peak."

I must have looked startled.

"It is not on any map, but that's what we call it," Mark said with a grin. "Or sometimes just Ike's Peak. You see, sometime before the Revolution, so the story goes, some branch of General Eisenhower's family had the idea for developing a tourist resort at Lake Baikal. They negotiated to buy a tract of land along this shore, but later had to give up the idea. When he was President of the United States, Eisenhower was supposed to come to Russia for a state visit and he particularly asked to be taken to Baikal.

"Well, you know, Irkutsk wasn't used to entertaining heads of big foreign states and we were not ready for him. So things began to hum. Special experts came in from Leningrad and Moscow to help. The first thing was to pave the road from Irkutsk to Baikal. Then they decided to build this special road to the top of the mountain so Eisenhower could have the best of views.

"Well, he never came. The American U-2 spy plane was shot down over our country and the visit was canceled. All the same, we in Irkutsk are grateful to Ike. Sometimes when we drive along this nice pavement to Baikal we give a friendly little thought to him."

5
IRKUTSK

During my first stay in Irkutsk I avoided visiting industrial plants. Such enterprises afflict me with a feeling of unease. However, when I returned to the city in 1969 with John deVisser, it became necessary to visit at least one plant so John could photograph people at work. Arrangements were made to tour the aluminum smelter at Shelekhov.

We were accompanied by a rotund little man we had hired from Intourist to act as John's interpreter. Sergei Saltikov had spent many years lazing about on Black Sea cruise ships with parties of European tourists, and he was furious at being dispatched to Siberia. He joined us only a few hours before we left Moscow and so we did not find out, until too late, that he was a lush, and that his concept of the English language was uniquely his own. Although perhaps capable of directing lady tourists to the nearest toilet, he sank into the absolute depths of obscurantism when he tried to explain something of any greater complexity.

Once when we were being driven across the taiga our Russian guide asked Sergei to draw our attention to something.

"Take your optic suspension position for observation independently in the reverse direction!" Sergei instructed us.

By the time John and I had worked *that* one out, whatever it was we were supposed to see had long since vanished astern.

Then there was the time we were being shown through a power house, one of whose turbines was out of action and under repair. As we approached the silent machine Sergei translated the guide's explanation: "His tubule is steady for the prophylactic," a statement which produced such an appalling mental image that I hustled past the unfortunate turbine without even a sideways look.

Sergei was cast in an unmistakable mold. His little pink hands were horribly reminiscent of trotters, and his pointed ears and enormous jowls heightened the porcine effect. At the table he was a sight to behold. He engulfed his food with a single-minded fury which suggested that the ultimate Worm Of The World was resident in his rotund tummy.

It was inevitable that we should privately give him the sobriquet of Piggy, and equally inevitable that he should get wind of it. From that moment he became our sworn enemy. His method of obtaining revenge was to intimate to others that, far from being what we seemed, we were in reality Yankee spies. Some of our Russian friends relayed this accusation back to us. They thought it hilariously funny, but there were times when the fun wore a little thin.

The night before we were to tour the aluminum plant Piggy engaged in a monumental binge. In the morning he refused to budge out of his bed. "I am too many strengths down for this work continually," he snorted, head buried in his pillow. "And which, therefore, is not in the para-

graphs of my estimation working to plus four hours in
the day!"

By this time experience had made interpreters out of *us;*
so we knew what he meant. According to the trade union
regulations, an interpreter is not obliged to work at his
profession more than four hours in any one day. However,
this day had only just begun, and we had our four hours
coming to us. The threat of being fired on the spot finally
roused Piggy, but we would have been wiser had we left him
in his bed.

We were trebly unfortunate that day because Mark Sergei was out of town, and his place had been taken by a failed
opera singer turned journalist who possessed the amiability
of a trained bear, but lacked the bear's native intelligence.
Yura, who might have saved the situation, refused to accompany us on the reasonable grounds that factories gave
him headaches.

After a twenty-mile drive through rolling forest we descended into a valley dominated by an immense sprawl of
factory buildings whose high chimneys spewed out the continuing pall of smoke and fumes I had noted with distaste
on my first arrival in Irkutsk. I had mentioned this blight
to my conservationist friends in the city, and they assured
me that the management of the aluminum plant had promised to install air filtration equipment "as soon as possible."
My friends probably knew as well as I that such promises
from industrialists, whether of the capitalist or Communist
persuasion, tend to be illusory.

There was a delay in the foyer of the main office building
while a sullen Piggy went off to find the official who was to
receive us. He proved to be a cool young man who was introduced as the Party Secretary for the factory.

He did not seem pleased to see us. For once the warm

welcome we were used to was notably lacking. In fact he looked at us as if he was of two minds whether or not to send for the militiamen — as policemen in the Soviet Union are called. John glanced at Piggy, and then at me with a wild surmise.

"My God!" he muttered. "Do you suppose the little bastard's done it again?"

We were ushered into the Soviet version of a boardroom, equipped with a T-shaped, green, baize-covered table, and there we were treated to a succinct résumé, at the high school level, of how aluminum is extracted from bauxite. My questions about the people who worked at the plant, or indeed about anything, were fielded. We were then perfunctorily dismissed into the care of a lesser luminary who treated us with the suspicious abruptness of a prison warden. There followed a truncated tour of one smelting room, but at such a rapid pace that I recall almost nothing about it except that the magnetism from the electric furnaces deranged my watch forever.

Before we left the office to see the plant, the Party Secretary put a firm hand on John's camera bag.

"You will take *no* pictures!"

Despite our best efforts to persuade him otherwise, he remained adamant. Appeals to the failed opera singer to contact someone in authority in Irkutsk and obtain permission fell on deaf ears. Through it all Sergei stood with his pink little paws shoved into his coat pockets, smiling to himself. Revenge was sweet!

As we drove back to Irkutsk without a single photograph to show for the expedition, John was building to a seething rage. When we reached the bridge across the Angara he ordered the driver to stop so he could shoot some pictures of the fishermen on the river. As he got out of the car, Piggy tapped him on the shoulder.

"Forbidden photographics to bridging is make with Soviet Union!" he said smugly.

Now John is a big man, and for one awful moment I was sure Sergei was going to perform an involuntary high dive into the river. It would have solved nothing. He would simply have floated safely to the shore like a toy balloon.

John evidently realized that violence was not the answer, but he turned on Piggy like a bull elephant at bay. "Listen, you little bugger! One more word out of you and we'll fix you with a new assignment. Intourist guide for polar bears on the New Siberian Islands . . . for ten years!"

This was the sort of language Piggy understood. He deflated so spectacularly one could almost hear the air hissing out of him. For the brief period he remained to burden us he was as innocuous as a tub of lard.

The visit to Shelekhov was a washout for John but it turned out reasonably well for me. That evening I described the incident to a group of friends and they were convulsed. After they had laughed themselves out, Lev Amisov undertook to repair the damage. He introduced me to a charming brunette named Luba Karamova, who had been one of the first shock workers on the Shelekhov project.

Luba explained that when the decision was first taken to build the aluminum plant there were no trained construction workers available in the Irkutsk region.

"It is the greatest problem we have — lack of manpower and [with a smile] womanpower too. Although now there are thirty million people in Siberia, it is not enough for the work we have to do. Hundreds of thousands of new people come every year but we could easily use millions more.

"When they planned Shelekhov they could only get a few

hundred technicians and trained people, so the Party sent out letters to all the Komsomol groups [Young Communist League] asking for volunteers who would help build the plant and the town. That was in 1959. I was eighteen then, and a student at Kharkov in the Ukraine. The idea of going to faraway Siberia was exciting. It would be a new thing, I thought; an adventure, and something worthwhile doing, too.

"There were nine hundred and five of us volunteers who started the work here. Few were older than nineteen and most were even younger than that. There were no professionals amongst us, and hardly any had special skills. We lived in tents pitched in the taiga and the first winter was rather dreadful. Sometimes it was forty-five degrees below zero. We kept the tents warm somehow, and we kept ourselves warm working, because clearing and preparing the construction site went on all winter. We learned skills as we needed them. Boys and girls worked at the same jobs and the girls worked just as hard as the boys.

"In the spring we began getting new crowds of Komsomol youngsters, and things looked up. We built log barracks, and that was the end of the tents. A few people got fed up with the summer heat, the flies, the winter frosts and the hard work, and went home; but others came out to take their places.

"By 1961 the factory buildings were nearly finished and there were several apartment blocks and stores and theaters and things in the new town. That autumn the first electric furnace was started up in the plant.

"The job of the Komsomol youth was really over then, but the new city had become our home without our realizing what was happening. It was the biggest and perhaps the best thing most of us will ever do in our lifetimes. We had done it together and we didn't want to let it go.

"New workers were arriving and we were jealous of the newcomers. After all we had built the place, and so we decided we would stay and run it too.

"So that is how it is, you see? We are Siberians now. We belong to Shelekhov and it to us. No regrets about it either! Although there *is* one thing I sometimes wish . . . now that we have everything for comfort, sometimes I wish I could do it all again. . . . I really envy the kids who are coming out to Siberia to start building their own cities, like Ust Illim, and in the far North. They've got a great job ahead of them. . . ."

Luba did not add much to my knowledge of aluminum production in Siberia although, like most Russians, she could probably have reeled off yards of imposing statistics if I had asked for them; but she did provide further confirmation for the existence of a phenomenon which seems to have escaped the notice of professional observers both inside and outside Russia.

While grudgingly admitting to the speed and scope of developments in Siberia, most Western observers assume that this fantastic efflorescence occurred primarily because Russia is a totalitarian state with absolute power to enforce compliance to its will. Setting aside the new technological capabilities common to both East and West, the experts conclude that the trick has been made possible by the manipulation and exploitation of servile labor. On the other hand the mandarins in the Kremlin seem to believe (or at least to want us to believe) that the Siberian transfiguration is entirely due to the righteousness of Communist doctrine, and its ability to spur its believers to the accomplishments of prodigious feats.

Neither conclusion is correct. The massive surge of human energy and effort which is transforming Siberia is substantially a phenomenon of freedom-seeking. Before the Second World War, and for some years after it, a major attempt *was* made to develop Siberia by the use of forced labor — and the results were minimal. It was *after* the virtual abolition of labor camps that the Sleeping Giant truly came alive.

The real reason for the explosion in Siberia is a compulsive desire on the part of many Russians to break out of the more and more rigidly mechanistic society which is dehumanizing the people of all "advanced" nations. It is an inchoate and instinctive urge to discover and to justify reality of self on the testing grounds of physical — which is to say, natural — adversity. Soviet people, and in particular the young, have become increasingly aware of the abnormal constraint the Brave New World is imposing on essential man. They are trying to find ways and means of again functioning as natural beings. In this way they are no different from young people in other technologically threatened societies — except that they have found an area of action where they can at least temporarily reject the concept that man is destined to be trapped within the confines of a machine-made and machine-dominated world. They have discovered the wilderness of Siberia, and they are flocking to it.

It is a sad paradox that the result of their struggle to avoid being obliterated by the machine should so often end with the addition of yet another gigantic factory or power plant to sustain and further strengthen the juggernaut. This is apparent to some of them. Here are the words of a young dam builder who, at twenty-four, had already spent seven years in Siberia.

"When we finished Bratsk they told us we had built the biggest power dam in the world. It was going to power enough industries to employ four hundred thousand people. We were supposed to be very proud of that, and some of the bright-eyed young Party people *were* proud of it. But you didn't hear much talk about that among my crowd. When the last forms came off and the cleanup was completed, we could have got jobs with big pay in the new industries, but that was not for me. I came here to get away from being the slave of some machine. There's a new power dam to be built up the Kolyma River, away into the arctic . . . a *really* tough proposition, that one. A lot of us are heading there. What'll we do when that one's built?" He took a long drink of beer. "Listen, with the electric maniacs we've got in Moscow, they'll go right on giving us power dams to build until the world blows up!"

Most of the freedom-seekers are not so articulate, and not so clear about their motives. Some, like Luba, are filled with nostalgia for a freedom briefly tasted then lost again — and without a clear understanding of why that nostalgia should still haunt them. But there is a group of young (and not so young) artists, poets, novelists and others who think they understand what is happening to them. They are rather disparagingly referred to by the established literary elite as the "nature kids."

Here are excerpts from a letter I received from one of them while I was still in Siberia.

We were all brought up to believe very much in the New Man who is the ultimate goal of Communism. Creating that Man was our sacred duty. He was to be the perfect human being. But as time passed some of us began to wonder about the kind of New Man we were trying so hard to make. When they sent Gagarin into space he was supposed to be the prototype, yet when we thought hard about it we realized Gagarin didn't matter much. He was along for the ride. It was the machine we sent into space that was the essence of the New Man!

We began then to understand that the New Man was going to be truly a creation of man! It was a short way from there to realizing we were creating a monster, and in so doing we would become monsters ourselves, taking on the character of the machine. . . .

Man is not a machine; he is a living thing subject to natural laws, and if he is going to prosper he must abide by those laws. This is the way we must understand ourselves. This is the "New Man" we must recover.

We talk very much about our Russian soul. Do you know what that soul really is? It is the primitive in us. This presence has been in constant conflict with the illusion we have been creating about ourselves. Out of this conflict came much of the agony that is the greatness of our music, of our best writers. . . .

Some people sneer at us. They think we are advocating a return to the idea of the Noble Savage! They are incapable of understanding! We do not want to "return" to anything; we only want to peel off the layers of paint and varnish, chrome and plastic behind which we human beings have hidden ourselves from ourselves, and so come to the true man buried underneath. . . .

One afternoon I met a group of students at Irkutsk State University. It was a brilliant winter day and the air had a peculiar lucidity as if there was no atmospheric roof at all over this ancient city on its high plateau.

We passed a great new hotel being built by Intourist, all

glass and glitter and slab concrete in the sterile style of new hotels the world over. However, this one had a peculiar anomaly. The Moscow designers had planned a huge canti-levered aluminum and concrete canopy to project out from the façade to the very edge of the roadway.

When construction began on this canopy it was found that an ancient tree stood in the way. In almost any other place in the world the tree would have been summarily con-demned, for it stood in the path of progress. Not, however, in Irkutsk. With some considerable difficulty the canopy was modified and a gaping hole was left in it through which the old tree could continue to thrust its massive trunk toward the pale Siberian sky.

As we walked past it one of my companions gave the tree a friendly pat. "Do you know who saved this tree? Not the planners, I can tell you! It was the workmen themselves. They refused to cut it down and the people of the city stood right behind them."

Perhaps this is only another example of incurable ro-manticism in the Russian psyche, but it may have a deeper meaning. Certainly some of my Irkutsk friends look upon the old tree as a kind of symbol of a new resistance move-ment — a peaceful movement directed at slowing the on-rush of the mechanical colossus, Progress, so that men can at least try to regain meaningful control of it.

I was still thinking about the tree when we climbed the broad stone steps of the main university building — a hand-some white limestone palace built on the banks of the An-gara about 1800, under the direction of an Italian archi-tect. For a century it was the home of the Tsars' governors and the seat of power for an immense part of Siberia. Now it remains as one of Irkutsk's most famous and beloved buildings, and the students who have inherited it are not immune to the effect of its pre-Revolutionary grandeur.

We had dawdled a bit during our walk and were twenty minutes late for the meeting; nevertheless, the earnest young student who met us in the foyer delayed us several minutes longer in order to point out some of the old building's glories. He seemed as passionately proud of them as some of his engineer siblings are of the power dams and factories they have built. I warmed to him immediately although I had not really been looking forward to the visit because it had been rather too carefully arranged for my liking.

Fourteen young men and women, mostly under twenty and all Siberian-born, were gathered in a pleasant commonroom around a long table. They greeted me politely and I took a seat between a beautiful Buryat girl and an equally attractive Evenki damsel.

These were the insatiable elephant children and I was soon swamped by waves of questions. Theirs was a specialized curiosity. They were not interested in Canadian living standards, politics or such trivia . . . they wanted to know about the Canadian North. I offered them generalities, acting on the assumption that they would know as little about my country as I knew about theirs. To my surprise and chagrin they demonstrated that they knew far more about the Canadian North than do most Canadians. They wanted details. What, for instance, was the material used for insulation in permafrost construction at our new arctic "city" of Inuvik? (I did not know). How many Eskimo students were attending universities? (That one made me choke a little, but in the end I forced myself to be honest and answered — two.) How much progress had we made in reindeer husbandry? (The answer to that one had to be —

nil.) and so on and on until I finally appealed to the chairman for mercy. He grinned and rapped for order.

"We have picked enough out of Gospodin Mowat's brains. Now it is his turn to see what he can find in ours."

His deliberate use of the pre-Revolutionary word for "mister" instead of the contemporary *tovarich* — "comrade" — drew a chuckle from several students.

The little Buryat beauty, Tania, came to my defense. She removed a little crimson and gilt badge from the cleft of her dress and pinned it on my lapel.

"Now you are honorary member of Komsomol. *Tovarich* Mowat!" She looked around the table and there was a challenging glitter in her eyes. "In Buryat we do not make jokes at honored guests!"

The conversation that followed was lively and surprisingly frank. I say surprisingly because most of these students were presumably Komsomol members and therefore potential Party members; and the chairman was, in fact, the Party Secretary of a student organization.

Several had spent the previous summer working in the arctic as part of a group of seventy Irkutsk students who went to Chukotka on their own initiative and at their own expense. Many of them worked as volunteers at a collective where the local people — Chukchee and Eskimo — had established an experimental processing plant to prepare and preserve fish, reindeer, and sea-mammal meat for export to Japan.

Most said they intended to go north again the following summer and some had already changed their personal long-range plans as a result of the first trip and were taking special courses to prepare themselves for full-time arctic work.

"Why the North?" I asked. "Much of south and central

Siberia is still almost virgin territory. Surely there's enough to do down here."

"I've read a lot of Jack London," a geology student replied. "I suppose I might have caught what he called 'the lure of the North.' It wasn't really like he described it when I got there, but there was a special kind of feeling you don't get anymore in southern Siberia where I was born. The South is filling up with people from across the Urals. Things are getting too busy down here . . . the cities are too big."

"It's the freedom of the tundra I liked," one of the girls interrupted. "The mosquitos may drink half your blood, but you still feel it's worthwhile to be able to walk in all that open space and see wild reindeer, and wolves, and watch the geese nesting."

"That's *one* kind of freedom — romantic stuff if you ask me," scoffed a male history student. "There's another kind. There aren't many bureaucrats in the North. You can make decisions without having to consult a hundred fine fellows sitting in their offices all the way between Irkutsk and Moscow."

"It's a frontier situation," the chairman interjected. "Then too there's the social responsibility of developing a big part of the world that hasn't really changed much since the last ice age. All Soviet young people are aware of the duty to accept this responsibility. It is reward enough for them."

Nobody backed him up on that one. A trifle impatiently one young man, an Evenki, even took issue with the chairman.

"That isn't right. Things have changed, and were changing before Soviet power [the almost universal phrase used to describe the arrival of communism in the North] came to us. Of course the change was slow, and now it has become fast; but we of the Small Peoples had already learned a great many of the secrets of the North."

"There are other rewards," said an engineering student, with perhaps a touch of cynicism. "The farther north you go, the higher the wages, the better the living conditions in the new towns, the longer holidays you get and the better the retirement benefits."

"In North America," I said, "Most young people head *toward* the big cities — not *away* from them. Isn't there a lot of that here too? Especially among people born in Siberia?"

"There is and there isn't," Tania said cautiously. "We do feel the attraction of the cities, and most of us enjoy visiting them, but although we value them very much, we value the freedom when we are away from them even more. Many of us will go to Moscow or Leningrad or Novosibirsk when we finish here — but not many will remain in the cities."

"The big cities are for old people," said a blond male student. "They are run by the old people and youth has to wait its turn. It isn't the same in the new regions of Siberia, particularly the North. That's young people's country. Do you know that the average age in Bilibino where I worked this summer [Bilibino is a new town in Chukotka] is only twenty-six years of age?"

"There is too much inflexibility in the thinking of some older people. Look at the way some of them go about smashing up the natural world just for a new factory or bigger production!" The speaker was a second-year zoology student. "Look what almost happened to Baikal! Well, it's not the only place. Some of the older people don't seem to remember there are going to be a lot of generations who will have to live in this world after they are gone. I think this is a condition of age — the inability *really* to see the future in terms of unborn people. Oh, of course, they can plan for future *production*, but what good is it if the world is just a wreck when they get finished?"

"That is why *I* will go to the North to live and work," said one of the girls. "Things are still clean there and not yet spoiled. We will have to fight to see the North is kept this way."

"The balance of age in government is not as it should be," pursued the zoologist, who was now firmly in the saddle and riding hard. "Young people see the threats of the future with clear eyes. It is true we need the wisdom of the older people but it should be only a counterweight — it should not outweigh the ideas and opinions of the young. After all, it is our world more than theirs."

This seemed to me to be cutting pretty close to the bone, and I glanced at the chairman to see how he was reacting. To my surprise he did not indicate disapproval; but disapproval there was. It came from one of those who had accompanied me to the meeting. He was a man who had spent four years in a corrective labor camp during the Stalin era. Getting to his feet he took firm command of the meeting, brought the discussion to an end and thanked the students on my behalf.

"Now," he said, "we must go. We have another appointment and we are already late."

When we were on our way back to the hotel I taxed him for his action.

"There was no other appointment. Why did you break up the meeting?"

He shrugged and looked a trifle ashamed. "I am sorry, Farley. Do you have in English the proverb about the man

70

who, once bitten by a dog, stays clear of dogs thereafter?
Well, I have a reflex action, you might say. The way those
young fellows talk — I must admire them — but perhaps I
am too sensitive."

Sensitive he may have been, and doubtless with sufficient
reason, but he must have felt some guilt about his abrupt
action at the meeting. A few nights later he introduced me
to three other students, and over cognac in a small café
they expanded on some of the themes discussed earlier.

"There is a very strong conflict in this country now between old and young," one of them explained. "It is not
yet an angry struggle but it is being waged very stubbornly.
The old Revolutionaries and Party leaders suffered a lot,
and they did good work, but things have changed, and
their thinking has not changed enough. We don't disagree
with them about the principles of communism. We are just
as good Communists as they, but we are of a different kind.
Their main job was to defend the vulnerable young Communist infant and improve the physical conditions of our
people, and they had to accomplish miracles. They did, too;
but that phase is nearly over. Now there has to be a new
way of thinking about the future — the long-term future.
For instance, they talk about a world without war, but few
of them really believe in such a thing. We, on the other
hand, not only believe in it, we know it must be brought
about. They are mostly 'battle'-oriented. They still see the
continuing survival of the socialist countries as a 'battle'
with nature. *We* think the period of 'battle' thinking has
to end."

"We know about the peace movements among students in
your country," a second student interjected. "We think
they feel the same way we do, but they have a difficulty.
They have no clear idea what can be done, or how to do it.

71

They don't trust their system and they want to reject it, yet they have nothing to replace it with. We may not be entirely happy with ours, but that's only because it isn't working well. We believe it can be made to work better and this is what we intend to do. We will make the Communist idea really serve man the way Lenin intended it should."

"Aren't you at all worried about talking this way to a stranger?" I asked.

"Would we talk to you if we were? Don't underestimate us. You won't read about us in *Pravda*, but there are many like us in the Soviet Union. And remember, we are not anti-Revolutionaries. We are perhaps the new Revolutionaries, helping the Revolution to evolve."

"About *Pravda*," I said. "Are you in favor of what we in the West like to call a 'free press'?"

The elder of the three raised his glass. "Here's a toast to free ideas, anyway," he said. We all drank, although I must admit that I first of all cast a glance over my shoulder to see if anyone was listening.

"We *do* have a free press but it doesn't use printing machinery; it uses ideas in conversation. Do you know the saying that, these days, half of Russia is on wheels and the other half on wings? It is really true, you know. Everybody is on the move and our 'free press' goes all over the Soviet Union. It is far more effective than most printed papers. Who reads them anyhow? Have *you* tried to read our papers?"

"The day is coming when the grandfathers will realize they can withdraw with honor. Then there will be a wider spectrum of ideas and opinions in our printed press too. If communism *is* right — and we believe it is — we have nothing to fear from even adverse ideas. They can only serve to strengthen our resolve."

They were an impressive trio of young men but I was not entirely convinced by their, to me, somewhat naïve belief that there is safety in numbers or that a rational dialogue such as they propose will be well tolerated.

For this reason I have not revealed these young men's names and, in fact, have placed the interview out of its actual context.

6
IRKUTSK

During one of my visits to Irkutsk, a catastrophe struck. The city went dry! Not a bottle of vodka, cognac or alcohol was to be had in the stores. The mood of the city changed perceptibly. Men one met on the streets looked as if the Last Trump had sounded. On the other hand women, and in particular married women, seemed exceptionally sunny, almost smug.

The truth is that Siberian men do tend to take a drop over the ordinary limit. As the Siberian saying goes: One hundred versts (roughly a hundred miles) is no distance. A hundred rubles isn't worthwhile money. And a hundred grams of vodka just makes you thirsty.

The cause of the drought seemed obscure. Yura attributed it to the presence of a huge convention of state and collective farmers. "They've drunk everything there is," he said gloomily. Someone else saw the drought as part of a dark plot on the part of Them — the bureaucrats — to force temperance on the city. Mark thought it was just a distribution bottleneck.

"Nobody in their right minds would deliberately try to deprive Siberians of their drink," he said. "The place would explode like an atomic bomb!"

Somehow our party seemed to be exempt from the general deprivation. We usually had a bottle or two, and as a result our popularity soared. One night we had fifteen people in our room, among them Lev Amisov and his nephew, a vivid, cheerful young writer improbably named Valentin Rasputin. During Lev's temporary absence on a search for more liquid refreshment, Valentin told a yarn about his uncle.

Lev is the proud owner of a summer house — not a dacha, but half of a log-built duplex in a little village near Irkutsk. Each July this house becomes the focus for a family reunion. The previous summer the reunion lasted five days — until the last bottle was consumed. The exhausted participants then slunk away to their own homes; but Lev was not yet in a mood to sober up. He had hidden a small barrel of home brew in the earth-walled cellar under his kitchen floor against just such an emergency as this.

Unfortunately his wife was privy to the secret. When Lev came thirstily into the kitchen after bidding the last guests goodbye, he found his wife standing at the kitchen table which she had placed squarely over the trapdoor leading to the cellar. She was busy with an immense pile of ironing. Not a word passed between them, but Lev knew *she* knew what he had in mind and that she was not going to be co-operative. The only advantage he had was that he retained freedom of movement. After an hour or so he went outside and relieved himself, then came back and sat on the kitchen settee with a ponderous tome of poetry on his knee, grimly prepared to wait until bladder pressure forced his wife to abandon her guard post.

"Ah," said Valentin, "but as usual he had misjudged my aunt! She had relieved herself before taking up sentry duty!"

They waited, silent, apparently engrossed in their own pursuits; the hours passed and Lev began to get really desperate. Finally he could stand it no longer. Throwing down the book he stamped out of the house.

As he paced miserably up and down amongst the birch trees, inspiration suddenly came to him. He snatched a spade out of his garden, raced to his neighbor's door and banged on it furiously. When the neighbor's wife answered he explained with an urgency which was not at all assumed that a large and evil-looking snake had just crawled under the duplex and would undoubtedly finish up in somebody's cellar. Would she let him into *her* cellar so he could search for and destroy the beast?

Would she? She practically thrust him down through the hole and slammed the trapdoor after him.

Lev went to work. It took him only a few minutes to break through from one cellar to the other. Settling himself in the cool darkness, he pulled the bung out of the barrel.

The first inkling his wife had that she was not alone in the house was a terrifying crash under her feet as Lev upset a shelf of pickle jars. The crash was followed by a full-throated roar of fury as he stumbled backward and fell into the cabbage bin. The sound was sufficiently muffled so she did not identify its origin, and she ran screaming out of the house.

In the garden she met the neighbor's wife, wringing her hands and equally terrified.

"What happened?" the neighbor's wife cried anxiously. "Did that big snake get into *your* cellar?"

At this moment Lev emerged from his own kitchen door, covered with mud, slathered with pickled mushrooms, and happily bellowing a patriotic song.

"Ulcers on your soul!" his wife shrieked, using a favorite Siberian epithet. "It's a snake all right! Wait till I get my broom!"

"Which is why," said Valentin winking broadly, "if you want to make my uncle turn pale . . . you only have to hiss!"

Lev returned empty-handed and so, as always in moments of dire emergency, we turned to Kola. Kola was a sight to behold. Every evening he would change out of his natty street clothes into a skin-fitting siren suit of chamoislike material in a gentle shade of fawn that zippered tightly at all orifices. Clad in this remarkable outfit, he would pad energetically around the hotel corridors looking like a dapper Martian. Whatever he may have looked like, his efficiency was unimpaired. The accomplishment of the impossible was routine for him, and in due course he rejoined us carrying three bottles of champagne and two of cognac.

He told us that a party of Germans had just arrived in the hotel. "Timber experts and pulpwood specialists from the Democratic Republic. *Very* big shots. I'm afraid these bottles may have been intended for their reception. . . ."

"Thank God the partisan movement remains alive! It's the Order of the Red Star for you, Kola!" Lev cried.

We talked about Germans and Germany for a while and I was surprised by the intensity of feeling which still remained a quarter of a century after the end of the Second World War. There was no overt hatred, but there was an adamantine determination that never again would Germany be allowed to become a threat to Russia.

"While the Soviet Union exists, Germany will remain divided," one elderly man said flatly. "Unless, of course, West Germany takes the socialist course, which is about as likely as the Angara River reversing herself."

"Why worry?" I asked. "Between us we beat them the last time, didn't we?"

"You Westerners delude yourselves that the Germanic will for conquest has been destroyed. That is your business, although if you look at the historic record it is hard to understand how you could be so innocent. As for us, we will never trust the old Germany to behave in a civilized manner, and the old Germany of the sword and the flame is still alive. The United States knows this. That is why they have helped West Germany become an armored camp sitting on the frontier of the socialist lands. How do you suppose Americans would feel if they had an enemy like that on *their* doorstep — in Mexico perhaps?"

"But surely," I said, "there is a time to forgive the sins of the past. Even some Jews have forgiven Germany. Look at Israel."

A young man who had not said much until then drained his glass and angrily replied. "*I* am a Jew. I have not forgiven Germany. The Israelis may appear to have done so but only so they can make use of German money and German weapons against the Arabs. Even if the Jew within me could forgive, the Russian in me never could. Do you know the fascists killed more than fifteen million Soviet people? Do you think all the black smoke from the crematoria was only from Jewish bodies? Maybe we will forgive them some day . . . but trust them? Never!"

"It is true," said the elderly man. "Here in this room I

am sure you will not find one person who did not lose a close relative to the fascists. You will hardly find a family in all the Soviet Union who did not suffer death or destruction at their hands. I can tell you the fascists destroyed over one thousand of our towns and cities — shelled, bombed, or just burned them to the ground. It will mean little to you. It means much to *our* people. In 1940 we were just beginning to master our economic problems, and the destruction brought by the German invasion set everything back a full ten years. For you it was different. The war *saved* you from your economic problems. North America became rich out of the war. You kiss and forgive, and take them to your bosom, but it is out of self-interest you have forgiven them!"

At this point Mark intervened to change the subject and let emotions cool.

"Well, anyway, things aren't so bad now. At least we have the Germans to thank that this isn't a dry evening. Fill up and I'll make a toast to Peace and Women — it's rare enough those two go together!"

Early one brilliant November afternoon Mark Sergei drove us to the airport to catch our flight to Yakutsk. However, the local weather proved delusive. Irkutsk was placidly sitting under its usual clear skylight (it has more hours of sunshine than any other city in the USSR) while western and northern Siberia were suffering under howling blizzards. Our flight was "indefinitely delayed" so Mark led us up a broad stairway to the Intourist lounge.

Because Irkutsk is the aerial crossroads of Siberia (the terminus or transfer point for flights from Mongolia, China, the Pacific coast, European Russia and the far North), Intourist has done itself proud in the facilities provided at the airport. These include a private bar, a luxurious lounge and an array of magazines, books and newspapers in a score of languages. Foreign tourists in transit under Intourist's omnipotent wing make use of these facilities; but so, happily, do a good many Russians who, through some magical process which I never did succeed in fathoming, somehow achieve special "tourist" status.

The lounge was almost empty when our party, which now included Nadia, who had elected to fly home to Yakutsk with us, arrived. Flights continued to come in from the south and east and since none was able to depart, more and more odd bods drifted into the lounge. They included two Czechoslovak journalists returning from North Vietnam, a Rumanian psychiatrist going home after a month's holiday trip through China, a young Russian engineer on leave from a dam-building project in Outer Mongolia, a bevy of Japanese businessmen bound for Moscow, and some exuberant army officers.

The bar was opened and in no time at all a general party was under way. Only the Japanese behaved as if they were in a North American airport and kept soberly to themselves. That was their loss. The rest of us were soon dancing to the record player or drinking and talking with one another as if we had been friends for years.

Claire was being ardently pursued by the Rumanian doctor. I attempted to corner Nadia, but she was as mercurial as a nymph and kept bouncing away to share a joke with someone or to snatch a gulp out of Yura's glass as that worthy dozed in an easy chair. I joined Kola, who was talking to the Czechs at the bar. The journalists had spent a month touring northern Vietnam and they confirmed that the country had been heavily damaged by the bombings and civilian casualties had been very high. What impressed them most was the steadfast quality of Vietnamese morale.

"After fighting for their independence for more than twenty-six years," one of them told us, "it has become a way of life. You can't reason with them about it. You can't make them see that the United States might some day, out of sheer frustration, try to wipe them off the face of the earth. They say they don't care. They say they will not give up even if they are atom bombed — and they are actually preparing for this to happen."

In distillation, the many conversations I had with Russians about Vietnam indicated a curious state of schizophrenia. On the one hand, there was an awe-struck admiration at the way the Vietnamese were holding the American military colossus at bay, coupled with a tremendous feeling of solidarity for a fellow socialist state in agony. On the other hand almost everyone I met wanted an end to the war — an immediate end, even if this meant that the Vietnamese would have to back down a little. There was a strong undercurrent of fear that this local war might spread and get out of hand, eventually triggering the Big One (a fear which appears to find justification in events in southwest Asia during the spring of 1970). Most Russians found it impossible to understand how the United States dared run such risks. They seemed almost more baffled by the American attitude than angered by it.

There are hawks in the USSR, of course, but most of the Russians I met, from all walks of life, were possessed of a deep-rooted and violent aversion to the very idea of war. The reasons are obvious. They know what war is all about. Furthermore, they realize that they have nothing to gain and everything to lose if their country should become involved in war again. The difference between ordinary Russians and ourselves seems to be that they live with this aversion uppermost in their minds, whereas we have mastered the art of putting it quietly away in the back of ours. I had expected the Russians to be a bellicose people — for this is the way they are usually portrayed to us — and it was a shock to realize that they are far more intensely concerned with preserving peace than we are.

I do not think their almost fanatical devotion to the cause of peace is something which has been impressed upon them by their leaders. If anything, the process probably works the other way. The hawkish urges of certain Soviet leaders have undoubtedly been dampened by an awareness that the masses are stubbornly opposed to war.

It can hardly be accidental that during the twenty-five years which have elapsed since the end of the Second World War, the USSR has not, despite several tempting opportunities, gone to war with anyone. I exclude such actions as the repression of the Hungarian and Czechoslovak revolts, since these can be almost exactly equated with similar "police" actions taken by the United States against Cuba or the Dominican Republic.

This is a rather remarkable record when compared with that of the Western powers. There has hardly been a year since 1945 when one or other of these powers (and sometimes several of them together) has not been directly engaged in warfare. The record of the United States in this regard is particularly depressing.

To suggest, as some do, that the USSR has been restrained from military excursions by the retaliatory threat posed by the United States is to embrace a dangerous illusion. If there is one thing Russians are *quite* confident about, it is their ability to hold their own if they are ever forced to fight again. The simple truth seems to be — in the words of a popular Russian song — "The Russian people don't want war!"

They are so fervently anxious to avoid it that propaganda designed to make them tolerate the idea would probably have little effect unless, of course, the Soviet Union itself was threatened with invasion.

This brings up another point. Our belief (it is almost a tenet of faith) that the Russians are mindlessly manipulated by their propaganda agencies like a bunch of automata is one of our more glaring misconceptions. In my experience most Russians are so immunized to the propaganda downpour that it runs off them like water off a duck. Furthermore, most Russian internal propaganda is so unpalatable, and is prepared by such unimaginative dullards, that nobody but a born fool would pay much attention to it. There are undoubtedly born fools in Russia but most Russians do not fall into this category. The real nature of the situation is summed up in the words of a Soviet correspondent who spent five years in the United States and with whom I once had a discussion about the relative effectiveness of propaganda in our mutual countries.

"I have the greatest admiration for your propaganda," he told me. "Propaganda in the West is carried on by experts who have had the best training in the world — in the field of advertising — and have mastered the techniques with exceptional proficiency. On the other hand," he added somewhat wryly, "we never had such a training ground because we had very little to advertise. Consequently, our propagandists are mostly old-fashioned and inept, and they try to make up by sheer volume of words for what they lack in ability. Yours are subtle and pervasive, ours are crude and obvious.

"This is one thing. Another is that we Russians are not, by nature, a gullible people. We are, and always have been, suspicious of what we cannot see for ourselves. You can call it the peasant mentality if you like. At any rate it is quite a different attitude from the rather charming naïveté which makes many North Americans incapable of doubting or assessing what they are told by their leaders and their communications media.

"I think the fundamental difference between our two worlds, with regard to propaganda, is quite simple. You tend to believe yours . . . and we tend to disbelieve ours."

The conversation at the bar was interrupted when a somewhat ruffled Claire elbowed her way into the throng and caught my arm.

"Listen!" she said urgently. "That Rumanian Romeo tried to inveigle me down the hall into an empty office so he could psychoanalyze me!"

I glanced over my shoulder and sure enough the Rumanians was bearing down on us, a beatific smile on his face and a determined gleam in his eye. Happily, at this juncture someone suggested we all adjourn to the restaurant.

Aeroflot waited until dinner was on the table before it jumped us. The loudspeaker boomed a call for the flight to Yakutsk. I leapt nervously to my feet, ready to run like hell, but nobody else so much as budged.

"Take it easy," Mark admonished me. "They won't go without you. Let *them* wait for a change."

Sure, I thought to myself, and the stars will stand still in the sky until we're ready. But the food was good and the cognac in copious supply, so I resigned myself to spending another day or two in Irkutsk.

When we were quite finished we leisurely made our way to the boarding gate. One of the little tractor trains was waiting and we climbed aboard. Suddenly I realized that the *whole* of the dinner group — more than a dozen people —

were on the train with us, and yet I knew most of them were heading for Moscow and points west, while we were going into the northeast.

"What goes on?" I asked Kola. "Don't they know this is the Yakutsk flight?"

"Of course they do. They're just coming along to see us off."

The lot of them boarded the plane, making light of the buxom stewardess's half-hearted attempts to head them off, saw us to our seats, had a parting drink with us and kissed us soundly, while the pilot gunned the motors just a trifle impatiently.

Polar Aviation's big, pot-bellied Antonov-10 (Soviet pilots call it the Pregnant Cow) lumbered off into the black night, and for the first time since leaving Canada I was aware of a real sense of dislocation. My prior knowledge of Siberia's southern tier had been sketchy enough, but at least I had known something about that region. My knowledge of what now lay ahead of us was effectively nonexistent. Although Yura and Kola had provided me with some basic facts, these offered only the most skeletal picture.

We were bound for the city of Yakutsk on the banks of the Lena River, 1,200 miles northeast of Irkutsk, at the same latitude as Anchorage, Alaska. I knew that Yakutsk was the capital of something called the Yakut Autonomous Soviet Socialist Republic, which embraced an arctic and subarctic area of one million two hundred thousand square miles, or more than a third the area of the United States. I knew, too, that Yakutia held the distinction of being the coldest inhabited region on earth and included within its boundaries much of the Central Siberian Plateau and a large slice of the Siberian Highlands. I knew it fronted on the Arctic Ocean with a shoreline more than 2,000 miles in length; that it almost reached the Pacific on the east; and that its southernmost point was just 160 miles north of the Chinese border. These were facts which would have been of value to a geographer but which left me helpless to envisage the place.

On one occasion when I asked Yura to describe it in more meaningful terms, he replied with some impatience, "How I do that? Is big forest; big mountains; big river; big tundra . . . everything very big. How you describe north part of Canada? Is like north part of Canada, except is different!"

My attempts to inform myself about the people of Yakutia had not been quite so unrewarding, although they fell short of preparing me for the reality. In Leningrad I had spent an afternoon at the Ethnographic Institute indulging my amateur interest in human prehistory. My mentor was Chumer Taksami, an archaeologist whose specialty was the ancient people of Siberia.

The origins of Siberia's natives are to be sought in millenia out of time when a mysterious human flood began to rise in the west-central Asiatic plains and to flow northeastward into the Siberian wilderness. At least forty thousand years ago this tide overflowed the Chukotka Peninsula and spilled across what is now Bering Strait into the waiting void beyond. The Western continents absorbed this influx until both South and North America became additional domains of ancient man. New tides continued to flow north and east out of the deserts, over taiga and frozen mountains until they reached the bitter fringe of tundra along the arctic coast. It was not until the beginning of the sixteenth century that the age-old migratory spasms ceased.

At the time the Cossack, Yermak, broke through the Ural wall, remnants of neolithic peoples of ponderous antiquity still lingered in Siberia, sharing its immensity with many later races. Chumer, who is himself a native Siberian — a Nanai — told me something of the fate of these many peoples as he led me past case after case of their artifacts.

"These relics are now all that remain of scores of tribes and nations who were obliterated by the European conquest of Siberia, even as so many of your native American tribes were obliterated during the same period and by the same cause.

"When the Cossacks first came among us there were about one hundred discrete peoples living in Siberia. Now there are twenty-nine; and some, like the Tophe and Yukagir, number no more than three or four hundred individuals. The vanished races managed to exist with one another in a state of 'barbarism' for thousands of years; but they could not endure the benefits of European civilization."

Among the tribes who managed to survive were the Yakut. A Turkic-speaking people of Mongolian physical type, they originated in the common heartland east of the Caspian Sea and drifted east and north through innumerable generations to reach the lands which were to become their home and which they settled more than a thousand years ago.

From being nomadic horsemen they transformed themselves into a sedentary people who made the most of their harsh new world. They developed an incredibly hardy breed of little horses which they raised as much for meat as for transport. They learned reindeer-breeding from those who had preceded them into the white wilderness. When, in 1620, the first boatloads of Cossacks drifted down the Vilyui River from the west and reached the Lena — the great central artery and sacred river of Yakutia — the Yakut, it is estimated, numbered more than half a million people occupying most of east-central Siberia. They did not occupy it exclusively but shared it amicably with many smaller nations.

By 1918, many of the smaller nations had vanished and the entire population of the Yakut region, including *all* the surviving natives *and* the European interlopers, was down to a quarter of a million.

"The decline of the native peoples of Siberia seemed to be irreversible," Chumer told me. "Then came the Revolution . . . but you will see for yourself what happened after that. It is modern history, and you and I are talking now about the ancient time."

As the Pregnant Cow plodded on above a world I did not know, I found myself creating mental images of what might meet my eyes when daylight brought an end to this flight. Would the Yakut, Evenki, Yukagir and Chukchee be the Asian version of the Crees, Chipeweyans, Hares and Eskimos of Canada — whose blood relatives they were? Like the North American natives, would these people I had yet to meet be debilitated, disoriented islands of human flotsam, nearly devoid of hope and of ambition, surviving on charity — when they survived at all?

Would the town of Yakutsk, and other towns I might visit, be repetitions of Churchill, Yellowknife, Inuvik, Frobisher Bay . . . thinly disguised colonial outposts whose sole *raison d'être* was to assist in the exploitation of the Northern territories for the enrichmment of distant Southerners?

Soviet propaganda which I had read insisted this would not be the case, and in the short time I had spent in the USSR I had heard a great deal of talk about "equal rights" and "special treatment" for the Small Peoples of Siberia. I had already met many representatives of the Small Peoples whose apparent success seemed to give substance to the claim that the natives were being treated with astonishing consideration. However, I had met these examples in Leningrad, Moscow, Irkutsk . . . I had not seen the Small Peoples in their own homes. Even in Canadian cities it is possible to find occasional Indians and Eskimo who have successfully transcended our society and who can be pointed to as evidence of our just and benevolent concern for native minorities.

The conflict between what I had been told about the treatment of minorities in the Soviet North and what I knew to be the truth about the treatment of such groups in the Canadian North and in Alaska was so great I could not begin to resolve it. There was no use guessing. Tomorrow I would begin to know the truth.

7

YAKUTSK

At 6 A.M. the Pregnant Cow bumped down at Yakutsk airport. The door opened and a blast of arctic air blew through the plane. The passengers hung back as if reluctant to face the frigid blackness; but the urgent beckoning of our stewardess brought Claire and me to the door.

"You have a welcoming committee!" Kola explained.

Waiting at the foot of the ramp was a half-circle of broad-faced, dark-complexioned men who looked vaguely like a group of Eskimo gathered to greet a plane at some far northern settlement in Canada — except that, despite the below-zero weather, they were impeccably dressed in European fashion.

"Who are they?" I asked a trifle nervously.

"Yakut, is who." Yura replied. "Famous Yakut writers and poets come to say hello. Very good fellows. You will see."

As we reached the bottom of the stairs Yura was pounced upon and soundly kissed. Claire and I had our arms vigorously pumped. A particularly dapper young man whose wide grin showed a gorgeous display of gold-capped teeth introduced himself.

"Efrimov Moisie Dmitrievich. Excuse please, my such bad English. Am secretary Writers Union of Yakut Republic. You are honored sister-men from north country. We give much welcome!"

The genders may have been a bit mixed, but the emotion was sincere. Moisie hustled us into a cavernous airport whose waiting room was filled with sleeping passengers. But this was not good enough for "honored sister-men." While waiting for our luggage to be claimed by Kola we were taken upstairs to a room normally reserved for the use of air crews of Polar Aviation (the writ of Intourist with its luxury lounges does not extend as far as Yakutsk).

The room was crowded with pilots, army officers and a few civilians, most of them pounding their ears. At the far end of the room stood a Chinese rose tree, some ten feet tall, looking wildly out of place. Northern Siberians grow potted trees the way we grow geraniums or African violets. They are to be found in almost every office and in many homes.

Despite having had to wait for us for several hours, our hosts seemed not the least fatigued. Champagne corks began to pop and we were swept into a torrent of talk about books and writing, travel and travelers. So much enthusiasm at such an ungodly hour was more than I could match, and in any case I was having trouble adjusting to these people. The contrast between the trim, dark business suits, white shirts and subdued ties worn by these ebullient little men, and their knee-length, beautifully embroidered reindeer-skin boots did not help the adjustment process. Nadia disappeared for a few minutes, and when she returned her stylish high-heeled shoes had been replaced by Yakut boots. Nadia was home . . . Claire and I felt we were a long way therefrom.

A big, burly Russian was snoozing in an armchair under the rose tree, his astrakhan hat tilted forward over a bulbous nose. The warmth of our reception stirred him to surly wakefulness. He raised his heavy head, glared at us with bloodshot eyes, and in a bull's voice demanded silence. He was obviously a Very Important Person.

For a moment I felt a return to normalcy. The natives had been put firmly in their place. But no! Far from relapsing into respectful silence, our new friends ignored the interruption. Yura, however, fixed the offending Russian with a hostile stare and in a loud voice explained:

"Huh! Big Chief in Moscow, maybe. Here is just another white man with loud voice. This is Yakut Republic. This is Yakut airport! Have a drink champagnsky!"

Our luggage having been retrieved, we were driven to the Lena Hotel, a five-story concrete structure which provided us with luxurious accommodation, including a bedroom, sitting room, and bathroom in which there was not only a workable flush toilet but sometimes running water too. Subconsciously I had been expecting to find myself installed in a log hut — and the luxuries of the Lena were a bit too much to take in all at one go.

It was Claire who restored my sense of reality with the discovery that, in Yakutsk, the always inadequate toilet paper which is the mortal lot in the Soviet Union, was simply nonexistent. When I delicately drew Yura's attention to this, he grinned.

"Not using toilet paper in real North. Is much better using reindeer moss."

This was not much help, but we soon discovered the local

drill. Each morning one made a rapid trip to a magazine kiosk and purchased a newspaper. Some people preferred *Pravda*; others were partial to *Izvestia*; but the *real* cognoscenti bought the *Red Star*.

While I am on the subject of minor inconveniences, I should mention the telephone. Claire and I went to bed soon after reaching the hotel, hoping to sleep until noon. At 8 a.m. we were awakened by the demoniac shrilling of a telephone bell. For some terrible moments I could not even locate the thing. I finally tracked it down in the depths of a big cupboard. It spouted an impassioned spate in an unknown language and refused to believe I could not understand a word it was saying. I hung up and crawled back into bed. The shrilling began again. This time the machine was vibrant with outrage at my obtuseness. I hung up. Instantly the bell rang. I took that telephone, throttled it with my scarf, muffled it in the depths of my heavy parka, wadded it into the cupboard and shut the door.

The difficulty is that, because of a mysterious shortage of paper in the Soviet Union, telephone directories are almost, if not quite, nonexistent. This means you must *know* the number you want to call or else engage in the trial-and-error method of tracking down your quarry. As one who distrusts telephones and hates the way they have come to dominate our lives, I have a sneaking regard for the Soviet method of outwitting them. On the other hand, one must occasionally get a little sleep. This cannot be achieved by taking the receiver off the hook, since this is construed as a distress signal and will bring a posse of worried hotel officials, probably accompanied by a doctor, pounding on your door.

We woke at noon and I had my first daylight glimpse of Yakutsk — out the hotel window. I looked down upon a spacious, paved square around which wheeled a line of buses, taxis and trucks. Backing the square was a series of masonry buildings. Most of them were five stories high but the one directly opposite was in the process of having an additional three floors added to it. This building would have been able to hold its own, for size, in Moscow, but here in the heart of Siberia it seemed positively gigantic.

I whistled tunelessly — a sure sign of inner perturbation. Claire, who was still abed, wanted to know what was bothering me.

"Nothing much. I'm just confused. Where in hell are the picturesque native huts of Yakutsk? And how in the name of all that's holy do these people get away with running up eight-story masonry buildings on permafrost?"

"Why shouldn't they get away with it?" Claire asked.

"Because, oh wisest of women, it just isn't possible! It's something you won't really understand, but permafrost means a permanently frozen soil which may be hundreds of feet in depth. It never thaws. That is, it doesn't until you build a house on it, whereupon the warmth seeping through the floor thaws the ground under the house, gradually turning it into a bog, into which the house slowly sinks. Permafrost is the bane of arctic engineers and construction people. It drives them mad. Our solution has been to build very little one- or two-story structures of wood or aluminum, flexibly mounted above the ground surface on blocks or on steel posts. This crowd must be clean out of its collective mind! These monstrous masses of concrete all over the place have simply *got* to founder and fall apart. Wonder if they're insured?"

Claire had joined me at the window. "Sometimes you can't see what's right in front of your nose, Farley. Look at the building across the street. There's your answer. As the buildings sink, they just add new stories on the top."

A brisk knock on the door announced Kola's arrival. It was typical of his thoughtfulness and attention to detail that he had brought us a copy of the *Red Star*. He announced that we were to have lunch with some of our newly met Yakut friends.

Our host was Basil Protodiakonov, a small, shy man with a winning smile and a face cast in the same mold as an Eskimo. He was the author of three novels and two books of poetry. He was also, he told us modestly, a professor of history at the Yakut State University.

Over a meal of black bread, caviar, pickled fish, *schi* soup and reindeer *shashlik* (equivalent to shish kebab), Basil talked about his city and his country.

For almost three centuries after its founding in 1640 as a Cossack fort, the settlement of Yakutsk changed very little. Essentially a trading post and later an outfitting center for placer gold seekers, it eventually came to be a minor administrative town of the Russian Empire. During the eighteenth and nineteenth centuries it acquired a bad reputation as a place-of-no-return for those political prisoners whom the Tsars felt were particularly dangerous; but for the most part it remained an almost unknown village, infinitely remote from the civilized world. It was inhabited by fur traders, a few unlucky government officials, a ragtag garrison of Tsarist troops, political prisoners, and an amorphous fringe of natives who were considered to be one small cut above the level of outright savages.

In 1917, Yakutsk had a population of seven thousand people and was the only "large" town in the immensity of north central and eastern Siberia — a region half the size of the United States. Essentially it was not very different from similar, if smaller, frontier settlements in the Ca-

nadian North and in Alaska, for it epitomized the general
state of inertia and neglect which characterized such places
and which still characterizes many of them to this day.

The blight of internal colonialism began to disappear
from Yakutia in 1919 when the Yakut people, in revolt
against the Russian Empire, took back almost the whole of
the original region they had owned before the coming of
the white men. They were encouraged by Lenin and other
Soviet leaders to form their own republic.

"This was not so easy to do," Basil explained. "At the
time of the Revolution our people, and the Evenki and others who lived with us, were not in good condition. Whole
communities in the taiga died every year from starvation,
from typhus, from tuberculosis and smallpox. A woman who
could raise one child out of every five she bore was very
rare. There were no schools for the children if they did survive. We had no written language of our own, and so we
were completely illiterate because we had almost no opportunity to study Russian. Many, many of our people had
become so hopeless it was nearly impossible to rouse them
even to try to help themselves.

"It was lucky all did not feel so hopeless; and the reason
they did not was because of something the Russian Imperial
Government did for us by accident. From the middle of the
eighteenth century they had the habit of sending condemned
political prisoners to live out their years and die in the
taiga of our land. These men were not criminals. Many
were aristocrats who had made the mistake of asking for
liberal reforms. They lived in our village with us and taught
some of us to believe in a future, to believe in ourselves, to
be willing to work for a better world even if it could not
come in our time.

"In 1914 we already had a revolutionary group called

the Lighthouse Keepers. It was their task to keep the light of hope alive. When the Revolution began in Russia, we too revolted. We took Yakutsk city and drove out the Tsar's men. Maxim Amasov, a young man of our people, was our leader. He was helped by Platon Oiyumski who became the first Yakut writer.

"We had to fight hard to stay free. First we were invaded by Admiral Kolchak's White troops, and we threw them out. Then Pepeleyov, a White general armed by the Japanese and the Americans, invaded our land, but we beat him too. There were raids into Yakutia from Mongolia until 1924, but all were repulsed. It is not easy to take freedom away from a people who have just escaped three hundred years of oppression."

Moscow recognized the autonomy of the country in April 1922, when the Yakut Autonomous Soviet Socialist Republic was formally constituted. Since that time the Yakut have governed themselves, although subjected to varying degrees of pressure and control from Moscow. When, on a later occasion, I questioned the degree of "autonomy" enjoyed by Yakutia, a young painter of the new generation gave this answer.

"Freedom is always relative. What we native Siberian peoples have now is the freedom to live — after having been condemned to death. We may grumble about 'ukases' from Moscow, but I tell you truly that if anyone tries to destroy the thing which gave us our new life, the Communist idea, there is not a man or woman in Yakutia who will not fight like a taiga devil to defend it."

Hitler discovered the truth of this declaration. Yakut soldiers were among the toughest and most effective troops in the Soviet army. They were used as shock troops and suffered astronomical losses in proportion to the size of their nation. One out of every five Yakut men of military age, and a good many women with them, died in battle against the Germans.

Basil Protodiakonov was less afflicted than most people in the Soviet Union by the compulsive desire to pour masses of statistics into the ears of visitors, but he was not totally guiltless.

"To tell you something about the progress we have made since the Revolution, there is the fact that we have almost tripled our numbers. There are now three hundred thousand Yakut of pure blood, not to mention the people of mixed Russian and Yakut blood. Our land now has a population of over seven hundred thousand, including people from almost every state in the Soviet Union; and our city of Yakutsk has one hundred ten thousand people. We welcome all newcomers and do not fear they will take our land away from us for we are so strong within ourselves.

"Knowledge has made us strong, and has given us back our pride. Since 1924 we have had our own written language. Our children spend their first years at school studying in their native tongue and using textbooks written by our own Yakut educators. In 1917, Yakut people were almost totally illiterate and now there is no illiteracy. We have eight hundred grade schools, seven hundred eighty kindergartens, eighteen high-level technical schools, and our own State University. Nearly fifty thousand Yakut now have higher-education degrees of university level. We have our own State theater producing Yakut drama, opera and ballet, and our own symphony orchestra. There are twenty-eight newspapers in the Yakut language. We have our own television and radio system; eight museums; more than six hundred libraries. We have . . ."

I felt a yawn beginning — not because of lack of interest but due to a simple reflex action which overcomes me whenever I am exposed to statistics. I tried unsuccessfully to stifle it. Basil glanced at me, paused for an instant, and went right on: ". . . now talked long enough about ourselves. So let us have one more toast. Dear friends! Please carry back with you the loving wishes of the Yakut people for the Small Nations of your North. Let us drink to their success and happy future!"

I managed to drink that toast, but any North American Indian or Eskimo will know why I very nearly choked upon it.

After lunch we were driven down the broad main street of Yakutsk to a not-quite-completed block of flats housing the Writers and Artists Unions. The main street was a study in instant change. Massive new masonry buildings alternated with ancient log structures, which had settled so deeply into the melting permafrost that the lower windows of some were actually below street level. Yakutsk is treeless but the skyline gained something in variety from the presence of scores of construction cranes all busily at work, despite the fact that on this November afternoon the temperature was fifteen degrees below zero. These cranes are the ubiquitous hallmark of modern Russia. We had grown used to their gaunt dominance over Moscow and other major cities; but it was a surprise to find them just as abundant here in the heart of Siberia.

Basil escorted us into a room where twenty or thirty writers, painters and journalists were waiting to welcome us. With one exception they were all natives — mostly Yakut but including several Evenki and a shy young Yukagir lad who looked to be about eighteen. The exception was a gentle-faced Russian who had lost a leg during the siege of Leningrad.

We all seated ourselves around the inevitable green, baize-covered table. In the Soviet Union indoor life revolves around tables. If it is not a conference table, it is a dining-room table or a sitting-room table. The North American kind of party where people mill aimlessly about a room engaging in competitive and transient conversations is virtually unknown in the USSR, where it is axiomatic that, if you wish to entertain friends, you do so sitting at a table. The system has its advantages. You never have to balance your glass and a cigarette in one hand while you jiggle a plate full of dainties in the other. You never need to wait for your host to carry your glass out to the kitchen to renew its contents — a bottle is always within reach, and if *you* neglect to keep your own glass topped up, your neighbor will do it for you.

There is nothing static about these tabletop soirees. It is permissible to play musical chairs if you happen to catch a stimulating glance from the lady across the way; but guests are not allowed to escape into exclusive little conversational compartments for long. The *tamadar* sees to that!

Tamadar means "Master of the Table," and the word is of Georgian origin. If the tamadar notes a tendency toward breakaway conversations, or a lull in the gaiety, he immediately calls on someone to propose a toast. Russian toasts are not mere sterile formalities; they are vital ingredients in social intercourse — ornate, involved, witty, and usually of considerable length.

Theoretically there are two kinds of toasts. If it is not a serious one, the proposer may elect to sip at his raised glass, and the others may follow suit. However, if it is a serious one, the proposer drains his glass, and so do the guests. Serious toasts include those to women, peace, friendship, absent friends, love, present guests, motherland, national heroes, and practically everything else you can name. I never actually encountered an unserious toast.

All glasses must be filled to the brim when a toast is proposed — not with wine (wine toasts are considered effete) but with cognac, vodka, or, if you are in the far North, pure grain alcohol. A good tamadar will accept no excuses for a guest's failure to drink up, unless the guest has already slumped out of his chair and disappeared beneath the table. This seldom happens to Russians but, I am ashamed to relate, it happens quite frequently to visitors from other lands, at least during the period of their initiation.

Between toasts one drinks champagne or any of the several excellent Georgian wines. These serve, instead of water, as chasers for the most robust liquors. By the exercise of superlative cunning it is sometimes possible to acquire a bottle of mineral water which, since it is colorless, can be surreptitiously substituted for vodka, thus enabling a neophyte like myself to remain compos mentis.

Our initial gathering at the Writers Union was not a full-fledged party. We were too full of curiosity about one another to consume more than a token number of bottles. Again I was amazed at the degree of interest in things Canadian and at how well informed these people were about North America. Most of them had read translations of such diverse writers as Hemingway, Dos Passos, Jack London, Steinbeck, Stephen Leacock and (I blush to include myself in such company) even Mowat.

Yura introduced me to the crippled Russian, who was a writer of nature books.

"You see?" Yura said wickedly, "no race prejudicial in Yakutia! Even they let white men in Writers Union!"

This sally was greeted with laughter, but it made me feel uncomfortable, perhaps because I could not imagine a situation even remotely comparable existing in North America.

Claire asked a question about the publication of Yakut children's books in which she, as an illustrator, was particularly interested. This led to a general discussion of local publishing and to another deluge of statistics.

The Yakut Writers Union has fifty-two full members (those who have proved their professional competence through their published work) and thirty-four associate members. The Union publishes a monthly literary magazine, *Polar Star,* with a press run of five thousand copies in Russian and twenty-five thousand in the Yakut language. The Yakut State Publishing House publishes an average of one hundred and sixty titles a year for a total run of about one million copies — all in Yakut. The majority of these books are translations from Russian and other foreign languages, but from thirty to fifty titles a year are original works by Yakut authors. It is a two-way street. Altogether about eighty books (poetry, fiction, nonfiction and plays) by Yakut writers have been translated into Russian. Figures for works in the Evenki language are comparable though quantitatively much smaller. Even the four-hundred-strong remnant of the Yukagir people can point to several hundred titles printed in their own tongue.

These figures have to be counted impressive if they are to be credited at all. Although I had no opportunity to examine the records of the publishing concerns, I did visit most of the ten well-stocked bookstores in Yakutsk, and their contents, and the crowds of Yakut of all ages waiting to buy books, gave me no reason to doubt what I had been told.

On my first meeting with the native authors there was little discussion of the subject matter of their work, nor did I bring up the question of how much freedom they had to write what they wanted to write. However, during succeeding visits to Yakutsk, and some long and intense conversations, I heard quite a lot about both subjects.

The prime motive of the Yakut writers has been the urge to sustain, revivify and glorify their native cultures. Yakut poets have produced long, epic verses devoted to legendary Yakut heroes. Novelists write with unabashed chauvinism about the strength, courage and pride which characterized the taiga and tundra dwellers both *before* and after the coming of Soviet Power. Men like Nikolai Yakutsky write ecstatic works of nonfiction extolling the beauties, the riches and the potential of the Yakut Republic. It all adds up to an outpouring of the strongest sort of nationalistic feeling. It is certainly not anti-Russian; but it is unabashedly pro-Yakut.

There is often an interlarding of stock praises of the Communist system, but these are such obvious interjections that nobody but a Westerner diligently seeking proof of the existence of a propaganda mill would take them very seriously. There are also the usual political books and articles which *are* pure propaganda and which sit in sad and lonely stacks in every bookstore and seldom seem to find a buyer. One role of such publications in Soviet society was described to me by a truck driver.

"Sleeping pills are hard to get, so if we can't sleep we 'hit ourselves over the head' with a bottle of vodka. If there isn't any vodka, well, for twenty kopeks you can buy a book about the glories of the last Five-Year Plan. Nobody needs to stay awake if he doesn't want to."

On the question of the writer's freedom to say what he

thinks, there was some ambivalence. The older writers gave no indication that they were bothered by a feeling of restraint.

"If we wanted to criticize the system in such a way as to make difficulties for it or to sabotage what it is doing, we would not be published. When mistakes are made, we do criticize just like everyone else has a right to do; but we see it as our task to support what Communism is doing . . . because of what it has done and continues to do for us."

The younger writers appear to be less affected by this sense of gratitude, as this comment by one of them suggests:

"Publishers and editors are usually old men. Some were Stalinists. Most of them don't like to see things change too fast. Many of our older writers agree with this, but we don't feel the same way. We have a lot to be proud of in our past but we cannot live entirely in the past. It is time we began to think hard, and write hard about what is happening to us now and consider the alternatives the future has in store. You don't get perfection in the future if you believe things are nearly perfect in the present. Consequently a lot of what we younger people write these days is written 'for the basket' [he meant the wastepaper basket], but it won't always be so. This is one thing we are quite sure about."

8
YAKUTSK

The anniversary of the Great October Revolution comes on November 7, by the new-style calendar, and during the first days of November 1966 the people of Yakutsk were busy painting their city red. Flame-colored cloth hangings bearing portraits of a benign Lenin, a stern Marx, or a fatherly Gorki appeared on the front of almost every building. These ranged from handkerchief-size through bedsheet size to an enormous portrait of Lenin hanging four stories deep on the face of the town's largest apartment block. Crimson pennants, banners and flags sprouted from rooftops and from every lamppost. Billboards and hoardings displayed garish pictures of workers and farmers marching triumphantly across red fields toward a newer dawn, and crimson bunting clung like Spanish moss to the upthrust skeletons of cranes and derricks.

Yakutsk was transformed and, if it did not become a thing of beauty, it was at least ablaze with color and vigorous with motion. It was overflowing with human beings. For

several days Polar Aviation's aircraft had been flooding the
town with people coming home for this, the greatest holiday
in the Soviet year, and with men and women from the far-
flung mining centers, industrial developments and electric
power projects scattered throughout the North. These latter
were mainly immigrants to Yakutia from distant parts of
the Soviet Union who either had no homes to go to or who
could not spare the time to travel to them.

The Lena Hotel became so crowded that scores of visitors
(mostly male, young, bearded, and loaded for bear) had to
be content with mattresses and couches packed cheek by
jowl in the lobbies and the halls. The hotel restaurant was
crowded all day long and far into each night. Although the
temperature plunged to 20° and 30° below zero in the small
hours before dawn, this had no perceptible effect upon the
groups of revelers who sang their way around the frozen
streets until the restaurants and cafés again opened for a
new day's business.

When we went down for breakfast (a table was thought-
fully reserved for us, otherwise we might have starved to
death), we would find the restaurant already filled with
slightly bleary-looking Russians, Ukrainians, Armenians,
even Lithuanians, restoring themselves with a magic elixir of
champagne and cognac mixed half-and-half in eight-ounce
glasses and knocked back with one convulsive gulp.

Yakutsk was becoming a distinctly boisterous place, but
it was notable that although the Yakut intermingled with
the newcomers in the restaurants and cafés and seemed to
drink as much as anyone, they showed no evidence of carrying a load. When I sought an explanation from Moisie, he
only shrugged, smiled, and muttered something about white
men not being able to hold their liquor.

Another notable thing was that no matter how stoned the merrymakers became, they never seemed to get ugly. On the contrary, they became terribly sentimental and full of boundless love for everyone, particularly for pretty women, of whom they counted Claire as one. Happily their expressions of affection stayed within reasonable bounds and I never had to take up arms on her behalf. This was lucky, since I cannot recall ever having met a brawnier bunch of potential bruisers.

By November 6 the normal life of the city had ground to a halt. Nobody was making even a pretense of working. The day brought a peculiar phenomenon with it. The temperature had dropped during the night to 30° below zero and not a breath of wind stirred the frozen air. When Claire, Yura, Kola and I left the hotel at midmorning, we found that Yakutsk had disappeared under an opaque shroud that, unlike ordinary fog, was eerily luminescent. It seemed to glow with a diffuse brilliance yet was so dense I could see only a few yards ahead of me. Cars and trucks growled along the roads, invisible except for the yellow cones from their headlights. The streets were crowded with holiday-clad people whose gay clothing reflected the mysterious glow as they slipped past us, disappearing like disembodied spirits.

Claire and Kola and I had experienced nothing like this before, but it was old stuff to Yura.

"Is people-mist," he told us. "Is same in all big towns in far North."

Yura's people-mist was later explained to me by a meteorologist, but he gave it a far less attractive name: human habitation fog. As I understand it, the fog is caused by a buildup of warm, slightly moist air from people's bodies, houses, vehicles and animals which, under conditions of windlessness and extremely low temperatures, forms a blanket over towns and villages. It only occurs during cloudless weather, and its eerie internal brilliance is due to refracted sunlight. It often endures for days on end, since calm, brilliantly clear and utterly frigid weather is the normal condition during the Yakutian winter.

The cold of Yakutia is proverbial — and with reason. The two coldest inhabited places on earth — the towns of Verkhoyansk and Oimyakon — are within its borders. Although they lie four hundred miles apart, each has registered an official low of 97.8° F below zero! Throughout most of Yakutia the inhabitants endure temperatures of 70° below zero during January and February. Such fantastic cold does not seem to bother people much. At Oimyakon I was told that small children are permitted to stay home from school when the temperature goes below minus 60°. But the city folk of Yakutsk are evidently of a softer breed; *their* younger children can stay home if it is a mere 50° below.

At 30° below, Claire and I experienced a pressing desire to stay home too; but fortunately the temperature began to rise. A light breeze blew away the people-mist and by midafternoon Yakutsk was basking in bright sunlight. It was not exactly Mardi Gras weather, and I felt somewhat annoyed at the Bolsheviki who so thoughtlessly gave birth to the Great Revolution at a season when good Soviet citizens in Siberia would have to celebrate under polar conditions. Claire and I agreed we were lucky to be under no obligation to join the multitudes who, so we had been told, would spend most of the morrow either marching through the streets in procession or, worse still, standing on the sidewalks to cheer the marchers on.

"We can watch it all from our little home away from

home in the Lena," Claire said. "Let's get a bottle of champagne so we can celebrate in style."

Of such stuff do we weave our mortal dreams.

On the evening of the sixth, Nadia and Moisie took us to a performance at the State Theater and I wore my kilt for the last time in Siberia. I am proud of my Scots ancestry and the wearing of the kilt is a symbol of that pride. But there are some things more precious to a man even than his pride. When we left the theater the temperature had slipped to 34° below and we were unable to find a taxi. Only prompt action by the ever-solicitous Nadia averted what could have been a major personal calamity for me . . . but all that came later.

The program began with speeches delivered by the high and mighty of the Party. The Mayor (a Yakut) introduced the most important man in Yakutia — the Communist Party Secretary, a dark, handsome, rather saturnine-visaged fellow who gave an hour-long accounting of the economic successes achieved in the Republic during the year. Except for the Secretary's impassioned delivery (he was, as are most Yakut, a born orator) it sounded startlingly like a progress report being given by the Chairman of the Board of some vast industrial empire to his stockholders. Perhaps the simile is not entirely inappropriate, since the Yakut people *do* consider themselves the real owners and beneficiaries of the resources and industries of their country.

Other speakers followed, detailing the progress made in social and cultural developments, and I noted that of the thirty or forty men and women who occupied the stage, only three were recognizably European.

Reaction to the speeches (which were being broadcast on radio and television) surprised me. The audience applauded almost every item of what seemed to be an endless list of statistics, with an enthusiasm which, I am convinced, was neither forced nor ritualistic. The excitement and pride on the faces around us must have been genuine.

There was a brief intermission and then we were treated to a play about Vladimir Ilyich Lenin. This was not one of the most exciting theatrical events I have ever seen and I noted that the audience seemed to feel this way too. The applause was polite, but not sustained.

The third and final part of the program was an oratorio in seven parts composed in the Yakut language and sung by a chorus of forty voices accompanied by the State Symphony Orchestra. It was based on ancient Yakut folk themes . . . and it was absolutely magnificent! Even Kola, who is a connoisseur of opera and symphonic music, was so moved by the splendor of this performance that, for once, he could find no words to express himself. He was not alone. As the chorus wove its way through the melodic but strangely alien and compelling music, people wept openly. At the conclusion the entire audience came to its feet with a roaring ovation.

I was still somewhat stunned by the emotional impact of the oratorio as we pushed our way through the lobby and out of doors. The sting of the bitter air soon brought me round. We waited ten minutes for a taxi and by then I was beginning to get worried.

"Farley, you grow cold?" Nadia asked sympathetically.

"My dear, I'm perishing!"

"Then come with me," she said sweetly. "All of you come. Soon we all make warm."

She took us down a dark and unprepossessing side street to an ancient wooden building. Padded double doors led out of the Siberian deep-freeze into a big, brilliantly lit room that was rocking with noise, hazy with smoke, and blissfully hot. This was the Red Star, a combined restaurant and dance hall, and it was swinging to the blare of a ten-piece band. At least two hundred people clustered around scores of tables piled high with festive food and bottles. Nadia led us to a table presided over by a blond Russian boy and we were welcomed to a party that had, even by Siberian standards, already reached an advanced stage of revelry.

Having been apprised of my dangerous state of chill by Nadia, the blond boy, Boris, poured me a full tumbler of what I took to be vodka, and shouted out a toast of the bottoms-up variety. I hoisted my glass . . . and the world exploded. These people were drinking pure alcohol — and drinking it straight! Not even Newfoundland fishermen, the toughest men I know, would dice with fate that way. I never quite recovered from my initiation into what is locally known as White Dynamite, and my memories of the remainder of the evening are hazy. Fortunately, Claire stuck to champagne and was able to remember and record some of her impressions.

"Over and over I was amazed by the high quality of Russian music. Even in this small arctic city the dance band was really excellent. It was also curiously folksy because of the combination of two accordions, a balalaika, trumpets, trombones, and a piano. . . . The dancers were extraordinarily gay, everyone smiling and nodding and laughing at everyone else. People danced close together in a sort of nondescript foxtrot, but in true Russian style everyone danced with everyone else. It was impossible for any girl to sit out even part of a dance. Somebody would come along and snatch her up. . . . The clothing of the women fascinated me. Some wore snowboots of thick felt with rough leather soles; others wore spike-heel pumps and some wore flat-heeled ballerina slippers. There were women with sheer nylon stockings, and others wearing black wool overstockings. There were girls in informal woolen dresses, others in sweaters and skirts, and still others elaborately turned out in party frocks. A number of them wore aprons, and it was some time before I realized they were waitresses who had simply stopped waiting!

"It was a good thing there were plenty of spare men, because our lot weren't up to much. Kola was the first to slump into a coma. Yura went to the toilet and never came back. Then blond Boris fell off his chair and went to sleep under the table. Farley stayed upright but he looked and acted as if he had been pole-axed. When it finally came time to go, we needed help and this was provided by two militiamen. They were both Yakut and looked like characters from an operetta, in their long black overcoats trimmed with red, huge felt boots, and shining leather cross-straps. They did not act like real policemen. They were too small, too round, too shy and far too amiable. It was impossible to imagine them seriously arresting anyone. They helped us all to the door, found our outer clothing for us, helped us get dressed and even tried to find a taxi, but there were none available. The Lena was nearly a mile away but somehow we all survived the stagger home — it must have been because of the antifreeze."

I was awakened at 9 A.M. the next day by an insistent rapping on my door. In no friendly mood I flung it open, and there stood a pale and distraught Kola in his siren suit.

"Farley, please be brave! We have been invited to be guests of the Presidium during the parade. Do not blame me! They will be crushed if we do not go. We have one

hour to get ready . . . and it is Fahrenheit minus 22°
outside!"

At ten o'clock sharp, Simeon Danielov, president of the
Writers Union, arrived to lead us to our fate. There was no
question of taking a taxi; the entire main street was one
milling mob of people. We threaded our way to the civic
square and to an impressive marble review stand backed
by thirty-foot-high portraits of the local Communist leaders. Several of these, in the flesh, occupied a podium in the
center of the stand which was crowded with officials, great
and small, stamping their feet, laughing uproariously, and
ecstatically embracing old friends. There was none of the
grim and paralyzing solemnity which hangs like a pall over
Moscow's Red Square on this date. On the contrary, Yakutsk was vibrant with a feeling of gaiety and warmth which
belied the bitterness of the weather yet did not belittle the
intense significance Soviet people attach to the birthday of
their Revolution and of their nation.

The Moscow celebration has a hollow, ominous, and depressing character, as if it is conceived and executed by au-
tomatons. One reason for this was given to me by a Soviet
journalist.

"The Moscow parade is really quite dreadful. I won't
watch it myself. There we show our worst face to the world
— a hard, unsmiling face. It is our showcase of power, intended to make our real and potential enemies realize they
had better leave us alone. We are a little paranoid, you
know, although after fifty years of unrelenting hostility
from the Western powers, and Japan, perhaps this is understandable. But the face we show in Moscow on November 7
is not the real face of Russia. To know what the Great October Revolution really means to us you must see the cele-
brations in some out-of-the-way town.

I think my journalist friend would have accepted Yakutsk as being sufficiently out-of-the-way.

As we stood chatting to some of Simeon Danielov's friends (he seemed determined to introduce us to every soul on the stand) there came a distant burst of cheering, followed by the dull roar of engines. My memory jumped sharply back to the night before our departure from Moscow and I braced myself in expectation of seeing the obscene gray snouts of tanks and armored carriers appear at the entrance to the square. A brass band began to play a stirring march (why the bandsmen's lips did not freeze to their instruments was a mystery I never solved) and the voice of the Party Secretary boomed out of the loudspeakers overhead:

"Comrades! Here come the shock troops of our Republic! Let us give them the greeting they deserve!"

The roar of engines grew louder, and around the corner came a column of more than a hundred tractors and farm trucks extravagantly decorated with red bunting, representing the state and collective farms from many miles around the city. The people in the square cheered wildly and threw paper flowers at the grinning tractor drivers, one of whom responded by waving a not-quite-empty bottle which may, conceivably, have contained tea.

Apart from a contingent of militiamen and a company of Red Army soldiers bearing no arms, this was the extent of the military flavor of the parade. It was also the extent of mechanization. Only the farmers rode — everyone else marched by on foot. And almost *everyone* in Yakutsk, with the exception of the few thousands in the civic square, and we people on the rostrum, must have been in the march. Someone told me later that the population of the city had swelled to one hundred and fifty thousand for the holiday.

After three hours on the reviewing stand, I believed it. I suspect I saw every single one of them with my own eyes.

Contingent after contingent marched by carrying banners and placards, sometimes pushing or pulling floats, and usually preceded by a flag-bearer carrying a portrait of Lenin. Each contingent was greeted by the Party Secretary, who must have been chosen for his high office at least partly because of his leather lungs and his apparent imperviousness to physical discomfort.

The fact was that the marchers were the lucky ones. They could at least keep warm. For those of us on the stand the affair soon became a deadly serious exercise in arctic survival. I could understand why the reviewing stand was built of marble and concrete. No wooden structure could have endured the pounding of hundreds of feet as their owners bounced up and down in a desperate battle to keep their blood flowing.

Claire, Kola and I would certainly have lost that battle and, tough as the Yakut people are, I think most of our fellow victims would have too, had not a life-support system existed. I first became aware of it when I noticed a steady drift of people commuting between the stand and the city hall which stood a hundred yards in the rear. At first I supposed these people were simply going off to relieve themselves, but this did not explain the joyous quality of the smiles they bestowed on all and sundry when they returned to duty.

The truth was revealed when Claire's face began to turn blue and she began to moan softly. Simeon gave her a sharp glance then hustled us off the platform and into the city hall. The first aid station was in the spacious lobby. It was presided over by six extremely busy waitresses who were serving tumblers full of neat cognac. A quick gulp followed

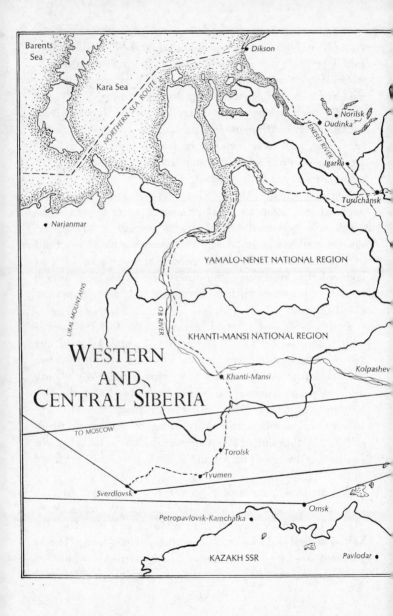

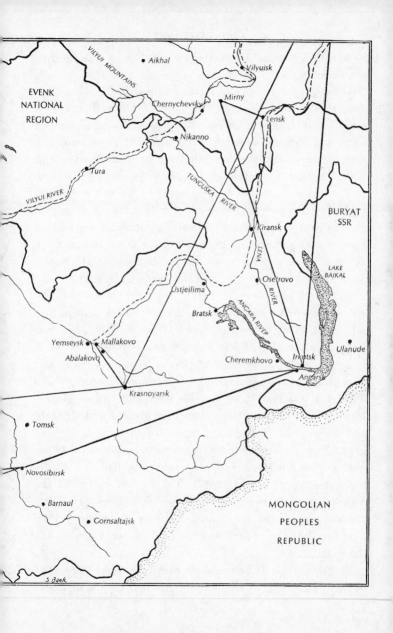

by a volcanic moment of instant thaw, then it was back to the Front again.

We regained our places in time to watch the schoolchildren of Yakutsk — every last one of them, I swear — march past in neat platoons.. They carried a multitude of signs and banners devoted to the theme of Peace; and the messages and exhortations were not only in Russian and Yakut but in many foreign languages, including English.

The peace theme was not restricted to the children. It recurred on banners and slogans carried by such disparate groups as a contingent of Aeroflot pilots, and a party of Evenki reindeer herders in native dress accompanied by a dozen of their deer. It was a major component of the slogans carried by students from the State University.

In this remote place, so distant from the eyes of the foreign press (or indeed the eyes of any foreigners except myself and Claire) Peace On Earth, Good Will To Men, was patently something of deep concern to everyone.

I have watched peace marches in North America, and they radiated the same feeling of passionate sincerity. The difference was that those marches were undertaken as protest against the government and were greeted with distaste and disfavor by significant portions of the public, whereas in far Yakutia the peace marchers must have had the blessings of their leaders, and they certainly had the wholehearted support of the people. The loudest cheers at the Yakutsk parade were not for boastful banners describing production miracles accomplished under communism — they were for the banners extolling the vital necessity of peace in the world.

Professional anti-Communists can make what they want of this incident. They can call me a dupe if they wish, but it remains my conviction that the people of Yakutsk are on the side of the angels, in this respect at least.

Many Russian friends assured me that what I saw in Yakutsk was a repetition of what was taking place in most parts of the Soviet Union on that same date. It might be an idea if, at the next anniversary of the Great October Revolution, Western press representatives eschewed the massive military parade in Moscow and dispersed into the Russian countryside. I imagine they would be permitted to do so unless, of course, the inscrutable gentlemen in the Kremlin decided that the passionate desire for peace among the Russian people was some sort of military secret, best kept concealed.

When the last marchers had passed the reviewing stand there was a concerted rush for the city hall bar; but Claire and I and Kola wanted only to get back to the hotel. As we parted from Moisie Efrimov, he called out an invitation for us to join him and his wife for a little snack later on.

Moisie's flat was, by Russian standards, a big one. There was a combined living room and dining room, lined with books, into which two huge tables had somehow been maneuvered end-to-end; there was also a kitchen, bathroom and two bedrooms. The "snack" turned out to be a full-fledged family party, and the other guests, all Yakut and about twenty in number, had already assembled. The men wore smartly cut suits in which they looked surprisingly debonair, and their sloe-eyed ladies were gaily dressed and elaborately coiffured.

By the time we arrived most of the men were crowded into one of the bedrooms playing cards upon the twin beds, while the women hustled back and forth between kitchen and dining room bearing plates piled high with Yakut culinary specialities. Moisie was soon called away from the game to prepare one of the more exotic dishes, *stroganina*, and he invited Claire and me to watch how it was done.

He produced an entire frozen fish about three feet long, stood it on its nose and with a razor sharp knife began slicing slivers off it exactly as one might peel shavings from a log of wood.

Claire was somewhat aghast when Moisie thrust a sliver into her mouth, but she got it down somehow and, after a thoughtful pause (during which I quite expected her to bring it up again) admitted that it was excellent. The fish, called *chir*, was a rather fatty, white-fleshed species from the arctic coast especially flown to Yakutsk for the holiday feast. The thin slivers seemed to dissolve in the mouth, leaving a rich, nutty flavor.

The guests were eventually herded into the dining room, crowding it far beyond its ordinary capacity; but that only made things cozier. The table had to be seen to be believed. Gleaming bottles almost obscured the vast array of food. There was French brandy, Armenian cognac, half a dozen kinds of vodka, grain alcohol, Polish, Hungarian and Georgian wines, and a large bottle of champagne between every two guests.

The food was as varied and as lavish. Several teen-age daughters of the guests acted as waitresses. The main dishes included cold, boiled cuts of young foal, hot mare's-blood sausages, hot marinated beef, roast chicken, horsemeat salami, stroganina, wild rabbit soup and pickled fish. The table was also loaded with side dishes of black and red caviar, Kamchatka crab meat, pickled mushrooms, smoked sausage and some ominous looking things that may have been strips of pickled rawhide.

The eating and drinking lasted three hours and there were toasts on the average of one every five minutes. Poor

Kola soon began to fail under the strain of trying to eat
and drink with the rest of us while at the same time having
to translate in three languages. The toasts got more and
more sentimental and we sang sad Russian songs, wild Yakut chants, and lugubrious Newfoundland ditties, until, carried away by the applause which greeted my rendition of
"Lukey's Boat Is Painted Green," I essayed an imitation of
the bagpipes and discovered I had hit upon an act which
was to bring me fame throughout northeast Siberia. My
imitation piping (particularly the "Pibroch of Donald
Dhu") roused such a response that I predict an absolutely
smashing success for any real piper who may care to try his
art in the highlands of Yakutia.

Before the meal was over Kola surprised us by fainting
dead away. A doctor was called upon to revive him with
spirits of ammonia while the rest of us adjourned to one
of the bedrooms for a little dancing. Moisie owned a big,
flashy record player but alas, it would only play 45 rpm
and all his records were of the 33 rpm variety. This made
but little difference. The room was so crowded we could only
move vertically. We jumped up and down to the weirdly
speeded-up music, doing what seemed to be a Yakut version
of the bunny hop. When that finally palled, three of the men
sang to us. They boomed out the ancient nomad songs of
their people with power enough to shake the building, and
they succeeded, where the doctor had failed, in bringing
Kola bolt upright in bed, wild-eyed and quivering.

I must admit that I did not have any deep and meaningful conversations during this party. Whatever I may have
learned about the people of Yakutia was accomplished
purely by osmosis. I am not at all sure this isn't the best
way.

9
YAKUTIA

Yakutsk is not Yakutia. Though it is their capital city, and they are proud of it, the allegiance the Yakut give to the taiga is greater than any man can give to a world of concrete and asphalt.

One September evening I arrived in Yakutsk after a flight from Moscow to be greeted by Moisie Efrimov, Simeon Danielov and Nikolai Yakutsky. They were in boisterous spirits as we drove to the hotel.

"The rabbits have come back!" Nikolai told me excitedly. "It is the peak year and they are in the taiga in their thousands. Are you very tired? If not we will go to the taiga in the morning and spend the day there."

"Yes, and the night too, and the next day . . . if the vodka lasts," Simeon added, laughing.

At dawn a hunting party of half a dozen men came for me. Gone were the dapper literary gentlemen I had known. Fur hats, skin boots, and bandoliers packed with cartridges had transformed them into a robust troop of forest dwellers who might have been resurrected from one of their own epic legends. We drove out beyond the city, across the broad flood plain of the Lena into the encroaching forest.

In spring and summer the Siberian forest is known as the Blue Taiga, because of the smokey blue-green hue imparted to it by the dominant larch trees. After the first frosts, it becomes the Golden Taiga as the larch needles take on the color of honey amber. In September the endless roll of the larch forest begins to glow with a lambent light, given texture by black swaths of pines and defined by the slim white lines of birches.

We drove to a parklike stretch of pines. Nikolai armed me with a double-barreled twelve-gauge gun, and we formed a skirmish line under his direction and set out to hunt for supper.

A heavy, wet snow began falling, and we had not gone fifty yards before we were absorbed into a timeless void. Nikolai came over to join me, and as we moved together into the depths of his inner world, I recalled some lines from one of his poems.

> *The taiga is a universe without an end*
> *Those that live within it are the stars.*
> *Bright stars are the eyes of the beasts*
> *And of the men who walk with the beasts.*
> *The space between the stars is infinite*
> *For the taiga is a universe without an end.*

This is a true poem. The map of Siberia can give no real concept of the immensity of that land. The taiga alone can give the sensation of illimitable space and distance. It is a somewhat daunting feeling, and it makes men walk softly and speak in subdued tones.

Several times I saw the ghostly forms of snowshoe rabbits

bounce through the veil of falling flakes, but I had no desire to shoot at them.

It was late afternoon before we returned to the thin slash of the road. The drivers of our cars had been busy in our absence. A huge fire roared amongst the pines, and suspended over it were pails of tea made from the same sort of tea bricks which for thousands of years were carried by caravans from Asia into Europe. Piled on a sodden newspaper were the ingredients for a hunter's feast; a red pile of horsemeat together with potatoes, tomatoes, onions, slabs of unleavened bread . . . and bottles of vodka.

We squatted Indian style around the flames, steam billowing from our soaked clothing, while we cooked hunks of meat alternated between chunks of onions and potatoes, skewered on freshly cut willow rods. The vodka bottles went around from hand to hand and we parboiled our gullets with mugs of boiling hot tea. The snow continued to fall and no one cared.

Fourteen-year-old Peter Danielov, Simeon's son, squatted opposite me, his wild black hair plastered all over his dark face; immobile except for the gleam and flicker of his eyes in the firelight. He seemed the epitome of a true forest animal, and it required a considerable effort to see in him a teen-age student of our world, already the winner of a major scholarship in mathematics and destined for a career in astrophysics.

After a while Nikolai began telling a hunting story.

When I was a boy of twelve I was hunting with my grandfather. It was winter and we had walked a long way from the village when we came to a thicket where many trees had been uprooted by a great wind. My grandfather stopped and sniffed the air like a dog.

"Ah," he said, *"there is a big fellow sleeping close to here."*

We went into the tangle and found a big mound. A tunnel half-filled with snow led into it.

"Well, boy, here is the bear's home. He is sleeping deep inside his house. I suppose we must leave him to his sleep for what can one old man and one small boy do against a bear?"

He was challenging me. I took my knife out of my sheath, tested it on my thumb and said:

"What we can do is kill that bear!"

He smiled and put his gun down — it was an old muzzle loader. He took his hatchet and cut a long pole and sharpened one end of it. Then he scrambled up on the mound and shoved the pole downward with all his strength.

"Now I've tickled his ribs! Hand me my gun!"

I gave him the gun and he cocked it and pushed the barrel down the hole. It went off with a rumble like an earthquake — then there was a roar that made my skin go tight all over my body. My grandfather scrambled off the mound and we ran back to the edge of the wood while he reloaded his gun.

We waited but there were no more sounds from the house of the bear. After a while my grandfather uncoiled the halter rope he carried around his shoulders and tied a noose in one end of it.

"Now," he said, *"we have another choice. We can go back to the village and get the strong young men to come here tomorrow and pull out that bear, or you can crawl down the tunnel yourself and tie the rope around him so we can pull him out together."*

It was hard to make up my mind. I was very frightened. I asked him to make the decision.

"That I cannot do," he said. *"I am an old man and my life means nothing. You are young and your life means*

125

much, but it will mean very little if in the long run you cannot decide when to take risks with it."

He was telling me I could become a man on this day if I chose. I put the knife between my teeth and took the rope and crawled down the tunnel, pushing the snow out of the way with my shoulders.

It was too dark to see anything. I moved as slowly as I dared, but I knew if I stopped I would not start again. It stank in that tunnel and I could hardly breathe. There was no sound except the drumming of my blood in my ears.

My hand touched something warm and I died a little. It was the paw of the bear. I lay there in the darkness for a long time and when I came to my senses I was stroking the bear's paw as if it was the head of a good dog. The paw never moved so I tied the loop around it and crawled out into the daylight. We pulled and we dug and we pulled and we dug for an hour before we got him out. Then we cleaned him and skinned him, and hung the meat in a tree out of the way of the foxes. Finally we put his skull on the end of a long pole and set it up above his house to honor his spirit and to calm his anger.

Then we went home. I was no longer a boy. I had become a man of the taiga, like all those who had gone before me.

As we drove toward the city that night through the endless cone of swirling snowflakes pinned in our headlights, Nikolai was silent. But when we reached the hotel and I was saying goodnight, he got out of the car and gave me a tremendous hug.

"Through many hundreds of years the taiga fed us, kept us warm, shaped our lives. It is the home of my people. I am so glad we could take you into the home of the Yakut."

YAKUTIA

In most areas of the world the impact of twentieth-century machine culture has shattered earlier and simpler cultures, forcing their people to abandon the old patterns of existence. Fishermen, hunters and small agriculturalists have either suffered a traumatic transformation into industrial workers, or they have been left to huddle on pathetic remnants of their own lands, despised and scorned for their inability to realize that the ways of industrial man are the God-given ways pointing to the heaven of ultimate progress.

Yakutia seems to be something of an exception. Leonid Popov, son of a horse breeder from the Namcy region, and a fine Yakut writer, gave me this description of what took place amongst his people when the industrial revolution came to Yakutia.

"At that time the remaining Yakut lived dispersed in small groups, often at great distances from one another. Our houses were mostly domed felt tents called *yurti*. In winter we traveled through the forest paths on foot or astride our ponies, and in summer we rowed our boats upon the moving waters. We were often out of physical touch with one another, but we were still one people although our ranks were sadly thinned.

"We had small herds of cattle, of horses and, in some areas, of reindeer. We cut hay in the natural meadows around the taiga lakes. There was trapping for fur and hunting for wild meat. Nevertheless, these things did not sustain us as they had sustained our forefathers. We could no longer work as hard as one must work in the demanding taiga. In my father's time almost everyone had tuberculosis, or some even worse disease, and the Yakut people were perishing.

"Then Soviet Power came to Yakutia. The tax collectors,

127

the merchants, the soldiers, the officials of old Russia were replaced by a different sort of Russian — mostly young men and women who said they had come to help us build a better world for ourselves. At first these newcomers were not trusted. We had learned very well not to trust white men. But they endured our suspicions, and in time we trusted them. I think this came about because they gave us no orders. They did not tell us: 'You must give up all the old ways and leave the taiga, where men live like animals. You must learn to build cities and factories and learn to live like us.'

"No. They understood we had the right to shape our lives to suit ourselves. And there was one thing in the heart of every Yakut — we did not want to leave the taiga. We told the new Russians this and they went to work to help us make the taiga life a better one.

"The majority of our people live in the taiga still. They are not forced to do so. Many young men and women leave to become doctors and scientists or anything they choose, but most return to us. They come back to the forests, the mountains, the rivers of our land.

"But Yakutia now has many modern towns, mines, power stations and industries. People who prefer town life and factory work come to us as citizens of our Republic from all parts of the Soviet Union, and we welcome them. Their work in the mines and plants helps to make a better life for all. And our work in the taiga, providing food as breeders of animals and husbanders of the soil, makes it possible for them to live in the new towns. It is a sensible division of labor.

"By using the new technology to strengthen the old ways of life we have developed a modern 'taiga culture' that is strong and durable. The Siberian taiga has not become a human desert, as you tell me has been the case with comparable regions in your country."

One day in mid-November Claire and Moisie and I visited Leonid's birthplace, a hundred and fifty miles north of Yakutsk. We drove there in Leonid's car, a black Volga, of which he was inordinately proud.

"I was a tank driver in the war but not many tanks could survive what my Volga does — the beauty! She's as tough as one of our Yakut horses!"

The Volga is the middle-priced Soviet car, although it costs about five thousand rubles. It functions equally well in any climate and in any terrain. In Siberia a Volga is expected to last six years without requiring major repairs. During very cold weather special batteries are installed; kerosene is mixed with the engine oil; low temperature grease is used; winter tires made of a soft, ultraflexible rubber replace normal tires; and a double windshield with a sealed air space between the two areas of glass is fitted to prevent frosting and fogging.

Although hardly a thing of beauty, and not renowned for the softness of its ride, the Volga is one of the most sensible automobiles to appear since the unfortunate demise of the Model A Ford.

We drove for many miles along the flat alluvial plain of the Lena valley, banging over frozen ruts and meeting many trucks bound for the city. Some were laden with coal from nearby mines and many bore macabre cargoes of whole, skinned carcasses of horses and cows.

There were herds of long-haired little horses pawing through the snow in unfenced roadside fields. These were "eating" horses. They are never worked because that would make their meat too tough. All year they forage for themselves except perhaps in March, when the snows are deep and hard; then they come to the farms and are given hay and grain.

We drove for almost an hour across the broad expanse of the Yakut State Farm, owned and operated by the Yakutsk City Soviet. State farms are really farm factories. Their workers are hired in much the same way, and on much the same terms, as workers in any other kind of factory. They are highly mechanized and, so I was told, are more efficient than the collective farms; but the man who told me this was a state farm manager and his opinion was hotly contradicted by the collective farmers I met. Collective farms are true cooperatives, with the land, equipment and stock being held in common by the people who do the work. Some years ago the Moscow bureaucrats mounted a campaign to replace collectives with state farms. The campaign has not had much success in Yakutia, nor do I think it is likely to.

"If I want to work in a factory I will go to the city and work in one," a young farmer told me. "But I'll be cursed before I'll be a factory farmhand living in a concrete apartment house in the middle of the country and not even be able to step behind a tree to have a private piss!"

Indeed the square blocks of masonry apartments set in the middle of an open field, which form the center of the Yakutsk State Farm, did not look particularly prepossessing, however efficient they may be. A troglodyte existence in the midst of the uncrowded taiga seems something of an anomaly.

We left the valley, climbed an ancient river escarpment, and plunged into the true taiga. It was no longer golden because, although larch is a conifer, it loses its leaves when winter comes. Flocks of ptarmigan, pure white except for the tips of their tails, exploded from the roadsides and bombed into the intricate tracery of the naked tree tops. The taiga seemed almost devoid of human works, but every now and again we passed a hitchhiker heading the other way. They are called "voters" because of the way they hold up their hands to ask for a ride. They seldom have long to wait. It is considered unforgivably selfish to pass one by if there is any possible way he, or she, can be squeezed into or on top of a car or truck.

About every ten miles we passed a little clearing containing three or four log houses and as many low-built barns heavily plastered with mud against the winter's cold. Leonid explained that these were the homes of "forest farmers." Paid by the State, it is their job to cut fire-breaks; fight small fires (or give the alarm in case of a major outbreak); carry out systematic reforestation; and detect and combat insect infestations.

"In the old days," Leonid explained, "people thought the taiga would last forever and could not be harmed by men. Now we know better. Now it is not allowed to cut a single tree unless two seedlings are planted in its place. Even in areas where there are no people and the taiga is thin and not much use for timber, pulp or even firewood, it is guarded against fire and insects. This is very costly for us, but we believe it necessary if the taiga is to survive."

Siberia contains the most extensive forests in the Northern hemisphere. Having seen quite enough of the fantastic wastage caused by forest fires in northern Canada, I was particularly interested to discover if similar catastrophes were of such routine occurrence here. My Yakut companions denied it. After having flown more than twenty thousand miles over Siberia without seeing a single fire, and having seen only a very few burns of any significant size, I am inclined to believe them. I was told that, apart from an extensive airborne forest protection service, massive use is made of military aviation and of troops to fight any fires which may develop.

"Why not?" Moisie asked when I expressed mild surprise. "We have to feed all those soldiers who are doing nothing anyway. Besides, it gives them pleasure since they are helping to protect what is their own."

A hundred miles from Yakutsk we entered the Namcy district and began passing village collectives — cozy clusters of single-family log houses with blue smoke standing straight above the chimneys in the subzero air. Occasionally we also passed small cemeteries sited on top of treeless knolls. Most of the graves were marked with the traditional double-barred cross of the Russian Orthodox faith.

I drew Moisie's attention to one such cemetery and asked if the Yakut were still Christians.

"Not now," he said. "In fact, not really ever. Russian priests came here almost three hundred years ago and we soon learned it was wise to kiss the cross and take the name of a saint. For generations the priests thought we were true believers — some people were, no doubt — but most Yakut kept secretly to the old beliefs. The shaman was stronger than the priest right to the end of their struggle, although few priests ever knew it. After the Revolution both lots went out of power. We bear no grudges. We have kept some of the traditional things brought us by the priests, just as we have kept the traditional things belonging to our own forefathers."

We passed through the broad, cleared fields of the Lenin Collective Farm and finally reached the town of Namcy. It is the home of about three thousand of the fourteen thousand five hundred people inhabiting a district of twenty-eight thousand square miles which, until a few decades ago, consisted almost entirely of virgin taiga.

The district is pure Yakut, and although it lies only two hundred fifty miles south of the arctic circle in one of the coldest regions in the world, it has one state farm and five flourishing collectives. Prior to the Revolution its scattered inhabitants owned less than a thousand scrubby cattle and about two thousand horses. There was no cleared land other than natural forest clearings, and no field husbandry of any sort. At the time we visited Namcy it boasted twenty-two thousand cattle; eleven thousand five hundred horses; about two thousand pigs and fourteen thousand, two hundred hectares of cleared land planted to new varieties of hardy northern wheat, barley, oats and vegetables.

The town was constructed entirely of wood, and its buildings (which included several multistoried structures as well as several hundred single-family dwellings) were laid out in a well-planned pattern in an elegant grove of pines and birch trees. Each house had its own garden containing ornamental trees and was surrounded by a picket fence. All were beautifully built of squared logs, meticulously dovetailed. Even in this modern era of streamlined construction techniques, the builders had taken time to add ornamental shutters and the decorative fretwork which is so characteristic of Old Siberia. I once thought the Finns built the finest log structures in the world; but the Yakut have nothing to learn from them, although a mere fifty years ago most of them were still living in simple *yurti*.

We stopped at the district administration building and were given an exuberant welcome by Vladimir Pesterov, a warm, stocky Yakut who is the elected Chairman of the district. Our arrival sparked a walk-out as secretaries and staff members abandoned work to catch a glimpse of the first foreign visitors to reach Namcy. Vladimir made a path for us to the boardroom and seated us at the familiar table. Twenty or thirty of the senior staff members, both men and women, joined us for a question-and-answer session. I was much impressed by the robust and stalwart look of the men, most of them in their thirties or younger, and by the dark glory of the Yakut women. Claire was spellbound by the decor of this boardroom in the taiga. An immense oriental carpet covered the floor almost wall-to-wall. The large windows were hung with heavy velvet drapes, and a flamboyant geometric design had been painted right around the room just below ceiling level. In each corner stood a potted cherry tree. In her notes, Claire defined the decor as: "Persian-Japanese-Taiga Modern."

The desire of these people to tell us all there was to know about their district was so untrammeled that poor Kola was driven frantic trying to interpret. There was indeed a lot to tell. Notwithstanding my distaste for statistics, it is impossible to avoid using some of them in an attempt to describe Namcy.

There were no schools in the district prior to the Revolution. Now there is no illiteracy and there are more than six thousand students attending elementary and secondary schools, a teachers college and an agricultural institute.

In 1917 there was neither doctor nor nurse in the district. Now there is a one-hundred-bed district hospital, four cottage hospitals, and twelve nursing stations, staffed by twenty-four doctors and one hundred eighty-four medical workers.

The veterinary service provides four doctors in Namcy settlement and one for each of the state and collective farms. Each doctor has a staff of seven veterinary technicians. The cattle and pigs of Namcy would seem to get better medical attention than do the people of many rural communities in North America.

There are twenty-two community halls in the district (a community hall normally houses a cinema, library, reading rooms, gymnasium, games rooms, and a display center). The central library at Namcy has a monthly circulation of seventeen thousand volumes. We visited the community center and found there a traveling art exhibit consisting of several hundred prints and paintings, many by Yakut artists but some from Moscow, Leningrad, Armenia and Poland. Although it was the middle of the day, the gallery was crowded with men, women and children. The district also has its own daily paper and a monthly cultural magazine.

Everything is bought and sold through consumer co-ops. Profits from the co-ops are either returned to the members or, by a vote decision, may be used for community projects. All goods and services are paid for in cash. The co-ops do seven million rubles' worth of business each year.

The average income for a farm worker doing an unskilled job is one hundred to two hundred rubles a month. Skilled workers, such as animal breeders in charge of the cattle and the horses, average two hundred rubles. In addition all workers get a share of the products of the farms (meat, grain, eggs, milk, butter, etc.) which is sufficient for the family needs. They also keep privately owned livestock and have their own gardens or small farms. They receive the usual benefits, including free medical care, pensions, subsidized living quarters (rental for a family dwelling, including electricity and heating, averages eight to ten rubles a month), paid vacations with travel allowances, etc.

For those who wish to build their own homes — and most rural Yakut do — the State provides one hundred percent of the cost on ten-year renewable and interest-free loans.

Hard consumer goods such as guns, radios, refrigerators, washing machines are also sold on credit with no interest or carrying charges, and Namcy did not seem to be suffering any marked shortage of these or related goods.

As we wandered about the town visiting schools, the hospital and private homes, I asked Vladimir if the district had experienced many serious problems in adjusting to the new system. He replied that there had been many difficulties in the past and some still existed. The prime problem during the initial stages of collectivization (this was begun in 1929–1930 and was not completed until 1937) was in persuading the independent-minded Yakut farmers of the value of working cooperatively.

"In some places, so I have heard, compulsion was used. There was none used here in Yakutia. It would not have worked with our people. They were slow to change and they did so only when they saw with their own eyes the advantages they would get. They watched the co-op experiments with as much suspicion as a peasant watching a fortune-teller at a fair. But once they were persuaded, there was no stopping them. They made quick progress despite a lot of stupid mistakes resulting from enthusiastic ignorance and a chronic shortage of technical advisors and good agricultural equipment. We still don't have enough technicians or equipment, but only give us time. . . ."

Moisie introduced us to his cousin, Peter Petrovitch Efrimov, who at the age of twenty-nine was the manager of a newly formed pig collective at Modusty in an area of virgin taiga sixty miles to the east. This collective included Peter's mother and father, both in their sixties, and seven other families. Although the farm was only a year old it already had two hundred pigs.

After graduating from secondary school Peter joined the

army (most native Siberian people are not subject to the draft but *are* encouraged to volunteer), emerging as an artillery sergeant after three years' service. He then enrolled at the Lvov Finance Institute in the Ukraine, where he studied farm administration for four years, graduating with a Candidate's Degree (equivalent to a Bachelor's degree). When he came home in 1965 he married, took over a small farm of his own, was elected chairman of his village co-op, begat two little boys and was then elected Deputy Chairman of the whole Namcy district.

He is the most enthusiastic pig man I have ever met. Getting him to talk about anything else was nearly impossible. If Peter has his way, the day will come when the entire taiga will echo to the squeal of countless porkers. They are a peculiar breed of beasts, "designed" for the far North by research teams in Yakutsk and Novosibirsk, and they apparently can endure any degree of cold and thrive upon it.

Another enthusiast was Ilya Tamarovo, a very dark, whipcord-lean little man in charge of fur breeding and forest trapping. He was particularly pleased to meet Canadians because, as he put it, "You gave us the most valuable animal in all the taiga — the *ondatra*. I hope you like Siberia as well as he did!"

Ondatra is the muskrat. Fifty pairs imported from Canada were released in Siberia in 1935 and they bred and spread at such a phenomenal rate that they are now found almost everywhere from the Pacific coast to the Ural Mountains. A raw pelt is worth two rubles, and muskrat now provides the largest single source of income for taiga trappers who, incidentally, have the highest average income of any group of people in the Siberian North, with the exception of truck drivers. Fur prices are supported, and there is none of the wild fluctuation that wreaks such hardships on Canadian trappers.

Ilya was happy about the high income his trappers made but not so happy about what they did with it.

"They have more rubles than they know what to do with. Some of them decide to spend it buying a car, but what use is a car in the taiga even if you don't mind waiting till the other three hundred people ahead of you in the quota lineup get theirs? A lot of the lads are spending their money on travel. They go off to the Black Sea and lie around on the beaches with the pretty office girls from Moscow; and when they come back they are too weak to carry a squirrel carcass! Never mind; maybe that's better than trying to turn all their spare rubles into white dynamite."

Ilya was determined to take us into the deep taiga to visit a colony of our one-time fellow Canadians, but the temperature had dropped into the minus thirties, and though the transplanted muskrats may have adapted to such weather, we had not. We opted for lunch in the town restaurant instead. Here we ate boiled horse brisket garnished with raw onions, cabbage soup and Yakut cookies. These cookies are made from a mixture of thick cream, sugar and chopped cranberries. The batter is dropped on a pan, but instead of being baked it is hustled outside and allowed to freeze solid.

After lunch we drove another forty miles northward to the Red Banner Collective Farm, where we were taken in charge by a blooming lass named Galia who, to our surprise, spoke French — and better French than either Claire or I, though we are citizens of a so-called bilingual country. We asked her where she had learned the language (Paris? Moscow? Irkutsk, at least?) and she replied that she had studied it in secondary school at Namcy. Why on earth had she bothered? Well, French has a nice sound, rather like the Yakut tongue, and you never can tell when a third language may come in handy.

Red Banner is a beef and dairy farm — on the same latitude as, but in a much more ferocious climate than, southern Greenland. It has about six thousand cattle and produces three hundred twenty tons of meat and one thousand four hundred fifty tons of milk and cream each year. Galia took us to visit one of her barns. It was a strange structure, very low, dome-roofed, with walls built of two-foot lengths of logs laid up in woodpile fashion and cemented together with a mixture of clay and manure. I assumed this was an ancient Yakut design. On the contrary, it was the result of recent experimentation into the problems of housing cattle in the far North.

"The research stations tried all sorts of new methods and new materials for barn construction," Vladimir explained. "None proved as efficient as this for the Yakut climate. The insulation is so good that the body heat of the cows keeps the barn comfortably warm even for human workers during temperatures of sixty below zero; and it is quick and cheap to build, using almost any kind of local wood. The weather is not cold now, of course; but come inside and see how warm it is in there."

Not cold? Claire looked at me and mumbled through blue lips, "He *has* to be kidding!"

There were two hundred forty milk cows in this barn, in two rows of spacious stalls. Due to a shortage of straw, no litter was used, but the hard-packed clay floor was kept in immaculate condition by the milkmaids, each of whom had twelve cows under her care. The air was kept clean and sweet-smelling by rows of variable ventilators set into the low roof.

Galia, whose major task was the scientific selection of the best breeding stock, explained that the rather shaggy beasts we were seeing originated from a type called Kholmogor, which were first bred at the orders of Peter the Great for use in the Archangel region of European Russia.

"Since 1925, Soviet science has worked to improve Kholmogor cattle even more. Now they are nearly as hardy as reindeer, and much better producers of milk and meat than the Yakut cattle used to be. Those being raised for beef can live out of doors all winter, but these darlings stay in the barns almost nine months of the year."

I wondered about the economics of keeping milch cattle under such conditions. Vladimir assured me it could be, and was, done at a profit. Perhaps so in this case, but it can hardly be true in all cases, particularly in regions to the north of the arctic circle such as Tiksi, where cattle are kept at 73° North Latitude! The answer seems to be that the USSR has made it a matter of basic policy for the development of remote regions that they should, as far as possible, be self-reliant in terms of food production. Kola admitted that the profit motive was not the essential factor.

"Much of our far Northern agriculture has to be subsidized, at least in its initial stages. But what is the alternative? If large populations are to live and work in the far North they must have fresh foods, and the best of foods, and if such foods cannot be produced locally they have to be imported from great distances at very high costs. It is better to spend the money to produce them locally so that food production adds a segment to the economic base of the developing region, and at the same time enables the native peoples to share in the developing economy more or less on their own terms."

We intended to head back to Yakutsk that evening, but the Red Banner Farm workers thought otherwise. We argued. Well, they said, the *least* you can do is stop long enough to have a glass of tea with us before you go.

We agreed to this much, but the moment we were ushered into the long log cafeteria, we saw that our fate was sealed. The farm workers were awaiting us along both sides of an immensely long table which was laden to the point of collapse with bottles and with food.

Kola's eyes rolled and he groaned dismally. "Yakut hospitality! Farley, I can't survive any more. I am only a weak Moscow man. Please tell my wife I died bravely in the cause. . . ."

IO
ETERNAL FROST

Although the taiga culture continues to be the preferred way of life for most Yakut and Evenki, they are not restricted to it. Many of them (Moisie thought the figure might be as high as eighty thousand) have chosen to move from taiga to town and from agriculture to industry. This transition has not brought about a break in their cultural continuity. Most of the urban Yakut are concentrated in Yakutsk, where they retain an absolute majority, set the city's cultural tone, control the local Soviet (town council) and in general maintain the Yakut "fact." They do not contribute many working people to the new mining and industrial towns and cities which, for the most part, are peopled by young European immigrants conditioned by, and products of, a technological society. The Yakut and Evenki seem happy to let these new people dig the mines, build the power stations, and generally do the work involved in the gargantuan natural-resource development which has made Yakutia a major element in the economy of the Soviet Union.

The urban-oriented Yakut have deliberately chosen to involve themselves in consumer industries, most of which have direct links with, and in truth grew out of, traditional skills and occupations. As Simeon Danielov put it:

"Our people are growing gently into the twentieth century. They are adapting to it without much strain in the same way all living things can adapt to change when it does not come upon them too abruptly or with too much violence."

I asked Simeon if this approach was the result of the far-sighted vision of Soviet policymakers.

"*They* may think so. No, it is something we Yakut worked out ourselves. You must realize our mode of thought is not your mode. Europeans often ignore this truth. We have survived for a long time in a world where survival was very difficult and we learned how to do it. When the blizzard lashes the taiga only a fool tries to face it and struggle with its power. But only a fool abandons himself to it and lets it blow him where it will. The wise man leans against it and lets it push him slowly, slowly, so he can pick his path and find his way to safety. This is what we are doing."

In Moscow I repeated this little story (suppressing its source) to a particularly energetic official of the powerful Council For The Productive Forces For The Development Of The North. He literally snorted with impatience.

"That's nonsense! There is too much nonsense like it talked in the Soviet Union. It is only another peasant proverb to excuse inaction. Anyway, it doesn't apply. For instance you've been to Yakutia and seen for yourself! Those people are among the most progressive of all the

Small Peoples of the North. *They* don't tolerate such backward notions!"

I did not disillusion him.

The industries in which the people of Yakutsk are involved include a clothing plant; a woodworking and furniture factory; a dairy product factory; shipbuilding; a textile plant; a big and effective (as opposed to the token type) handicraft industry that not only supplies products to all of the USSR but also sells abroad; and the Yakutsk Leather Treating and Processing Combine. In 1969 Nikolai Yakutsky took John DeVisser and me to visit the leather plant.

The combine had been conceived forty years earlier when the city was facing a desperate shortage of winter boots. However, there was no shortage of cow hides and horse hides or of homemade felt, and there were a number of old Yakut men living in town who were skilled at bootmaking. The town Soviet hired a dozen of them and set up a factory consisting of a decrepit log shed fitted with crude workbenches and heated by a broken iron stove. Within the year old men had trained a work force of sixty young people, and although everything was done by hand (including stitching), the plant had become a going concern. The work appealed to the Yakut and the place grew rapidly, if in a somewhat haphazard manner which is still reflected in the mélange of wooden buildings and spanking new concrete structures which today house the republic's largest manufacturing enterprise. In 1969 it employed seven hundred workers and produced two hundred thousand pairs of boots and shoes.

On the day of our visit the director, a Yakut, was away in Moscow at a conference so we were received by a pale, craggy-faced, intense and very nervous Russian, Dmitri

Maslov, who was the combine's chief technician. He was exceedingly embarrassed at finding himself cast in the role of guide to a pair of foreigners.

Our tour of the plant turned into a happy rumble as we discovered that most of the employees were young and pretty girls. *They* were not the least bit shy. I suspect our visit may have had a bad effect on the day's production figures, but no one seemed to mind. The workrooms had a pleasantly casual air about them. The girls had filled the place with potted plants, and despite the fact that most operations were being done on complex modern machines, the aura was much more like that of a home industry than a modern factory. It certainly seemed free of the tense, impersonal, pressurized atmosphere which both we and the Russians tend to equate with maximum efficiency.

"When I first came here from Leningrad," Dmitri told us, "I was upset because I did not think we were getting the best out of the people or the machines. Everything seemed too relaxed. I did some studies on three or four processes, thinking I would gather figures to demonstrate this to the director. It was a surprise to me to discover that, unit for unit, production and quality were higher than in the modern plants in Leningrad. People here, even if they appear easygoing, are the best workers one could want because they really seem to like what they are doing."

I chatted with a number of men, women and girls in various departments. Most were Yakut, with a sprinkling of Evenki, Buryat, and native-born Russians. These latter, incidentally, appeared to be at least as fervent Yakut patriots as the Yakut themselves.

By the time John had fired off all his film, Dmitri had relaxed. We went back to his office where he unstoppered a bottle, and himself, and told me far more about the shoe business than I really wanted to know; but although his facts and figures may be less than scintillating, they are revealing of what is happening to the Yakut as they "lean against the wind."

The one-time shoemaking shed is now a fully integrated operation, receiving raw hides from the collectives and state farms and turning out fully finished leather products. It employs sixty-eight "upper level" technicians, of whom exactly half are natives. The remainder, mostly Russians and Ukrainians, are employed on four-year contracts, and it is a major part of their task to train native people to take over their jobs.

Although winter boots are the primary product, a team of Yakut women was engaged in designing fashion shoes. Their work had already been exhibited and well received in Brussels and in Paris. Specialty boots of reindeer hide (with the fur on) were being made to ancient Yakut patterns and exported to high-fashion markets in western Europe. In 1969 the demand greatly exceeded production, and by the end of 1971 the combine hopes to be exporting fifty thousand pairs of reindeer boots a year. By that time total annual production is expected to reach six hundred thousand pairs of boots and shoes, fifty thousand leather jackets and two hundred thousand pairs of gloves. Employment should have topped the thousand mark.

In many cases all the working members of a family were employed in the plant. Girls of eighteen and nineteen worked by day on a reduced shift and went to technical school in the evenings. After graduation a number of them will go on to university. The management considers it part of its duty to help its employees better themselves, even if it means losing them.

The plant works on an incentive basis. Basic wages for

women average two hundred rubles a month, but there are a whole series of bonuses for "overfulfillment of the norms" which can almost double that amount.

Maslov: "In the new economic climate of the USSR, we must be interested in profit; and so we must provide the workers with greater and greater incentives."

Ordinary workers get an annual holiday of thirty-six *working* days which, with the inclusion of weekends (they work a five-day, forty-hour week) and other holidays, gives them fifty to fifty-two *consecutive* days off. Skilled workers, and those in hard jobs, get forty-two working days off. Every third year, established workers (those who have been on the job four years or more) get free holiday transportation to any place in the Soviet Union, and their trade union pays one-third of their other holiday costs. After fifteen years in the plant, women can retire at fifty and men at fifty-five, on full pension. The pension base is one hundred twenty rubles a month, scaling upward depending on length of employment.

Dmitri Maslov is a good example of the European Russians who are voluntarily becoming Siberians. He was born in Middle Russia and at seventeen went to work in a Leningrad shoe factory; but he studied in the evenings and in 1964 graduated as a full-fledged engineer.

He chose to go to Siberia because: "The job sounded exciting . . . in Leningrad factories there were no innovations; the problems were mostly solved. So when this factory offered me a contract, I jumped at it. The life is good out here. The people are the finest in the world. My wife, Ludmilla, and I have not been sorry we came. All that nonsense about the terrible hardship and isolation in Siberia was old woman's talk. There *is* some hardship, but isn't that what a man needs if he is going to bring out the best in himself? My two boys were born here in Yakutsk and they will be Yakut."

His wife, also an engineer, works in a furniture factory. The family has its own house and a half-acre garden where Dmitri grows ornamental trees and tomatoes. He is an ardent cook, an amateur artist and, being a good tenor, sings in the factory choral group. In summer he enjoys mushroom hunting in the taiga and boating holidays on the Lena. On his first "three-year holiday," he and Ludmilla went back to Leningrad and to the Black Sea . . . then, with the holiday only half spent, they returned to Yakutsk.

"We simply got sick of it. Too many people. Too much confusion. Too many regulations. Not enough time to stop and talk and smile a bit. Who knows if we'll ever go west again? Our Yakut friends say the taiga has claimed us, and they may well be right."

There is an apparent paradox in the Yakut approach to modern society. Although most of the ordinary workers show little desire to become cogs in a technological machine, their intellectuals display a phenomenal ability in all fields of knowledge, including the most esoteric realms of science. They go after higher education with a single-mindedness and concentrated effort which appears peculiarly at odds with their devotion to their Yakut heritage and their desire to retain their national singularity.

The explanation for this purposeful pursuit of knowledge turned out to be both obvious and simple. It came to me from a rather remarkable source — a Yakut Communist Party member holding a high post in the State hierarchy.

"Knowledge is power. This is a truism but it is something which must never be forgotten by a Small People. As a Small People we have the choice of turning our whole destiny over to a stronger people — letting them direct us

where to go — or we can try and keep the leadership ourselves. If we are going to do this we must have as much
knowledge as they do and, since we are weaker in numbers,
we must be even more effective in using it.

"The willing horse may lead a good life — but the driver
leads a better one! What is even more important is that the
horse cannot choose the path he wishes to follow. Although
we are happy to share our sleigh with our good friends and
brothers from other places in the Soviet Union, and though
we all hope to arrive some day at the same haven, we intend
to keep a hold upon the reins."

As far back as 1921 Lenin proclaimed the policy of preserving national entities within the Soviet Union and of
helping them make the most of their own cultural resources
for the ultimate enrichment of the entire State.

Lenin's vision has not always been in favor with subsequent arbiters of Soviet policy. There have been powerful
men who espoused the melting-pot principle with such vigor
that a good many "nationalistic" leaders of Small Peoples
(and some not so small) simply vanished from the scene. It
is impossible to know exactly how Lenin's principles of self-
determination for minority peoples are now viewed in the
Kremlin but, hopefully, the proponents of the melting pot
seem to be losing ground. If so, it is probably because so
many of the Small Peoples have demonstrated that Lenin
was right and that the Soviet Union as a whole has been
the gainer from the tremendous efforts the Small Peoples
have made in their insistent and largely successful struggle
to survive as spiritual, cultural and ethnic entities.

"Without the existence of a vigorous native population
led by their own knowledgeable elite, the Soviet development
of the far North and the near North would not have been

possible or, at least, would not have been practicable on anything like the present scale."

This flat statement was made to me by a director of the Arctic and Antarctic Institute in Leningrad, himself one of the most knowledgeable men in the Soviet Union on things relating to the North.

"In their search for ways to maintain their identities while moving out of the past, the so-called Small Peoples needed a thorough understanding of all aspects of modern life. We could have made it difficult for them to obtain this but we did not choose to do so. Instead we went to great lengths to make higher educational facilities available to them, and they, in their turn, went to great lengths to take advantage of them. The result is that there now exists a very large cadre of native people, inured to the North, almost instinctively understanding it as we never can, and equipped and trained to use the most sophisticated instruments and information of modern science. It is these people, as much as any, who are solving the essential problems of how we can grow and prosper in the polar regions of this planet. They are helping their own people to prosper in the changing world; but they are helping the rest of us even more."

I did not have to take his word for this. I saw it demonstrated in many places, but perhaps most spectacularly in the Yakutsk Eternal Frost Institute.

"Eternal frost" equals "permafrost" in our less romantic terminology, but by any name it is the most important single factor bearing on the development of arctic and subarctic lands. One fifth of the earth's land surface; three-quarters of Siberia; and the *whole* of Yakutia, sits on a crust of ice, frozen bog, soil, gravel, and rock — a crust with a maximum frost depth of fifteen hundred meters in northwest Yakutia and an average depth under the whole of the republic of three hundred and twenty meters.

It is hard to conceive of the ferocious climatic conditions which froze the earth to such a depth — froze it so thoroughly that it still remains at a constant temperature of minus 4° C, despite the efforts of the planet's hot interior and of the sun to melt it. The sun does have some effect, but a minimal and transient one. Near the southern limits of permafrost the surface may thaw each summer to a depth of several feet and, in the far North, to a depth of a few inches. In winter, however, it all freezes into one solid block again.

The effects of this underlying shield of frost are tremendously far-reaching. For one thing, there is no drainage through it, and so all precipitation must escape by running off the surface or, if it cannot do that, it remains to form gigantic morasses like those which characterize the West Siberian Plain. The presence of permafrost is responsible for the size and flow of the great Siberian rivers and, in Northern Canada, is largely responsible for the astronomical numbers of lakes and ponds which in some regions cover more than two-thirds of the tundra surface. Paradoxically, it is also largely responsible for the existence of the immense Northern forests, since it acts to conserve the rather scanty precipitation. Without permafrost as a basement sealant, much of the Northern interior of America and Asia would probably be desert. These are only a few of the ways permafrost affects the polar world. It affects human activity in that world just as strongly.

Much of the upper level of the permafrost structure underlying Siberia is a mixture of soils, gravels, shattered rock and other unstable materials cemented by frozen water into something approaching the consistency and strength of bedrock. However, strong as it is, this cement must melt if its temperature rises above freezing point. When this happens, an area that appears to be as stable as a granite plain turns into a jellylike bog which, in summer, absorbs more water and then, on refreezing in the winter, expands and bursts upward like a miniature mountain range being born.

Anything which disturbs the delicate temperature balance protecting permafrost can bring about a horrendous change. A tracked vehicle grinding over summer tundra and breaking through the thin insulating layer of moss and lichen can create vast, heaving ditches which will endure for centuries. Casual damage to the forest floor during timbering operations can cause a fatal thaw which leaves the shallow-rooted trees with no hold on anything but quaking bog, and finally sends them toppling into chaos. And structures built by man can, through the slight temperature rise created by their own weight, or by heat radiated from them, create a local swamp into which the buildings sink, totter and collapse. The same thing can happen to roads, or in fact to anything man tries to build upon the frozen ground.

Sitting in the office of the Director of the Eternal Frost Institute, I listened to Senior Research Scientist Marina Kuzminichna Gavrilova, talk about this curious world in which she, and her ancestors through countless generations, had been born.

"The idea of a rock-solid frozen arctic is terribly misleading," said this middle-aged Yakut matron. "Everything on the surface of the land is delicately balanced on the edge of potential disruption. We people of the North have always understood this, but since we never attempted to change the surface it had no great effect upon our lives. Now all is different. There is hardly one single thing modern man wants to do, or hopes to do, in the far North that is not influenced by the eternal frost, or which cannot influence it. Man has had to learn to come to terms with it, to understand it. At first he tried to fight it, and every time he failed. The engineers who tried to build one of the first power dams on Siberia's eternal frost were sure their hundreds of thousands of tons of concrete would withstand any stress of nature. An earthquake would probably not have hurt their dam, but its weight melted the frost in the frozen rocks on which it stood. The rocks crumbled and the dam split open.

"People finally realized that here was an antagonist which would not be conquered so easily. Studies were begun, but I can say it was not until some of the people who were born on eternal frost began to join the studies that the attitudes really changed. Instead of trying to conquer the frost, our scientists began to learn how to make friends with it. We are still doing that, and it is a successful effort."

The Director, Pavel Melnikov, who is a Russian although he has lived in Siberia for more than thirty years, took up the story.

"Marina Kuzminichna is correct. Eternal frost used to be considered the worst enemy to those developing the North. Now it has become our biggest ally. Instead of trying to destroy it, we protect it. Instead of trying to push it aside, we use it. Whenever planners or constructors come to Siberia to begin work on a new project we tell them: 'Be nice to the Eternal Frost Queen. Keep her well covered under nice thick blankets and she will let you do anything you wish. But if you strip off her clothes, you had better watch out!' "

This was a somewhat risqué simile in the Soviet Union, where prudery in conversation is something of a fetish. I got the point. I was to see the "be nice" principle demonstrated scores of times before I left Siberia.

Meantime I toured the Institute and I was as fascinated by the people I met as by the work they were doing.

At the age of forty, Marina Gavrilova, born on a reindeer farm near Oimyakon, commands some thirty scientists and two of the most important laboratories in the Institute — Geophysics and Heat Dynamics.

At the age of nineteen, she resolved to spend her working life studying the eternal frost. After graduating from the Yakut State University (in one of the first classes), she went to Moscow and then to Leningrad for advanced studies. Her doctoral thesis on arctic climate won her a Gold Medal and was published in scientific periodicals abroad. In 1958 she returned to Yakutsk and got down to work, but as a married woman with a family to raise. Her husband, Vasily Gosikov (it is common for married people to keep their own last names), who is the Director of the Yakutsk Music Theater, told me something about the marriage:

"A very good woman, Marina. But when we were going to get married some of my friends did a bit of joking about it. Better to marry an iceberg, one of them said. All the same, it works out very well. She has so much of cold in that underground laboratory of hers, she really appreciates a warm-blooded chap when she gets home at night."

Marina's staff was about a third European and two-thirds native. All held degrees of Bachelor or Master value. If there was any racial tension, it did not show, and the respect and regard which the European staff members demonstrated toward Marina could hardly have been contrived.

There are fourteen major labs in the Institute. Eight are headed by Siberian natives and three of these by Yakut women! There is a lab devoted to permafrost and ground transportation; one to airfields; and one to deep mining in permafrost; several to theoretical research; one to agriculture on permafrost; and so on.

Another Yakut lady, Lilia Everstova, who holds her doctorate in advanced mathematics, showed me the computer lab, which is her domain. Her staff was assembling a monstrous digital computer to support two other digitals and an analog computer which, she told us, were so overworked they were getting tired. I could understand that, if the way she worked her human staff was an indication of the way she drove her electronic slaves. Her second-in-command, a lean young Evenki named Leonid Lee (also holder of a mathematics Doctorate) told me he pitied the new computer. "Lilia will give it a nervous breakdown in six weeks, poor thing!"

Since I have small affinity for laboratories, no matter how sparkling and complex they may be (and these were both), and none at all for computers, I was glad when Marina took me into her holy of holies — a lab built thirty meters underground in the permafrost itself. This was a fascinating maze of tunnels entered through heavily insulated doors, in which a variety of experiments under natural conditions were in progress. It was an eerie place, ice-cold of course, with feathery ice crystals clustering like hibernating butterflies on the frozen sand of which the roof and walls were composed. Marina proudly showed me a carbon-14 apparatus for dating permafrost samples which she and her staff had designed and built themselves; and she lingered long over a working model of a method of piping natural gas through unlined tunnels drilled deep below the surface.

"You see," she explained, "in eternal frost there is no need for shoring or supports for a tunnel. And, since the material is homogeneous, gas can be pumped through it without danger of its leaking out. The biggest problem was how to keep the gas at a temperature below minus 4°, and this we solved by compressing the gas and so lowering its temperature. We will soon build our first experimental transmission line here in Yakutsk and some day gas from the big new fields at Vilyuisk (three hundred miles north-west of Yakutsk) will flow over, or rather under, much of Siberia in eternal frost tunnels bored by mechanical moles."

Impressive. But I was more intrigued by one of Marina's personal projects. She wants to build an Eternal Frost Museum in which will be preserved samples of plants, fruits, animals, and other perishables, for the edification of our descendants in some distant future.

"Think how exciting it would be! Nature did the same thing with the mammoths that have been found preserved in eternal frost here in Yakutia. We could have all sorts of things — not stuffed, but *real*. Of course, we should have to have some people, too — after they had died naturally, of course. Would you like to represent the people of your country? We would make a very special niche in the Hall of Northern People, and you could wear that lovely Scottish skirt I've heard about."

"Why not?" I replied, suppressing a shiver at this macabre suggestion. "I'll put it in my will."

On several occasions I had long talks with Director Pavel Melnikov, a loquacious man whose enthusiasm for eternal frost has grown stronger with the years. He is also a very forthright man.

"I do not understand you Canadians and Americans. Almost your whole North is eternal frost country, yet you made no real attempt to study it until the 1950s when it became a military problem at the time you were building your Distant Early Warning Line. From what your scientists have told me, it is still largely a military problem for you, and only a few of your best men are studying it.

"We, on the other hand, have been actively studying the problem of how eternal frost affects economic and human development of the North for the past forty years. I myself have done nothing else for thirty-four years. This Institute employs three hundred and twenty people, of whom seventy-five are scientists with high degrees, and one hundred and thirty are engineers and technicians; and we will have twice as many people in three or four more years. We are building branches all over the Soviet North. There is one in Chernychevsky devoted to the construction of power dams using eternal frost in place of concrete; there is one in West Siberia for studying problems concerning the production and handling of oil and gas. We are building others in Irkutsk and Magadan, on the Pacific coast.

"We think it extraordinarily stupid that you people and we should be duplicating the same work. The problems are essentially the same in your country as in ours. The efforts you have put into solving those problems are fractional compared with ours, so you would hardly be the losers in a reciprocal exchange of information and a sharing of research work. We have tried to bring this about. I have twice visited Canada and have shared all possible information with your scientists, but have received little in return. We invited your Minister for the North, Mr. Chrétien, to send two or three Canadian scientists here to spend a year studying our methods. He has not done so. Last year we held an International Symposium here and invited eight Americans from the small U.S. Permafrost Lab. It was agreed it would be a reciprocal visit. Well, the Americans came and saw all we had to show them, but we are still waiting to be invited to visit their country.

"Overall total planning is the only way to *develop* the North as opposed to simple *exploitation* of its resources. And even in exploitation, which is the North American approach, everything you do has to take eternal frost into account. There is a terrible danger that if we interfere with it without sufficient knowledge, we will bring calamities to the Northern regions. With all our efforts we don't begin to have enough knowledge yet. You people have far less. It is not a matter of politics or competing economies; it is a matter of simple common sense that we should work together to ensure the preservation of a great part of the earth for the use of future generations.

"In earlier times man used to learn by experience what he could and could not do with his environment. I don't believe he learned very much by that method. Now it has become dangerous to his survival to follow such absurd procedures. We think this is a criminal way to act!"

II

MIRNY

Thirty-seven years after Yermak broke through the Ural wall, a band of Cossacks rowed rough-built boats along the wide Yenisei to the mouth of an unknown tributary flowing westward out of an immense mountain plateau. This region was inhabited by a forest-dwelling people whom the Cossacks called Tungus, but who called themselves Evenki. The land of the Evenki was full of fine sable, which drew the Cossacks up the new river (Tunguska they named it), over rapids, around roaring falls, deep into mountain valleys and finally to the height of land. A small party crossed the height of land, built new boats, launched them on a mountain brook, then descended it toward the east. They had discovered the headwaters of the Vilyui River, which was to lead them to its mother stream, the Lena, and so open the whole of northeastern Siberia to Cossack depredations.

In the autumn of the year 1618 or 1619, these Russian voyageurs were stopped by ice and forced to winter on the Vilyui bank near the mouth of a small stream called Malaya

159

Bortuobuya. They somehow survived the winter and when the ice went out launched their boats on the spring flood and were flung down the foaming Vilyui to emerge upon the placid Lena.

With the founding of Yakutsk a few years later, the difficult Tunguska-Vilyui route was abandoned. For two hundred years the Vilyui wilderness was forgotten except by the Evenki, whose home it was. As the centuries passed the Evenki shrank to a scattered remnant and the Vilyui region became a void of white rivers, dark forests and looming hills into which only a handful of placer gold seekers ever penetrated.

This was how it was on a June day in 1955 when Yuri Kabardon, a young geologist, set up a portable radio transmitter near the site of the long-vanished Cossack winter camp at Malaya Bortuobuya, and tapped out a message:

HAVE STARTED SMOKING PIPE OF PEACE TOBACCO GOOD

The "pipe" was a tube of gray-blue rock a mile in diameter extending down toward the earth's molten magma core. The tobacco was diamond-laden kimberlite.

Fourteen years after Kabardon sent his message, I stood beside a table in the city of Mirny (Peace) near the site of Kabardon's discovery camp and watched two young women sifting through a pile of glittering jewels which, although worth several million dollars, represented only a minute part of the riches that lay at the end of one of the longest and most frustrating treasure hunts in human history.

Soon after their arrival on the Lena some of the Cossack intruders heard of certain strange Fire Stones prized by the Yakut for their miraculous powers. Alas, most of the stones proved to be embedded only in Yakut legend, although a few real examples apparently fell into Russian hands. At any rate, something gave birth to rumors which grew and spread until they reached St. Petersburg. In 1736, M. W. Lomonosov, an erudite intellectual of scientific bent whose dictum, "The power of Russia will grow as Siberia grows!" is now one of the guiding principles of the Soviet Union, flatly stated that diamonds existed in *Sibir*, and predicted they would be found in quantity if men would seek them with proper diligence.

Men sought for them all right, but for a long time only a few small gems, of no great value, were discovered.

In the middle of the nineteeenth century a group of merchants from Irkutsk and Yakutsk organized a major and continuing search in the Lena valley and along its tributaries. Lured on year after year by the discovery of occasional scattered gems in gravel bars, these men spent fortunes without any real success.

After the Revolution, success, though still elusive, became increasingly desirable because of a "gentlemen's agreement" among the non-Communist countries which was intended to prevent the new Soviet states from buying diamonds from the international diamond cartel. Since industrial diamonds were vital if the USSR was to transform herself into a modern nation, or even if she was to survive at all, the search for a source of domestic diamonds began anew . . . and failed again.

The Soviet Union was forced to buy what stones she could get on the world's black market at fantastically inflated prices.

In the middle 1930s Vladimir Sobolev, a young graduate of the Leningrad Mining Institute who had meticulously studied everything available concerning the structure and character of South African diamond-bearing zones, went to Siberia and spent several years exploring the taiga-covered hills and the deep river valleys of the wild country lying between the Lena and the Yenisei. Early in 1941 he presented a report to Gosplan — the Soviet master-planning organization in Moscow.

"The Central Siberian geological platform," wrote Sobolev, "is to all intents and purposes identical with the South African diamond-bearing region. Here, if anywhere, we will find diamonds. I particularly direct attention to the valley of the Vilyui River and recommend that detailed prospecting be started there at once."

Unfortunately, Hitler invaded Russia shortly thereafter, and Sobolev's report was buried under the debris of war.

During the next few years it hardly mattered. The Western nations relaxed their restrictions and sold industrial diamonds to the hard-pressed Russians, who had now become their allies. When the war ended and the West reverted to its tactics of denying the Soviets whatever might be of help to them, diamonds were high on the new prohibited list.

Once again the age-old search was renewed. Someone recalled that Sobolev had specifically suggested trying the Vilyui basin. On August 12, 1949, Gregory Finstein, a young Jewish geologist, panned six diamonds on the Vilyui sand bars, and before the season ended the largest collection of gems ever taken from Siberia had been assembled.

It was still a pitiful handful, and there was still no sign of a pipe; but because the shortage of industrial diamonds was now gravely hampering industrial development, the search for the source of the Fire Stones was intensified.

It was an infuriating and frustrating business. Scattered stones continued to be found, but their source remained hidden. As one of the diamond seekers of that time described it: "The whole country was blanketed by taiga and muskeg. If any pipes existed, they gave no indication of their presence beneath the forest floor. The chances of selecting just the right spot in all that wilderness were astronomically small unless we happened on a pipe cut open by a stream or a river and exposed to view. That's what we were looking for. It seemed a hopeless search. The few diamonds we found offered no really useful clues, because diamonds are practically indestructible and are dispersed by river action, glaciers, or other natural forces over huge areas. What we needed was a tracer of some sort; a pointer to tell us when a pipe was near at hand."

Now it happens that almost everyone in the USSR is a science fiction fan. A pair of young Leningrad geologists, Natalia Sarsadskikh and Larissa Popugaeva, were no exceptions. One day in 1952 Natalia was thumbing through a tattered science fiction magazine published in 1944 when she came across a story called "The Diamond Pipe," in which the author described the imaginary discovery of Siberia's first diamond mine. In order to flesh out his account he wrote a paragraph describing certain reddish crystals called pyropes. He referred to them as the "poor cousins" of diamonds because, although the two gems are often found in association, pyropes are practically worthless.

By coincidence Larissa and Natalia had recently examined some sand samples taken from diamond-bearing bars on the Vilyui River, and Natalia remembered that a number of these samples contained pyropes. The two women discussed the matter and began reexamining the samples. They noted that although the size of the pyropes in each sample was rather uniform, the pyropes in some were larger than in others. It seemed like a meaningless fact until Larissa recalled that, unlike diamonds, pyropes are very soft. Considering this, they reasoned that pyropes ought to be significantly affected by the erosive action of sand and water; consequently, the farther they were carried away from their origins, the smaller they ought to become. If this was indeed true, then the poor cousins of diamonds might be made to betray the common home of both.

Nobody paid much attention to their idea. There was one notable exception. Twenty-two-year-old Nikolai Bobkov was excited by it. In 1953 he set out to see if it was possible to trace a pyrope trail on the Vilyui. The spring flood was still on and the river roared in spate, sending white water spewing over the rapids. Nevertheless, Bobkov picked up a pyrope trail and began following it. In his journal he noted that the pyropes grew larger as he approached the valley of the Malaya Bortuobuya. Two days later Bobkov was dead, drowned when his boat was swept over the rapid known to the Evenki as Big Blood Falls.

The following summer Larissa Popugaeva herself led a prospecting party to the Vilyui. Although Bobkov's journal had been saved, she chose her own path, following a trace of pyropes upstream, watching the reddish specks grow larger until they abruptly ended. At this point her party abandoned the river and began searching outward into the taiga. Within a week they had uncovered the first Siberian diamond pipe.

They called it Dawn. It proved to be too poor in diamonds to be an economical mining proposition, but it was composed of true kimberlite and so gave promise that other, perhaps richer pipes existed.

A year later the search which had extended through almost three centuries came to a triumphant end. Following the pyropes, and Bobkov's lead, Yuri Kabardon discovered Mirny. A hundred and fifty miles to the northeast the pyropes led Vladimir Shukin to the pipe called Udachnaya. Both were extraordinarily rich in diamonds.

Early reports about these finds were derided in the Western press. It was assumed they were propaganda; but even if there was something to them the experts concluded that the difficulties of trying to mine diamonds in permafrost and in such an utterly remote area would preclude production on any significant scale.

The West was whistling in the dark. By 1969, with the help of airborne magnetometers, Soviet geologists had located, but had not yet had time to evaluate, more than three hundred pipes in a vast region now known as the Yakutian Diamond Province. Four pipes which *have* been evaluated, Mirny, Irkholt, Dachna and Udachnaya, have a potential equal to the best South African mines. All the needs of Communist countries for gemstones (gemstone production at Mirny is twenty percent of total production) and for industrial diamonds are being met from limited production at just three mines, and there is a considerable export (nobody will say just how considerable) to capitalist countries. The Fire Stones of Yakutia have come into their own.

I asked the Director of the Yakutian Diamond Combine, Lev Soldatov, an urbane and dynamic Muscovite, whether the Soviet Union had ever thought of flooding the market and putting the DeBeers syndicate right out of business.

He smiled. "It's been a temptation, one can't deny it. We don't forget how your diamond merchants squeezed us for fifty years, and we have a lot of money to recover. But we can do that better while prices remain high. No socialist countries now suffer from high diamond prices; but capitalist countries do. Why should we ease that pressure? There is an even more important thing, of course. If we flooded the market all the ladies in the world would find their diamonds worth very little. We certainly wouldn't want to rouse the fury of world womanhood against us. I am not sure even the Soviet Union could cope with that!"

When John deVisser, Yuri Rytkheu and I boarded a plane for Mirny at Yakutsk airport, we stepped directly into another dimension of the Siberian story. The plane, an Antonov-24, was of new design and construction, with a modern decor that shone icily with space-age plastics. There were no Yakut or Evenki passengers aboard, except for young Sasha Yakimov, the editor of *Polar Star* and our guide for the trip. The remainder of the passengers were men and women from all parts of the Soviet Union who, with one exception, reflected the gloss of our brave new world. They were all quite young. Most of the men wore well-cut suits and overcoats and some even carried briefcases. The women were dressed in the height of Moscow style and were redolent of the pungent but pleasant Russian perfumes that are a symbol of Soviet affluence.

Sasha seemed slightly ill at ease. As we climbed high above the taiga and headed for Mirny, five hundred miles to the westward, he unburdened himself a little.

"These people are the new Siberians. They are not yet a part of this land. Perhaps the years will change them. In the meantime they are changing the world we knew. These are the people who are building the new cities in new places. We admire them, of course. Like us, they are good Soviet citizens, but they are not *quite* like us."

"You mean they seem like foreigners to you?" I asked pointedly.

Sasha looked at me for a moment then appeared to change the subject. "Did you notice the old man who got on last? He too was a Russian once; but now he is a true Yakutian."

This old man fascinated me. He seemed incredibly ancient, with a face so seamed and lined it was almost featureless except for his pale blue eyes. He had come staggering
across the tarmac bent almost double under a tremendous
load; a huge and blackened packsack with a bedroll poised
on top of it; two great bundles of steel traps; a worn and
filthy gun case; and half a dozen miscellaneous bundles
hanging by strings and straps from his narrow shoulders.
The stewardess, a bandbox beauty, immaculately uniformed
and totally impersonal, had not greeted the old fellow with
noticeable warmth. Her disapproval did not seem to bother
him. As he bumped into people in the process of trying to
stow his huge load under and on top of seats, he grinned a
toothless, friendly grin and joked in so heavy an accent
that few of his fellow passengers seemed to understand him.
Or perhaps they simply did not want to understand.

"Tell me about him, Sasha."

"He is Yakob Mashukov and he was born in Muktuyak,
an ancient little village on the Lena not far from where I
too was born. His people came from Russia, but so long
ago they do not remember when their ancestors first reached
Yakutia. Yakob is a trapper. Once he was among the best
in our country. Now he is seventy years old, but still he
goes every winter into the far taiga. He says it is the only
place he still feels at home. We will be landing at Muktuyak.
When you see it, perhaps you will understand what Yakob
means."

"But why is he going to Mirny?"

"Because the world has changed. Once he would have
taken his boat and gone down the Lena to the Vilyui and
then up it to the Markha River and up that until he reached
his trapping grounds beyond Udachnaya. It would have
taken him a month or more. Now he can fly to Mirny, and

from there to Udachnaya in half a day. He and I were talking about the diamond mines not long ago and he said to me, 'Sasha, it is true that the Fire Stones work miracles. Is it not a miracle that, because of them, I can reach my taiga cabin in two days?' "

We began to lose altitude. Mounded hills and heavy forest lay below us, lit by the afterglow of the fallen larch needles. The broad coils of the Lena appeared, rolling heavily between high, wooded banks, and then we were over a large town sprawled along the river bank. A maze of docks fronted on the water, and scores of ungainly, bargelike vessels were tied up to them. Concrete and multistoried wooden apartment blocks marched row on row back to the edge of the taiga, pushing the forest remorselessly away from the moving waters. Trucks crawled busily along the streets.

"The town of Lensk," Sasha said. "Thirteen years ago there were twenty-six cabins here and the name of the village was Muktuyak. It had only a few Evenki families and a dozen of the Old Russian families. Now that Muktuyak has become Lensk it has twelve thousand people. It is a new city in the North. Yakob Mashukov liked Muktuyak better."

Lensk, too, is a product of the Fire Stones. In little more than a decade it has become a major transportation center serving the sister cities of Mirny and Chernychevsky, which is the site of a major hydroelectric development on the Vilyui. Supplies and equipment of all kinds, including immense turbine rotors and prefabricated ships up to one hundred tons' displacement for use on the newly created Vilyui Sea (the reservoir created by the Chernychevsky dam), pass through Lensk. These things come from all parts of the Soviet Union via the Trans-Siberian Railway to yet another newly built city, Osetrovo, on the upper Lena not far from Bratsk. All during the summer a great river fleet is busy moving freight from Osetrovo down nearly seven hundred miles of river to Lensk, where it is stockpiled until winter comes. Then snow and ice roads are opened up to Mirny, two hundred miles due north, and the freight moves on to its final destination in fleets of trucks.

However, with all its shipyards and its storage depots, Lensk is more than a transportation center. Obedient to Soviet principles for Northern development, it has already produced viable secondary industries. Among these are a number of state and collective farms operated by the Evenki, producing cattle, milk products and a surprising quantity and diversity of vegetables, including cucumbers, for Lensk, Mirny and Chernychevsky. The success of these farms is due to the fact that the Lena has thawed the surface permafrost for a distance of as much as three kilometers back from its banks, so that the deep alluvial soil has been freed for cultivation.

Timber resources are also being harvested both for construction at the new city sites and for export. Diamonds do not take up much freight space, and there is no point in sending the river ships back to Osetrovo empty, so they carry lumber. During the summer great timber rafts go north down the Lena to satisfy the needs of Yakutsk and other communities along the river banks. Some of the rafts continue down the full two thousand miles to the river's mouth and to the arctic seaport of Tiksi, where the timber is loaded on ocean-going ships that travel east and west along the Northern Sea Route into the Atlantic and Pacific Oceans.

Seen from the air the region around Mirny looks like the point of impact of a meteor. In the center of a broad plateau of muskeg taiga is a titanic hole, well over a mile in diameter. Surrounding it, and stretching for miles in all directions, the thin forest cover has been incinerated, reduced to a tangle of blackened skeletons. Radiating out from the crater a star-burst tracery of survey lines runs through the debris of the dead taiga. To the north lies a huge area of a different kind of desolation; there the land looks as if it has been churned up by giant plows and then flooded by a mighty inundation.

Sasha and I stared at this appalling spectacle together — this example of what man can do to the natural environment in his frantic haste to rob the earth of buried riches.

"Do you call *that* the New Siberia?" I asked in disgust.

Sasha shook his head. "No. That is a mistake. It is a tragedy. They were so anxious to get the diamonds that nothing else seemed to matter. In order to make the survey work easier, the taiga and ground cover were deliberately burned. Because very many diamonds were needed in a hurry, there was no attempt to plan the work in order to save the land. Opening the mine itself was slow, so when they discovered diamonds spread about in the nearby muskeg, they brought in converted gold dredges to speed production, and these turned the valley over there into a swamp.

"When our government (he meant the government of the Yakut ASSR) saw what was happening, complaints were made to Moscow. At first nobody listened. The Russian engineers and technicians said it was the only way things could be done. They said Siberia was so big, a little mess here did not matter. But our President carried the matter to the Presidium of the Supreme Soviet, and in the end we won. It will not happen again. I have visited all the new diamond-mining centers and there is none of this destruction. Now we will watch carefully those who are not always concerned enough about the consequences of their actions."

Sasha seemed subdued as we landed on a paved runway long enough to take the largest Soviet aircraft. During our entire visit to Mirny he remained subdued, only speaking when he was spoken to. Although he never said so, there was no doubt in my mind: for him, this was alien territory.

We were met by a suave, heavyset young Russian sporting a Vandyke beard and dressed as if he had been fitted out on Saville Row. His manner was efficient and remote. Pavel Vecherin, deputy editor of the local paper, and public relations man for Mirny, would have fitted easily into Toronto or New York.

Vecherin showed me all of Mirny I cared to see, but for the first time in the Soviet Union I was unable to establish rapport with the people of a community. This was not entirely Vecherin's fault — even though I could not persuade him I was more interested in people than in statistics — it was mostly due to the fact that the inhabitants of Mirny seemed to live within their own personal solar systems. Almost all of them were young. They had great energy, great ambitions — and little common ground. Having come here from all over the Soviet Union, they had created an efficient artificial environment in the midst of the taiga and within it were living artificial lives. By Soviet standards they were extremely well off, and they were proud of the fact. Most of those I talked to had visited Yakutsk and were disparaging in their comments about it.

"An old-fashioned, ugly, uncomfortable place," one of them called it. "I'm grateful I've never had to stay there overnight."

There was certainly nothing old-fashioned about *their* city. Mirny is one of the avant garde cities of the USSR.

Beginning as no more than a few log shanties thrown up by the first construction teams in 1956, it grew rapidly through an adolescent period of timber barracks and apartment houses and then exploded into a welter of masonry and metal buildings embodying the latest refinements in Soviet Northern building techniques and design.

Mirny has everything. Its thirty-eight thousand people have a TV and radio station, daily newspaper, library with two hundred thousand volumes, two theaters, five cinemas, the most modern hospital I have ever seen, paved roads, a brewery and a vodka distillery, an advanced educational system including a technical school with eleven hundred students, dance groups, choirs, children's musical schools and . . . you name it, Mirny has it. Most of its citizens live in cleanly designed five- to seven-story apartment blocks, intelligently sited, and tinted in gentle colors to take away the blight of naked concrete which disfigures so much recent Soviet (not to mention North American) architecture.

The wages are 2.5 times the going rate for equivalent jobs in European Russia. Air transportation (there is no other kind except for the winter truck convoys) is so good and so cheap that people think little of flying eight hundred miles to Irkutsk or twelve hundred to Novosibirsk for a short weekend outing, or three thousand miles to Moscow or Leningrad for a long weekend.

Food is good and cheap and far more varied than in Moscow; and the same applies to all consumer goods. And what is very important in the USSR, the citizens of Mirny enjoy a special prestige throughout the country. They are the hardy pioneers who produce the diamonds without which the great (and never-ending) industrial leap forward would be impossible.

Young, vigorous, athletic (men, women and children play

hockey on outdoor rinks with fanatical enthusiasm through eight months of winter), the people of Mirny quite evidently believe in the image of themselves which is presented to the rest of the Soviet Union. They seem to have everything required from life — except the inner certainty which displays itself as an outward tranquility and which belongs only to people who have, for a long time, been in harmony with the world around them.

The feeling of impermanence, of not being rooted, was apparent in conversations I had with several residents of other new Northern cities. A gifted young interior designer summed it up this way:

"Our new cities are built by the young and they belong to the young. They are full of challenge and excitement and quick change. But, you know, even in the ones that were started thirty or forty years ago there are very few older people. When a man or woman gets on a bit, something seems to happen. The city they helped build doesn't have any place for them any more. They begin to feel uneasy in it. So when retirement time comes — it comes early for us Northerners — many people don't stay on. They go back to where they came from, hoping they'll feel wanted there."

I discussed this attitude with Nikolai Yakutsky.

"Yes," he said, "this first generation of New Siberians are a nomadic people. Perhaps most of them will never be real Siberians . . . but *their children will*. It will happen to the children as it did to the Old Russians who came out here hundreds of years ago. They will become part of this land. There is one danger. It is that the new people may forever alter the nature of the land through carelessness or by trying to reshape it in the way they shaped the European country. We don't want that to happen. We want things to remain uniquely Siberian until the youngsters who are born here can grow up and learn to love it as it is, and to protect it for others as we are trying to protect it for them."

The Russians who came to Yakutia centuries ago did not change the character of the new lands. Heavily influenced by the Yakut and Evenki cultures, they conformed to the country and became part of it. Whether modern men can or will follow the same pattern remains to be seen. If they do not it will hardly be the fault of the Yakut people, who take their role as conservators of the human and the natural heritage with deadly seriousness.

As we drove out of the city toward Diamond Factory No. 3 — a monstrous, aluminum-sheathed, windowless monolith standing fourteen stories tall on the desecrated tundra plain — Vecherin was still spouting statistics. "Our city is a league of Soviet peoples. There are forty-six nationalities working and living here."

"Yes," I said, "I've noticed the variety. But I haven't noticed many Evenki, Yakut or others of the Small Peoples. Can you tell me why that is?"

Vecherin gave me an answer that I had heard in substance many times before from white North Americans.

"It is *not* because we practice discrimination. But it *is* true that these people are only a few generations away from the Stone Age and most of them don't take kindly to city and factory life, perhaps because they are not ready for it yet."

However, there are some spectacular exceptions in Mirny, and I am still wondering how Vecherin manages to fit them into his glib evaluation of the native peoples.

One of them is Alexei Nikolaievich Stepanov, a smiling, compact Yakut thirty-six years of age. He is the Director of Diamond Factory No. 3. Alexei was responsible for the design and construction of the factory (the largest diamond-processing plant in the world) and not only supervised its construction but was the leader of the team that. worked out the novel separation and processing system and designed the equipment which makes the plant so efficient it runs day and night, summer and winter. Undeterred even by 70°-below-zero weather, it sometimes produces enough diamonds in the space of a single day to pay the whole of the annual operating expenses.

Alexei Stepanov was born on a cattle farm. After graduating from the Yakut State University, he took his Master's degree at the Moscow Mining Institute, and came to Mirny in 1958. His rise was meteoric. Sasha, who knew him in Yakutsk, described it to me.

"When Mirny was started there was nobody in the Soviet Union with specialist knowledge about diamond mining or processing. Alexei probably didn't know any more about engineering technology than the others who were working on the problem, but he did know more about Yakutia and conditions here, and he thought every difficulty through in detail as a Yakut would. In a very short time the other technical people were coming to him for answers, and his solutions almost always worked. They worked so well that he became manager of Factory No. 2 (No. 1 was a pilot plant). There he originated the advanced processes which are now standard in all our diamond factories. But, you know, it isn't so surprising. Remember that the Fire Stones of Siberia were discovered by the Yakut before there *was* a Russia."

Alexei Stepanov showed us through his plant, which was cavernous, unbelievably noisy, filled with gigantic machines, and almost totally automated. He seemed amused at my anxiety to get out of the place. When he had seated me in the comfort of his office, he showed me a Tsar's fortune in uncut diamonds and seemed even more amused at my attempts to appear properly impressed. As we were parting he drew Yura and me aside.

"Sasha has told me something about you, Comrade Mowat. Fire Stones are one thing — but hunting a bear in the taiga is another! I'll take a few days off work and we'll go to a place I know . . . Sasha and you and me and Yura. You will like that more, I think."

It was the nicest offer I got in Mirny; and I shall be eternally sorry that I was unable to accept.

12
CHERNYCHEVSKY

If the glossy modernity of Mirny failed to move me to any marked enthusiasm, Chernychevsky did. The town was born in 1960 on the banks of the Vilyui about a hundred miles northeast of Mirny and soon became the home of some twelve thousand people engaged in building a most unusual hydroelectric project.

We drove to it through rolling taiga on a newly built road, hard-topped by nature with glare ice. The skating rink surface did not seem to trouble our driver. Siberians do not bother spreading salt or sand on icy roads, nor are the tires of their vehicles equipped with special treads. Survival depends solely on the driver's skill.

We reached the deep and shadowed Vilyui valley and turned along it. Suddenly our view of the dark gorge was shuttered by a towering gray shape. Although recognizable as a dam — and a mighty one — it was quite unlike any of the great dams I had ever seen. Instead of the usual shining walls of white concrete lifting in precise lunar curves, here was a jumble of huge rock fragments rearing skyward in such apparent confusion that at first glance it seemed as if a natural cataclysm had stoppered the gorge.

The Vilyui dam is two hundred feet high, a third of a mile long, and built almost entirely of materials found in the immediate vicinity of the site. No concrete was used in the main construction. The cement which binds rocks, clay and gravel into a unified whole capable of withstanding the pressure of a reservoir three hundred and twenty miles long is natural too. It is eternal frost. The dam is a staggering demonstration of how Siberian builders have learned to collaborate with a primordial force which they once thought of as their mortal enemy.

The leader of the Vilyui dam builders was a graying, rather ordinary-looking man, a bit pudgy but with clear eyes and an expression as relaxed and amiable as his manner. Gavriel Bijanov had spent thirty years building power dams, but he looked as if he might have spent those years as a gentle schoolteacher.

He met me at the door of the big log building that serves as construction headquarters, and in lieu of the cool handshake I had received in Mirny, he hugged me hard.

"Welcome!" he said. "In 1962 I visited your country and traveled in your North — now I am happy to be the host to Canadian friends!"

The key people of his staff had gathered to meet us in the usual conference room. All save Gavriel seemed very young. Most were men but there were several women among them. Most were of European extraction but there were a number of Siberian natives. Gavriel's second-in-command, Nikolai Atlasov, was Evenki. We were greeted with the kind of warmth I had come to accept as characteristic of all Siberians.

These people were unregenerate enthusiasts and each was determined that I should hear every detail of the story of Chernychevsky. Gavriel's attempts to quieten them were the half-hearted attempts of a proud father in the presence of his precocious offspring. Nothing could wait. I had to hear everything and see everything immediately — if not sooner.

I listened for two hours straight until someone leaped to his feet and insisted we go and look at the dam itself. No matter that it was pitch dark outside and the temperature was 24° below zero. Off we went, slipping and slithering along the unfinished crest of the huge structure. Gavriel suggested that we might knock off for a little supper; but the chief of the powerhouse, Ivan Drobishev, pleaded with us at least to take a glimpse into his house of wizardry tunneled into the solid rock beneath our feet. The glimpse took an hour, and even then he was loathe to let us go.

We eventually snatched a bite to eat in a cafeteria and then went at it again until well after midnight, viewing an excellent film record of the building of the dam. Finally we were driven to the guest house — an elaborate A-frame structure beautifully sited on a wooded hill, designed, built and decorated by the dam builders themselves. It was the most comfortable and attractive hotel I encountered in the Soviet Union.

But were we allowed to fall into soft beds and die a little — as Nikolai Yakutsky would have said? By no means. Instead, we were served a banquet which extended through another couple of hours of talk. When Gavriel finally took pity on us and declared the party at an end, he got reproachful looks from several of his assistants who claimed they had only *begun* to tell the story. I went to bed exhausted — paralyzed would be closer to the truth — but I did not mind. I had listened to a splendid saga, a very human tale, and had seen at least an indication that modern men may yet manage to reverse the attitudes which are making us outlaws on our own planet.

Some years prior to my visit to Chernychevsky I spent a winter day in the Moscow offices of the Institute of Northern Planning. This agency, more than any other, has been responsible for originating and implementing the policies which have revolutionized Northern development in the Soviet Union. The staff consisted of dedicated Northerners who talked about their work with great frankness, beginning with an explanation of why the Soviet Union has become so deeply involved with Northern regions.

Apart from the natural inclination of any country of pride and energy to develop its own resources, the USSR has, ever since its birth, been under additional pressures to do so because, wherever possible, the capitalist powers have denied it access to world sources of raw materials. The Soviets were forced to make the most of what they could find in their own territory. Since over half of that territory lies in the North (arctic and subarctic), Northern development early became essential to survival.

There were other factors. As far back as the late 1920s there was concern over the steady buildup of industrial concentration, and consequently of human populations, in already densely populated regions of European Russia. This concern originally arose out of military considerations but later became a matter of urgent social consciousness. Through the years more and more Soviet planners in every field were converted to the concept that the dispersion principle must triumph over the agglomeration principle. As one of the Institute's members put it:

"Although we knew it would be difficult and costly to reverse the worldwide trend toward population concentration, we believed dispersion was a more natural and reasonable principle and would produce a better environment for human beings. People would have breathing space, for one thing. For another, the entire country would share a similar economic level. There would not be any areas of economic and social backwardness and so there would be no tendency toward a continuing depopulation of peripheral areas because of economic deprivation.

"Decentralization and dispersion were taking place as early as the 1930s but many people then thought only the Central and Southern portions of the Soviet Union could be treated in this way. It took much hard work to convince everyone that the Northern regions could absorb and support modern habitation centers on a large scale. Now we have reached the point where we have devised a Northern technology capable of creating living conditions almost anywhere in the North which are as good as those in, let us say, Moscow, and in many ways are even better.

"Those of us who fought for the development of the North had additional reasons to inspire us. There was the question of the future of the Small Peoples. We never did believe it was permissible to leave them to decay in ignorance and apathy in regions which were to lie outside our new society; nor did we think it wise or right to take them out of their Northern world and transplant them into our Southern way of life. Lenin insisted, and we agreed with him, that it would be much better to take the modern world to them.

"The wisdom of this is surely clear from the fact that, instead of being a burden on the State, the Small Peoples are now full partners with the rest of us in developing the New Life in the North."

A young woman in charge of social planning for the North added this comment:

"Human beings must have challenge! That is understood by any thinking person; and we know the best challenge is the one which is the most natural. If men do not have such challenge they find it in unnatural ways — perhaps in a fierce competition for power or money; perhaps in internal struggles that tear a society apart; perhaps in external struggles that become bloody wars. We know all this, you see; and so we have deliberately offered to our people — particularly the young — the challenge of the North, which is a challenge of nature. They have responded with enthusiasm. It is not good to give people security of body alone . . . we must also make a valid and good purpose for life. Those who go North find such a purpose."

It was early recognized that Northern development on a big scale required careful planning, but until the end of the Stalin era the planning was rather haphazard and sometimes bungled. Stalin was a Georgian and apparently never had the feel of the North. Under Khrushchev things were different. Tremendous efforts and vast sums of money went into planning and into research to back the plans. At the same time tens of thousands of scientists flooded out over Siberia to conduct the most intensive surveys and to compile the most complete inventory of resources ever undertaken by any nation. This resulted in the discovery of nearly every important raw material required by modern technology and, to the perturbation of some Western powers, it assured the Soviet Union of internal self-sufficiency in raw resources, if it proved possible for them to develop these resources on an economically realistic basis. And that was the rub. No country, communist or capitalist, can remain healthy if the things it purchases with its labor or its money are worth less than what it cost to get them. However, the Russians found sound economic methods for developing their Northern resources while at the same time turning an almost empty wilderness into a suitable habitat for modern man.

Here, paraphrased and much condensed, is how it was explained to me by the Director of the Institute of Northern Planning:

"We had four basic considerations before us when we worked out our policy. First: we had no intention of just exploiting the North for the benefit of the Southern part of the country. Second: whatever we did had to ensure it would bring people into the North on a permanent basis. Third: development had to pay its own way, and had to recover the very heavy cost of the initial planning and surveys, which amounted to over six billion rubles. Fourth: everything we did had to be predicated on conservation of resources so the future would be assured, not only for the new Northern communities, but for the whole of the Soviet Union. We could not afford to be profligate with what we had, as the United States and other capitalist countries have been.

"The first step in implementing these criteria is to examine the surveys and the inventories with special reference to resources of particularly high value such as gold, diamonds, uranium, and particularly rich concentrations of less valuable minerals. Such resources we call *valuta*. We then conduct exhaustive further surveys in the regions around each valuta to assess the potential of all secondary resources. When a valuta shows it could be a focus for the development of other resources — and most of them do — we are ready to go to work in earnest.

"We spend money as freely as needed to begin an intense

exploitation of the valuta. In the case of Mirny it was diamonds; in the case of Kolyma, gold; in the case of Norilsk,
a concentrated base metal deposit. As soon as production
begins, the profits are used to transform the original temporary mining town into a planned community designed in all
essentials to care for a much bigger population than is required to work the valuta alone. The town is built for per-
manence and has all the facilities needed by a modern city,
together with excellent communications with the rest of the
country. In addition the valuta pays for the installation
of a power base with a capacity far in excess of current requirements. In as little as five to ten years we create the
essentials for a human habitation center which has all the
amenities one could want; and this very heavy capital in-
vestment is provided directly from the profits of the valuta.

"The new community now begins development of its secondary resources which could not, on their own, have paid
for the initial installation of the new community. At the
same time local industry is beginning to develop. It is a
principle with us that raw materials should be processed as
fully as possible at their point of origin. This means construction of smelters, refineries, reduction plants in the new
center, and these provide a base upon which heavy industry
can later grow, while at the same time much reducing the
costs of transporting the resource material to other regions.

"As local processing of the several resources expands,
the new center finds itself in a position to begin manufacturing. At this stage it is approaching maturity as an integrated economic unit with many diverse activities; drawing
on many sources of raw materials; and capable of support-
ing a large human community in perpetuity and in modern
style.

"If the original valuta resource should now become exhausted, it will not fatally affect the life of the community. If the valuta continues to be productive, the State continues to benefit from it and the money can be used to finance the beginnings of yet other new communities."

The Director ended his explanation with a little homily:

"I believe you know better than I that your country, Canada, has an even bigger proportion of Northern lands than the Soviet Union. So why, may I ask, are you ignoring it as a place for men to work and live and build new cities? Why do you treat it as a distant colony to be exploited but not to be occupied? Well, perhaps you will someday see it differently — if you have not already lost it to your big southern neighbor.

"*We* think of the North as a land to be lived in. *We* do not go north just to fill our pockets. We are making it a part of our whole nation — and the North is making a new kind of men and women out of us."

There is not always unanimity of opinion among the hydraheaded organs of state in the USSR. In the summer of 1958 a battle developed in Moscow over the most suitable type of electric power source for the valuta center of Mirny. The hard-nosed industrial economists, who were only interested in diamonds, plumped for a coal-fired plant which would be fueled from nearby surface deposits and which would be quick and cheap to build and economical to operate. However, representatives from the Northern planning group insisted on a hydroelectric plant. Gavriel Bijanov, who was summoned away from a dam-building job in central Siberia to support the view of the Northern planners, explained the situation to me.

"There were a number of reasons for wanting hydroelectric generation. The obvious one, and the one we used as our main argument, was that we not only needed a great deal of power for the development of the Mirny complex in its secondary stages, but we also intended to supply the goldfields at Bodaibo, five hundred kilometers to the south; the diamond pipe at Udachnaya; and a new pipe at Aikhal, five hundred kilometers to the north. In order to do this we would need at least one and a half million kilowatts and it would have been impracticable to build a thermal station to produce that much power at Mirny, where everything had to be brought in by boats and winter roads.

"While this was true enough, we had still other reasons, ones which were not so likely to meet the approval of the economists. We had been thinking for years that something must be done to stop the severe air pollution caused by thermal plants, so whenever we could we tried to substitute hydro power. Also we had long dreamed about building cities in which everything would be done by electric power — not only lighting and cooking, but all heating as well. This would mean little pollution of the air; power would come entirely from a renewable source; and much more of the nonrenewable supplies of oil and coal could be reserved for gradual consumption in coal and petrochemical industries. Why go on burning the stuff when it can be converted into hundreds of useful products? So, you see, we needed lots of power for the Mirny development if we were to make the town fully electrified, and we wanted the nearby coal deposits saved as the basis for an extraction and manufacturing industry.

"Another reason for refusing a thermal plant was that we wanted a chance to design and build a hydroelectric plant under the most adverse conditions of Northern climate and inaccessibility — a plant which would be the prototype for many more to be built across the whole of the arctic to solve the very serious problems of power supply

in the far North. Such a plant had never been built anywhere before. Mirny was our chance to do it, because we
knew this first one was going to cost a fortune, and only
something as valuable as diamonds could pay for it."

The Northern planners won their case, and Gavriel was
given the job of directing the project. It was hardly an en-
viable prospect. He was faced with the task of having to
dam a major river in a region subjected to eight months of
winter and temperatures that plunged as low as 80° below.
Because of the inaccessibility of the site, he knew he would
have to forget about concrete and steel and build the dam
of local materials. Furthermore, everything he did would
be subjected to the iron control of permafrost.

The first workers arrived on the site by helicopter in the
fall of 1960 — twelve men and one horse! They threw up
log cabins banked to the eaves with mud and moss against
the terrible Vilyui frost. As fast as the huts were built they
were occupied by new arrivals. During that first bitter winter a trail paved with compacted snow was blazed through
the taiga to Mirny. During the ensuing five years this was
the only ground link with the outer world, and it was only
usable in winter. In summer all transport had to be by air.

Because of the incredibly difficult transportation problems, and the distances involved, major items had to be ordered from European Russia at least eighteen months in advance of the time they would be needed. Nothing that was
not absolutely essential could be brought in from outside.
The new town of Chernychevsky grew in the manner of a
classic pioneer community, its homes and buildings constructed of logs cut in the nearby forests and chinked with
mud and moss. They were heated with wood, too, and in
many cases were roofed with moss and mud that gave so
little protection against rain that in summer everyone

moved out to live in tents, despite black flies and mosquitos in plague proportions.

The unique nature of the Vilyui River itself posed special problems. In December it carries a dribbling 1.4 to 3 cubic meters of water per second; but by June the flow has leapt to 13,000 cubic meters a second. The fact that the future power drain would be at its greatest during the winter, when there was the least flow of water in the Vilyui system, necessitated the creation of a tremendous reservoir and a much higher and bigger dam than would have been needed to produce the same amount of power in the South. Also, because of the consequent enormous pressure in the penstocks, special propeller-type turbines had to be designed as a substitute for the normal radial-action type.

So complex were the preliminary problems that work on the main structure — the dam and the west bank powerhouse — did not begin until 1963. By then the initially high cost estimates had tripled, and Mirny, inadequately supplied with electricity from diesel generators and a "portable" coal-fired plant, was screaming blue murder. It looked for a while as if the whole Chernychevsky project might be abandoned in favor of a big coal-fired station. The great experiment was barely saved when Gavriel risked his neck by guaranteeing he would deliver power within four years.

As the work force began blasting a power canal and turbine hall out of the frozen granite (making use of the debris to begin pushing rock wings for the dam out from the canyon walls), a new difficulty appeared. The frozen bedrock which had seemed sturdy enough to support almost any weight, was found to be underlain by a cracked strata full of ice lenses which could easily be deformed by the great weight of the dam and so lead to its collapse.

The solution to this was to increase vastly the breadth of

the dam at its base and so spread the load over a much greater area — a solution which meant *trebling* the amount of rock fill that had to be blasted and trucked to the site.

The solving of each problem seemed only to lead to new and worse difficulties. As the riverbed was blasted, in mid-winter, to form a foundation trench, it was discovered that even the upper layers of bedrock were cracked. Although they were cemented together by permafrost, there was the likelihood that the weight of the dam would temporarily generate enough pressure to melt the ice and so again threaten the entire structure. The solution this time was to design a tunnel which would run along the basement rock through the full length of the dam and from which workers could inject cement grout under very high pressure into the fissures as the ice melted. It was estimated that this local melting process would continue for at least six years until permafrost had seeped back through the underlying rock and reasserted its sovereignty.

The bulk of the dam was to be of stone, but the inner core was to be a water-impervious mixture of clay, sand and fine gravel. The core was designed to contain the water of the reservoir while the thick layers of rock around it would act as ballast to keep the core in place and to insulate it from summer heat and from the warmth of the water in the reservoir. The real strength of the dam was to be provided by the Vilyui winter, which would freeze the core into one monolithic block.

Material for the core was found five miles from the site but, of course, it was solidly frozen. The clays and sands had to be thawed, thin layer by thin layer, under the summer suns, then scraped into great, flat-topped mounds for storage. In order to keep these mounds from freezing when winter came, electric heating rods were inserted into them in a rectangular pattern and connected to a series of diesel generators.

The core material had to be hauled to the dam site and placed in position during the coldest months of the year — the colder the better, from Gavriel's point of view.

"We did not like to place core material unless the temperature was at least 30° below zero. We had to be sure it would freeze absolutely solidly. The rods in the storage mounds raised the temperature of the material just high enough so it could be loaded on trucks, driven at top speed to the dam, dumped, spread and compacted before it turned to icy stone. At temperatures of 60° below, we had trouble with it. It insisted on freezing too fast. We fixed that by building big mobile flame throwers and also by saturating it with very high concentrations of salt water."

"At 60° below you surely must have had trouble with your workers too," I said. "Did you use flame throwers and brine on them as well?"

Gavriel laughed. "No, they had something better. They called it Spirit Vilyui and I am not sure how it was made. They tell about one fellow who dropped a two-liter bottle of it on the frozen ground outside his house one cold winter night. The next morning there was a mudhole there a meter in diameter and, when they tried to find how deep it was, they couldn't get a probe long enough to reach the bottom.

"We had the toughest and best-humored crowd of people in the Soviet Union. Most were just youngsters. They came from all over. There was an Azerbaijanian from Baku who had never even seen snow before. He had a wonderful voice and you could hear him singing all over the dam site. He would sing curses upon the ice and snow so they sounded as beautiful as love songs — but the words were the worst I've ever heard. At least once a week he'd roar that he was going home on the next plane. But, you know, he is still here. Even the women — and there were a lot of them — mostly held out. The wives did not have to work, but most of them did and a lot worked right on the dam alongside the men. I really don't know what kept people here, unless it was some special kind of Russian stubbornness. Perhaps, though, they shared our feelings. Here was a job most people in the South said couldn't be done; but it had to be done if the North was going to develop the way we felt it should."

By midwinter of 1965–1966, the builders were ready to close the gap in the center of the dam. It was one of the worst winters on record in central Siberia, and working conditions were appalling. Nevertheless, the task was completed a few weeks before the spring breakup unleashed the terrific Vilyui floods. The films taken at the time show thousands of people standing silent on the edge of the canyon watching the waters rise behind the dam. There are no scenes of cheering or flag waving, no bands, no rockets in the air. I asked one of the engineers why there was so little apparent excitement.

"It is difficult to explain. Instead of feeling like cheering, most of us felt closer to tears. It was not a feeling of victory so much as a feeling we had lost something — the thing we had done together, so many thousands of us; the life we had led together in this isolated little world buried in the taiga . . . it was coming to an end. Perhaps we would find it again in some other place, building some other dam, but here in Chernychevsky, the great times when we felt like giants and lived so closely with one another, and relied so much upon one another that we were all brothers and sisters, that time was running out."

There was another moment of a different kind in June

1967, when the great steel gate of the inlet lock rolled up and the Vilyui roared into the penstock and fell two hundred feet down into the frozen rock to begin spinning a turbine. There *was* a band that day, and red banners flying, and people in holiday dress, and a delegation of stolid, black-suited gentlemen from the Olympian heights in Moscow who looked, nodded their heads, congratulated the dam builders, and flew off back to their own peculiar world.

Chernychevsky was on the line.

The story does not end there, however. Now a second powerhouse is being built on the opposite side of the river. When both are operating at full capacity they will generate one million six hundred thousand kilowatts of power. Already electricity is turning Mirny, Chernychevsky and Lensk into electrified cities which will soon be devoid of chimneys, growing cleanly in clean air. It is powering the first of the manufacturing plants; a factory for producing exploded stone fiber for insulation; one producing prefabricated cement apartment units; another to process waste timber into fiberboard. The pylons march north now to Aikhal and to Udachnaya, and east to the new gas fields on the lower Vilyui where they will supply electricity for a gas-chemical industry.

The dream of the Northern planners — of men like Gavriel — is also becoming a reality elsewhere. During 1970 a dam and power station on the Chernychevsky model will be begun on the lower Kolyma River and two or possibly three more will be started in Chukotka. All will be built far to the north of the arctic circle.

The town of Chernychevsky will not wither away and die when the power plants are completed. Already its log buildings are being replaced by masonry apartments. It has begun to serve in a new role as a transportation and road-building center from which an all-weather highway is beginning to crawl north through the hundreds of miles of taiga to Aikhal. Before that job is completed, Chernychevsky will have undergone its third metamorphosis, changing into a manufacturing town with a number of low labor-intensive, high power-intensive industries to support it in the future.

In 1955 the Lensk-Mirny-Chernychevsky region had a population of fewer than four hundred people. In 1969 there were more than sixty thousand in the three sister cities, plus another sixteen hundred on the new state and collective farms. The overall population will not increase much above one hundred fifty thousand, which is the planned total for this particular complex.

But, far to the north, new cities are already being built — cities which will owe much to the pioneer dam builders of Chernychevsky.

13

YAKUTSK
and Mother Lena

One morning Simeon Danielov and I were walking beside the banks of the Lena near Yakutsk. Scattered across its gleaming surface were dozens of river boats, and as I watched them I began feeling homesick. Ships and seamen are a major part of my life and I am most at home when I can look out to a limitless horizon of open ocean. In Yakutia I was beginning to feel landlocked.

Simeon listened sympathetically as I explained my feelings.

"But Farley, you are mistaken about Yakutia. In the North we have 2,000 miles of ocean front. And connecting to the ocean we have an inland sea reaching into almost every corner of our country. It is narrow but with its major arms is more than eight thousand miles in length. You are looking at it now — *Elueneh* — mother Lena. She is our inland sea."

"A river is a river is a river." I replied. "The trouble

with all you poets is you get carried away by your own imagery."

"And the trouble with you is you can't see beyond your beard." Simeon said with a smile. "Tomorrow we'll open your eyes for you."

He was as good as his word. Next morning, in company with several friends, we drove out of town in brittle, crystalline weather under a low, cold sun which was proclaiming the near approach of winter.

We passed through a guarded gate on the river plain and abruptly found ourselves in what appeared to be a major seaport. Ahead of us a forest of gantry cranes swung their jibs against the sky. Lift trucks and straddle trucks crowded the road we were following, heaving and hoisting mountains of freight that partially obscured the view of nearly two miles of docks lined with ships. The illusion of having been miraculously transported to a busy ocean terminal was so strong I thought I could smell the salt tang of sea air. Perhaps I really could, for the whole of the terminal area (about twenty-five square kilometers) sits on a plain heavily impregnated with brine oozing up from deposits left by a primordial sea.

I had only a confused glimpse of the place before we stopped at the Yakutsk port authority offices, where we were greeted by a big blond Viking with a chin like a dredge bucket who wore the uniform of a captain in the Soviet merchant marine.

At forty-four, Victor Rukavishnikov had the weathered look of a man who had spent a lifetime on the water. Born of Old Russian immigrant stock in a small Yakutian village, he had spent twenty-four years on the Lena, as deckhand, mate, pilot and finally skipper. At forty he "swallowed the anchor" to become Chief of Port for Yakutsk harbor.

He had, however, avoided becoming a bureaucrat. When I started to sit down at the conference table in his office, prepared for the usual briefing, he stopped me.

"What's the use of talking in here? Let's go out on the docks. But wait a minute. What time is it? After ten o'clock. Ah hah, we'll have a quick one before we go."

When we were properly fortified, Victor led us at a lope through the complexities of the docks and terminal. Hundred-ton mobile cranes grumbled and whistled overhead, emptying the bellies of a score of big, awkward-looking vessels whose like I had never seen before. Women checkers kept an eye aloft as the cargo swung inshore. They were too busy to more than glance at us.

"Summer is over." Victor yelled in my ear. "Soon comes the ice. Our shipping season is only about one hundred and seventy days, and in that time the Lena river fleet has to handle nearly five million tons of freight. No time to stand around and think about your love life!"

The noise and confusion did not make for easy conversation. I managed to yell something back about how impressed I was by the magnitude of the place.

"Yakutsk port is nothing. Only in the third rank of Soviet harbors. You should see Osetrovo on the Upper Lena. It is in the first class . . . one of the biggest ports in the Soviet Union."

Victor's modesty was commendable but, I think, ill-founded. Yakutsk port is at least equal in size, modernity and apparent efficiency to any medium-sized seaport on the coast of North America. The thing is that it is not *on* a coast. It lies seven hundred air miles and about fifteen hundred river miles from salt water. As for Osetrovo — *it* lies another thousand miles upstream from Yakutsk, in the very heart of Siberia and less than two hundred miles from Lake

Baikal. Osetrovo is now Yakutia's main connection with the Trans-Siberian Railway, and in 1969 its harbor handled more than three million tons of freight, much of it "containerized," bound north down the broad waters of the Lena.

Victor yanked me to safety as a straddle truck waddled up carrying a loaded container about the size of a freight car between its widespread legs.

"Have you had enough of this? Simeon Danielov says you are homesick for the sea. How about a little voyage?"

Somewhat dazedly I nodded assent. We fled from the pandemonium of the docks and drove downriver to the passenger port. Here it was mercifully peaceful. Although the Yakutsk fleet of big diesel vessels carries up to half a million passengers a year, most of the ships were laid up for the winter. Alongside the main pier rested a most peculiar looking vessel. Built of gleaming aluminum and shaped like a flattened cigar, she seemed to be a combination of an airplane and a submarine.

"Byelorusskiy hydrofoil," Victor said proudly. "You have good luck. The river air observer reports no skim ice today — although it's overdue — so we'll take you traveling in our 'water bird.' "

Dubiously I climbed aboard this most unseaworthy-looking contraption. Her passenger accommodation, which ran the full length of the hull, was more like the fuselage of an airliner than a boat's cabin — chrome trim, reclining seats, aircraft-type windows — all that was missing were the seat belts and the No Smoking signs.

We were settling ourselves in the deep-padded seats when Victor remembered something.

"Ulcers on my soul! No vodka! Simeon! Kola! Leonid! Come with me!"

A few minutes later all four returned aboard laden with the spoils of a raid on a nearby canteen, and the boat's skipper, a short, taciturn Buryat named Vladimir Stepanov, ordered his two Yakut crewmen to cast off. A nine-hundred-horsepower aviation diesel snarled into life and we swung heavily and clumsily out on the glass-calm river. Then abruptly we were flying! Climbing up on her foils until only they and the propeller were still in the water, the vessel flashed downriver at sixty knots and I, who am used to traveling on my own Newfoundland schooner at six knots, began to wish I had stayed home in bed.

Sensing my unease, Nikolai Yakutsky came to my rescue. Corks snapped and bottles began to circulate. There were only six of us in a cabin designed to hold thirty, so there was ample room to have a breakfast party, complete with cold sausages, caviar, canned crab and other oddments seized from the canteen.

Ten miles downstream we approached a new river settlement. Our hydrofoil slowed and sagged sloppily into the water as Victor told me about the town of Zhataj.

"This is the base for the Middle Lena fleet. Here we have ten thousand people living. They work at vessel maintenance and new ship construction. There was nothing at all here fifteen years ago. Up until then all our steel vessels were built in Russia and brought out along the Northern Sea Route. Russian marine architects said we could not build our own boats here. We said we could. What is more, we said we could design them too, and do a better job than they.

"We started small, designing and building one of the first self-propelled steel barges to be used in Siberia. It was a success. It had to be, because we *knew* this river. We went on to bigger things. Eventually we got permission to do it all ourselves. What really convinced Moscow was when we designed and built a one-thousand-ton self-powered barge that only drew one meter, forty centimeters of water when it was fully loaded.

"Now we have eighteen types of river craft in serial production, and we supply them to all Siberian river fleets. The only ships we do not build are heavy-duty tugs, hydrofoils and passenger boats. We leave those to the Russians, just to keep them happy!

"We are proud of what we have done on our Lena. Forty years ago the whole river fleet consisted of thirty little wooden steamboats and a couple of hundred wooden barges. Fifteen years ago there was still not a single self-propelled barge, and very few steel boats of any kind. Nowadays just four of our three-thousand-ton self-propelled barges can carry as much as the whole Lena fleet of the 1930s — and we have scores of those big fellows.

"Mother Lena has always been the front street of Ya-kutia. They used to say in the West we would never be any-thing but a wilderness because we had no railroads, and no-body could afford to build them through the taiga and the mountains. Well, we don't need them. Almost all our coun-try lies along the 'coast' of the Lena and its tributaries, and there is hardly a stream of hers we cannot turn into a highway. On the rougher ones we use air-pillow boats that skim along a few feet above the surface of the rapids. If there is never a railroad built into our land, it won't matter in the least."

Victor stopped to wet his whistle and a middle-aged Yakut journalist took up the theme.

"It isn't only in summer that the Lena works for us. Once the ice thickens, her surface becomes a highway for truck transport. Convoys drive all the way from Osetrovo to

Mirny and Yakutsk, and trucks from here go even farther down the lower river."

"Trucks!" Victor interrupted contemptuously. "If the idiots who make up the supply orders for the year knew what they were doing, the trucks could stay at home and sleep all winter. *We* can carry all the freight Yakutia will ever need. That's *our* job, friend!"

I distracted him.

"How many vessels are there on the river, Victor?"

He gave me a calculating look and then his red face split in an immense grin.

"Military secret! Not for the ears of capitalist spies! To tell the truth, I really don't know. The fleets on all big Siberian rivers are pooled, and each river can draw on the pool according to its needs. If there is a lot of work to do on the Yenisei, then we send vessels there to help out. Other times, they send ships to us. Tankers, refrigerator ships and all the bigger self-propelled barges are dual-purpose, designed for coastwise passages as well as river work. Because of their shallow draft they can hug the arctic coast and find open water when the bigger ships can't move because of ice offshore."

We turned away from Zhataj with its dry-docks, marine railways and shipyards, and the boat reared up on her foils again. This time we flew upstream, passing Yakutsk, which was wreathed in a purple haze of woodsmoke from the chimneys of its older sections.

It was a superb autumnal day. The river rolled as smoothly as oil and seemed to be as wide as the horizon, although in fact it is only twelve miles broad at Yakutsk (it is thirty miles wide near its mouth). The banks were low, with occasional great buttes rising from the dark water. The current was swift but the channel was well buoyed, taking us between willow-covered islands, clear of the ever-shifting sandbars. Despite the lateness of the season there was an amazing amount of shipping, ranging from one-thousand-horsepower tugs (built in Poland) pushing or towing long strings of barges, to a two-thousand-ton tanker so deeply laden that her decks appeared to be awash. Here and there we whipped past dredges still busily at work deepening the channel. Occasionally we passed small craft carrying river fishermen and hunters bound upstream to look for geese and ducks.

I went forward to visit the skipper and found him perched in an aircraft-type cockpit, plexiglass-enclosed, in front of a formidable panel of instruments. He offered to let me take command, but I know my limitations. I can sail a boat adequately but I would be bound to make a mess of flying one!

After an hour's run the banks began to rise until we were whistling past high, forested cliffs. A low mountain appeared ahead and Nikolai Yakutsky pointed to it.

"Tatar Haia. The sacred mountain of the Yakut people. In the middle of it lies the valley of Tuey Nada where the Yakut nation was born. Very long ago a chief named Elai, son of a great leader in middle-Asia, led his people north and east until they reached the banks of the Lena under Tatar Haia. Elai carried with him the maxims of our people engraved on a stone tablet. When he saw the flowing waters of the river he flung the tablet in and gave the order to his followers to drop their saddle blankets. The Yakut had found the land they sought."

Nikolai also told me that in 1787 an American traveler came downstream to this place in an open boat from the vicinity of Irkutsk, then went on to Yakutsk where he spent the winter. This man's name was Ledyard. When I returned home I dug out the account of his journey and found this description of the Yakut people:

The Yakut is a man of nature, not of art. He is a lover of peace. No lawyers [are needed] here, perplexing the rights of property. . . . Never, I believe, did the Yakut speak ill of the Deity or envy his fellow creatures. He is contented to be what he is. Hospitable and human, he is uniformly cheerful and tranquil, laconic in thought, word and action. Those that live with the Russians in their villages are above mediocrity as to riches, but discover the same indifference to accumulating more that a North American Indian does.

The Yakut have not changed all that much since Ledyard's day.

Nikolai also talked about a United States naval expedition which sailed through Bering Strait in 1879 in a quixotic attempt to reach the North Pole. The expedition ship, *Jeannette,* under Lieutenant DeLong, was caught in the polar pack and spent two years drifting aimlessly in the ice until she was finally crushed not far north of the New Siberian Islands. In September 1881 word reached General Tschernaiyev, the Governor of Yakutsk, that Evenki reindeer herders had found eleven white men, all close to death, at the mouth of the Lena. These were the sole survivors of the *Jeanette.* Nurtured by Evenki and Yakut people, the eleven were brought to Yakutsk and finally restored to their homes. Strangely enough, the tragedy of the *Jeanette* is well remembered in Yakutia but is all but forgotten in the United States.

Apart from river traffic, the world we were flying past seemed as wild and uninhabited as it must have been in

Ledyard's time. It came as a considerable shock when we rounded a great bluff and saw a complex of modern resort hotels clinging to the slopes of a wooded valley. Called Tabaga, these hotels belong to the Railway Workers Trade Union and in summer house about eighteen hundred people from all over the USSR who prefer to spend their vacations in the far North rather than on the shores of the Black Sea!

"Tourism is important here," Simeon explained. "All-Union river tours sail throughout the summer from Osetrovo on big cruise ships. They even go northward past Yakutsk. Next year they will go to the mouth of the Lena and to Tiksi, where, if they wish, the passengers can transfer to oceangoing ships of the Northern Sea Route fleet and sail west to Archangel and Murmansk, or east and south to Vladivostok. The authorities think it important for people from European Russia to have a chance to see for themselves what the northlands are like."

A little more than a hundred kilometers south of Yakutsk we came to the town of Pokrovskoe, founded by immigrant Russians two hundred and forty years ago. Through almost all that time it remained unchanging; a cluster of log houses strung along the high bank of the river and known to the outer world only by the fearsome stories told by the few exiles who escaped from it during Tsarist times. Now, although it is still a town of wooden houses, it will soon be a city of concrete apartment blocks. A huge factory is being built here to take advantage of a limestone deposit and of a newly constructed cement plant. The factory will manufacture prefabricated building panels, concrete blocks and similar materials for shipment all over Yakutia on the waters of the Lena.

We went ashore on the beach, climbed the bluff and wandered through the old town's meandering, tree-lined streets.

Victor and Nikolai headed for the liquor store to replenish our supplies. I followed Simeon to the co-op store to see a friend of his, and I was startled to find a sporting goods department which offered, among other items, fencing foils and masks. Whatever the shortages in Moscow, there appeared to be no dearth of consumer goods in Pokrovskoe.

Nor was there any shortage of reading matter. The bookstore, in an old log building, had a stock of books, prints and paintings which would have been impressive in any Canadian city — but the population of Pokrovskoe was just under three thousand people. Simeon found copies of his newest book here and happily bought one and inscribed it for me on the spot:

For my dear sailor friend who on this day made the acquaintance of Mother Elueneh and took his first voyage on the inland sea of the Yakut Republic.

One of the great joys of Yakutsk, as opposed to almost every other place I visited in the Soviet Union, was that although the people were immensely proud of their city, and anxious to have me see it all, they never forced the pace. There were no conducted tours, no tightly scheduled attempts to cram me so full of information it would come running out my ears. Things just seemed to happen in Yakutsk, and they were always the right things, at the right time.

My visit to the Yakut State University was a case in point. I had decided not to bother going there, assuming it would provide me with nothing more than additional masses of statistics. But one cold morning in October as I was walking down the main street I became aware that a slight, beautiful Yakut girl who seemed to be no more than seventeen was dogging my footsteps. I slowed, turned and smiled.

She drew alongside and very shyly asked in English what time it was. I told her, but she made no move to go on her way. Then she said:

"Tovarich Mowat, please. We students at the University wish you to visit us. Will you come? Many have read your books, and we have heard about your travels in our country. We admire you so much. If it would not be too much trouble? . . ."

Moisie Efrimov was waiting for me at the hotel. He asked what I would like to do that afternoon — if anything. He did not seem at all surprised when I replied that I simply *had* to visit the University.

Yakutsk is a students' town. One out of every three of its inhabitants is enrolled in one of the innumerable schools, institutes or colleges, either for day or for night classes; and the University is the students' citadel. Although it was founded only in 1956, it has already become the heart of the city. Physical construction cannot keep up with its growth and, apart from its massive three-story central building (which is still uncompleted), classrooms for the forty-three hundred students are scattered all over the place in any structure which can house them.

"What do the buildings matter?" a second-year Evenki student asked me. "The important things to us are the best books, equipment and instructors; and we have those. We would come here for those things alone even if we had to sleep in tents all winter."

I wandered around the main building with a group of students. The science labs were filled with esoteric equipment, all brand-new and much of it made in Czechoslovakia and Rumania. The library occupied the largest single portion of the building, and it bulged at the seams with nearly half a million volumes. The professors and instructors of the sixteen departments (there are seven faculties, including medicine) held surprisingly high qualifications. One of the department heads (all of whom are Yakut) explained:

"When it was announced we were going to start the University, we were buried under applications from teachers all over the Soviet Union. Even when we explained that living conditions would not be so good at first and we had not too much money, it made no difference. So we took the best and today our standing shows us near the top in the Soviet Union. However, that is not all due to the volunteers. Sixty percent of our teachers are Yakut."

It is really a students' university. All regular students (there are an additional three thousand night students and students taking correspondence courses) are on scholarships. Most of them live in residences which they run themselves by means of elected councils. Those who live out receive extra grants to cover the higher cost of board and room. All textbooks are free. The Central Students' Council, the Student Trade Union and the Komsomol Committee all have representation, with full voting rights, on the Governing Board, where they exercise a strong influence on policy. The Prorector, Ivan Mikhailovich Bruhanov, a Yakutian-born Russian, was a little rueful about that.

"We have been reading about student power in American universities and the complaints of their boards about students trying to take a hand in too many things. Here the students already have a hand in everything! Sometimes I don't know who is running this University, they or we. Do you know every student group has an elected monitor who can challenge any of his Dean's decisions and bring it to the Governing Board? Not only that, but a Dean cannot even take disciplinary action against a student without permission of the monitor. It was not the same when I was a student. But never mind, it isn't so bad. They are a head-strong lot, and they make mistakes, but they are loyal to the University and as determined to make it a good place as any of the staff."

Later I talked privately to three students, two Yakut and one Russian. I asked whether they really felt they had much freedom to determine how the University was run. A twenty-year-old Yakut girl, studying history and languages, answered.

"Youth needs freedom. If they don't get it they become frustrated and then bored, or worse. This would be bad for the State, would it not? Here we have no more freedom than we need, but we do have what we need."

"In political thought and action too?" I asked.

A Yakut biology student answered that one. "That doesn't come into it. Those who are really political join the Komsomol. Most of us don't. We think it is our first task to get the best education we can. Only then will we be prepared to consider what needs changing; and only then will we be prepared to go about it sensibly."

"But can you dissent in any meaningful way from what we in the West might consider an imposed political doctrine?" I probed, feeling my way.

The young Yakut looked puzzled. "Is there any other kind of political doctrine?" he asked. Then he smiled. "We have a proverb in our country. When a horse is going the right way, why kick him in the ribs?"

These three students had all studied English for several years but had never before spoken to someone whose native tongue it was. Although their grammar and command of idiom was not as good as my transcription makes it appear, none of them would have serious communication difficulties if they were to find themselves magically transported to Canada.

Classes were small — I saw none with more than twenty students and many, including all the science classes, were smaller. There was no crowding or feeling of crowding. If the buildings were shabby and somewhat unkempt, the atmosphere was a pleasantly homey one.

To a surprising degree the construction of new university buildings is in the hands of the students themselves. Undergraduates in architecture design the new structures. Student engineers draw up the working plans and select and test the materials to be used. Students from all faculties work on the actual construction during the summer vacations and receive standard wages. This sort of thing undoubtedly helps create the feeling which was implicit whenever students spoke about the University. Almost always they referred to it as "our" or "my" University. They seemed to be happy with their involvement in the place — except for one young man, a Komsomol member, who took some pains to draw me aside.

"You should not believe all the students tell you," he told me in a conspiratorial tone of voice, "particularly the Yakut students. They still have many primitive opinions and ideas. Socialism has not yet fully reconstructed their thinking. There is much laxness — not enough discipline. This University would be better if the students held more political convictions and if they were subjected to stronger Party control. We are working on that; but at the moment do not get the impression there is here any tendency to the decadence of Western education practices."

I assured him I would heed his warning and shook free of him as fast as I could. I had noted two things about him. First, he was a new Russian immigrant from near Moscow.

Second, he spoke of "this" University instead of "our" University.

On several occasions we ended an evening in the apartment block which housed the Artists and Writers Union, the living quarters of many of the writers and painters, and the artists' studios. These were times to talk far into the night about the mystical subject of "North," peoples of the North, and sometimes to become involved in heated discussions about the thorny path of art.

The thirty-three members of the Artists Union represent, as they say themselves, the first generation of Yakut artists trained in Western techniques. Their dean is Ivan Machasynov who, at thirty-eight, is the eldest amongst them. Born on the taiga, and orphaned at the age of nine, Ivan went to school in Yakutsk, then on to Leningrad, where he studied for six years, spending long days at the Hermitage collection and trying to contain his yearning for Yakutia. His work during this period was good enough that he was asked to stay on in Leningrad, but he would have none of that. So back he came, and now he is the Director of the newly formed Yakutsk Art College.

Although all the artists work in watercolor and in oil, their natural genius lies in graphics — a medium closely akin to the old artistic skills of their ancestors who never made even the smallest wooden utensil without engraving intricate designs upon its surface. Wood prints, lino prints and steel and copper engravings preoccupy them, and when they are working on subjects from their own heritage they produce dramatic, beautiful and imaginative prints.

Unhappily, the same cannot be said for works based on modern subjects — mines, electric power stations, factories, or farmers driving tractors. These works are stiff, uninspired, unemotional and, like so much Soviet art of the "accepted" mode, depressingly clouded with propaganda overtones.

One night when we had spent some hours sitting on the floor of one of the studios, eating sugared wild cranberries, sipping cognac and examining prints, I commented on the disparity in quality between works inspired by tradition and those inspired by "other considerations." Why was one group so good, the other so bad, I asked?

There was an embarrassed silence. I had clearly hit upon a nerve. Someone changed the subject and I got no answer from his group — perhaps because it was a group. However, on another occasion in the home studio of a young Russian painter, there was no such reticence.

"Politics and art simply don't mix. We have always known this and the authorities ought to realize it. Just the same, they go on insisting it is an artist's foremost duty to serve the propaganda needs of the State. We have no wish to work against the State, but unless we are free to interpret things as they appear to us, we will never be more than hacks. And that is exactly what most of our recognized artists appear to be . . . in public anyway. In private almost all of us do our own work as we like, but it is impossible to have it hung. This is too bad, but not so serious, because our private works sell very well — much better than our public ones. The whole situation is foolish because our so-called private paintings are often better known than the works hung in the State galleries. Visitors from your countries who think Soviet art is still in the 1920s are not seeing what is really being done. Don't worry. We are making progress, and one day our work will be seen by all the world."

Having seen a fair amount of this private work, I can

believe him, but there is no question in my mind that the official attitude has greatly retarded the development of the visual arts in the USSR. It is unfortunately true that the political animal is usually antipathetic toward the artistic animal, perhaps because he is simply too stupid to comprehend the meaning and value of true art.

14
YAKUTSK
and Madame Presiden

On my last day in Yakutsk, Simeon Danielov took John deVisser and me to see a rehearsal at the National Ballet Theater. Fiodor Potapov, Director of the Yakut National Drama Theater, joined us, and as we sat watching the dancing he talked enthusiastically about the performing arts in Yakutsk. I found his presence rather distracting and wished I was John, who had nothing to do but scuttle about onstage and backstage among the ballerinas looking for good camera angles, or just looking.

The Drama Theater began in 1925 and now has a company of thirty-five professional Yakut actors, many of them Moscow-trained. It performs dramas written by Yakut playwrights in their own language. In 1947 the National Opera Theater was founded and it now employs several Yakut librettists and composers. The National Ballet Theater came later but already has five full-length Yakutian ballets in its repertoire. It also has as beautiful a *corps*

212

de ballet as any balletomane could hope to see. The dancing was somewhat erratic, but the two featured ballerinas, Evdoki Stepanova and Natalia Christoforova, made up for that. I could contentedly have watched them all day long had not John run out of film, a disaster which reduced him to a state of utter frustration. In common decency to an old friend, I felt obliged to take him home before he began to weep openly.

That afternoon we were the guests of Madame Elene Eremevina Amosova, a retired schoolteacher living in a log house which had been built by her grandfather in one of the older sections of Yakutsk. Decorated outside with traditional fretwork, it was light and airy inside. It contained three bedrooms, a large old-fashioned kitchen with an immense samovar and a masonry heating and cooking stove, a living room, a dining room and a glassed-in sunporch. Except for the presence of an electric sewing machine, television set, washing machine and other such modern gadgetry, it was typical of the homes of most urban Yakut families. Soon a modern apartment block will be built nearby and Elene Eremevina and her husband will move to a flat with running water, sewage system and central heating. They are in no hurry.

"My family has lived in this house for three generations, and it is a good house and we love it deeply. When my husband and I do move, the house will go to my eldest son. He is an engineer and could have a nice new flat but he would rather have the house. A family should have a house of its own in which to raise the children."

Born in 1910, Madame Amosova is still an exceptionally handsome and gracious woman, her sleek black hair untouched by gray and her wide, expressive face unlined. At the age of eighteen she became one of the first Yakut teach-

ers, spending many years in the far North with the Red
Tents — the young volunteers who traveled from village to
village and from camp to camp teaching reading and writing to the illiterate country folk. At fifty she retired on full
pension to devote herself to her great passion — the preservation, as a living art, of Yakut craft traditions. Working
with reindeer skin, native furs, natural felt and chamois
(most of which she prepares herself), she produces superb
examples of the womanly arts of her people. Her gorgeously
embroidered handiwork, and that of her many pupils, is exhibited throughout the Soviet Union and was shown at
Expo '67 in Montreal, and Expo '70 in Osaka.

"You see," she explained, "it happens sometimes that
when a people of ancient culture come into the modern
world, they are in such a hurry to catch up they throw away
all that reminds them of the past. I, too, felt like this when
I was a girl and the young Russians joined us in the Red
Tents. I wanted to dress like them and look like them. But
one day it happened that a Russian girl from Leningrad,
who had become my close friend, asked me to make her a
pair of our embroidered boots and a reindeer fur jacket.
She said her people had nothing so beautiful. Afterward I
began to think perhaps we were being too hasty. Over the
years I came to realize we must remain Yakut; to turn ourselves into Russians would be to lose ourselves, as some
stranger might lose himself in the depths of the taiga.

"Now Yakut handicrafts are an important part of our
education system. All little girls learn those arts and practice them too. The old things have again become fashion-
able, and a young Yakut girl who goes to Moscow to study
is proud and happy to display her embroidered boots and
gloves. She is envied — not laughed at; and she feels good
to be a Yakut girl."

Over glasses of tea we talked about the life of the Amosovas. Elene and her husband had raised four children, two daughters and two sons, all of whom have attended or are attending university. The youngest girl, Augusta, arrived home from classes while we were there, looking radiant in a fur capote which she had made and decorated herself. Shyly she talked to us in English about her ambitions to take a special degree in art in Leningrad so she could continue the work her mother had begun.

In the early days of their marriage, when they lived near the arctic coast, the Amosovas worked alongside the people they were teaching. Elene became a reindeer herder. She ran traplines, skinned and tanned the furs she caught, and, wherever she went, she talked with the old women and gradually amassed a huge collection of ancient Yakut, Evenki and Yukagir designs and patterns for embroidery and insert work. These were not deposited in one of the several Yakutsk museums — they were put into everyday use in the growing Yakut handicraft industry.

It was with reluctance that I left the Amosovas late in the winter afternoon. But I had another date to keep — with yet another remarkable woman.

Soviet journalists (from west of the Urals) have christened her the Snow Queen. This is a title which gives Alexandra Yakovlevna Ovchinnikova, Chairman of the Supreme Soviet of the Yakut Autonomous Soviet Socialist Republic and a member of the Presidium of the Supreme Soviet of the USSR, no pleasure at all.

"It makes me sound like a white-haired grandmother; and see, there is not a white hair on my head! Or worse, it makes it seem I am queen of some frozen fairy-tale realm at the North Pole. Well, of course you know I *am* a grandmother

and very proud of it, but I am much prouder of my country
— of Yakutia — and it is shameful to make people think
it is nothing but a waste of snow and ice."

I met her first at a very dull official reception at Expo '67
in Montreal. Simply dressed, her jet hair combed close to
her head; dark eyes very alert, and her face devoid of cos-
metics but glowing brown, she was a natural woman, and a
handsome one, in a swarm of vastly unnatural diplomats,
officials and their ladies. She seemed so alien that I — also
an alien in that gathering — was immediately drawn to her,
and before long we were having a little party of our own.
She introduced me to *kumiss* — fermented mare's milk —
of which she had brought a supply with her from Russia. I
had no clear idea who she was until after she left the reception and someone from the Soviet Embassy asked me how
I had enjoyed meeting the lady President of Yakutia.

When we met again it was in her office in Yakutsk. She
beamed at me from behind her uncluttered desk and asked
if I had come for more of her kumiss. It was a bitter day
and the heating in the government building was inadequate,
so she had draped a huge shawl around her shoulders and
was toasting her stockinged feet over a small electric
heater. She looked even less like the President of the Soviet
Union's largest republic than she had in Montreal. Soft-
voiced, attentive when anyone else was speaking, full of humor and with an almost constant smile at her lips, she was
certainly not my conception of executive authority. Nevertheless, she was, and had been for more than a decade, the
most important woman in her country.

When I made some joking remark about the advances of
feminism in Yakutia, Alexandra Yakovlevna took me up
quickly.

"There is no such thing in my country. There has never

been any need for such a movement. Yakut men and women have always understood each other very well, and we women are greatly respected. We try hard to earn that respect. In the old days the wisdom of women was held to be the true wisdom of the people, and it was seldom the men failed to be guided by it. This regard for us has not changed, you see. It explains why a foolish old women like me comes to be Chairman of my Republic. How do you like my dress? You *should* like it. I bought it in Canada."

The regard in which Alexandra is held is shared by both men and women, and a visitor encounters it wherever he goes. A Chukchee student at the University described to me how she had almost quit her course as a result of an unhappy love affair with a young Russian mining engineer.

"But," she said, "before I did, I thought I might as well ask Ovchinnikova for her advice, so I went to her office, and she told me she would be so upset if I spoiled my career she would cry all night. I knew she would, too. And so I stayed."

To Western eyes this incident may read like a saccharine-coated episode from a bad nineteenth-century novel. However, the Yakut (and, indeed, most people in the Soviet Union) do not have the emotional reserve which characterizes Anglo-Saxon society. For one who knows her, it is not difficult to believe that if the Chukchee girl *had* quit, the lady President would indeed have wept.

Alexandra Yakovlevna has many facets to her character. Not only young girls in love but hard-nosed experts in the new technology consult her freely when they find themselves in trouble.

"If I can't find an answer to a problem," said a young engineer engaged in installing a natural gas distribution system in Yakutsk, "I just slip up and ask Ovchinnikova's advice. If she doesn't know the answer herself, she always knows just how to go about finding someone who does. But usually she can put me on the right track herself."

There is a strangely ingenuous quality about this woman who blushed like a schoolgirl when John DeVisser wished to take her picture. She had to be coaxed into it because, as she said, "Women of my age should perhaps sometimes be heard . . . but not so often seen," an attitude somewhat at variance with the most unpolitic shape and content of a remark she addressed to me a moment later.

"When are you Canadians going to start acting like real men and women and stop behaving like simple little children? Don't you realize you are giving away your country to anyone who wants to steal a piece of it? Haven't you the will to fight for what is yours and, much more important, for what belongs to the generations not yet born? Oh, you make me furious!"

It so happened that she had recently played hostess to a delegation of Canadian government officials and politicians, and she showed a most extraordinary disregard for protocol as she told me what she thought about these men who set the policies for, and administer, the Canadian North.

"When I visited Canada they refused to show me any of your native people, or where they lived and worked. The authorities would not even take me to the Canadian Indian-Eskimo pavilion at Expo. Nevertheless, I made up my mind that when they came here I would be sure to show them how our people lived. Can you believe it? They wouldn't look! All they wanted to see was how we manage to build mines and mining towns in eternal frost! Don't they care at all about people? Are they only interested in the quickest way to turn their country into a colony for exploitation by the Americans, the Germans and Japanese? Such foolish little men! You really should get rid of them!"

When I asked her if these were private comments, she laughed gaily.

"I know the diplomats don't like it, but it is a woman's special privilege to say what she thinks and feels. I make the most of it. You can publish anything I say . . . if you feel brave enough."

I felt brave enough to ask her a pointed question. "You're pretty hard on our politicians, but don't you think Yakutia is being exploited by European Russia in much the same way we are?"

She gave me a charming smile. "Tovarich Mowat, you have beautiful blue eyes. However, they are not entirely meant as ornaments. I'm sure you know how to use them. You have been to Mirny and Chernychevsky and a dozen other places in my country. How would you answer your own question?"

She left me to fumble over that one for a moment, then continued: "The Soviet Union is many countries, but it is also one country. In the past some parts were rich and others were very poor. It would still be that way if the people from the various parts had not learned how to help one another. Yakutian diamonds and gold, for instance, help the whole people of the Union; and in return we have received the help we needed to become a strong and happy nation in this modern world. No one is exploiting us . . . it may even be the other way around, but don't tell that to the Moscow people, please."

Two days before I was to leave Yakutia, Moisie Efrimov brought me a supper invitation from Alexandra Yakovlevna. I felt some trepidation in accepting. Dealing with a forthright woman is never easy, but dealing with one of such uncompromising directness as Madame President for an entire evening promised to be something of an ordeal. In preparation for it I asked Moisie to tell me more about her.

"Like all good Yakut she was born in the taiga. Her father raised cattle for a living, and children on the side. I don't know which job he liked best, but he fathered sixteen daughters and two sons. That was before the Revolution, and of all those children only four survived. Alexandra was one, of course; but then nothing in the world or beyond it could have prevented her from staying alive.

"Please don't ask exactly when she was born. She won't tell anyone; but she was still a child when Soviet Power came to us, and she was one of the first Yakut children to go to school. She studied very hard because, she says, she felt the most important thing to be done at once was to make roads and connect up all the isolated little places so they could share the Revolution better. After grade school she enrolled at the Road Building Institute, graduated as an engineer, and spent twenty years building roads and bridges all over the place. While she was at that she took correspondence courses and got her diplomas in history, economics and several other subjects.

"Everyone came to know her, so it was inevitable we should elect her as our Chairman. You won't find anyone in Yakutia who has done more for our country, who is more modest about it, and who is better loved. Of course, she does speak her mind rather plainly, but we are used to that."

I said I hoped I would get used to it too, but my fears proved groundless. Madame President showed another side of her nature at the party. She is an ardent Yakut traditionalist, and one of the great and inviolable traditions of her people is that hospitality transcends all other things.

She had chosen the dozen guests entirely from native peoples and had selected individuals whom I already knew and liked. From the moment we sat down to table, she directed the evening with masterful subtlety, setting the tone for one of the gayest gatherings I can recall. We drank enough, but for the first and last time in Siberia not too much. The toasts were frequent and emotional, but not sentimental. Conversation was controversial and witty, and almost completely apolitical. My good companion, Yura Rytkheu, was so lifted out of his rather gloomy self (he had then been on the wagon under doctor's orders for some weeks, which is enough to make any Siberian gloomy) he was moved to stand up and sing a Chukchee song — and a love song at that!

Somewhat carried away myself, I inadvertently committed a dreadful gaffe. Alongside everyone's plate stood a wooden kumiss drinking cup and a champagne glass. Now kumiss is very nearly a sacred drink in Yakutia, and one simply does not take liberties with it, but in an absent-minded moment I poured champagnsky (as the Russians call it) into my half-filled kumiss cup.

I realized what I was doing only when a dead silence settled over the table. Greatly flustered, I jerked the bottle away, spilling champagnsky into Alexandra Yaklovlevna's lap. She laughed — a lovely rippling laugh — reached over, picked up my kumiss cup and tasted the contents. For a moment she closed her eyes then she stood up and proposed a toast.

"Comrades, friends — for many thousands of years the Yakut people have made the most beautiful drink of all — our kumiss! We thought nothing could taste better. Now our good friend from Canada shows how wrong we were. He has invented a drink so good it will change everything. It will be a peace drink to link our two Northern countries together in the future. Please, all of you, do as he has done . . . then drink with me to our benefactor and to this new drink which we will henceforth call . . . *kumpansky!*"

Because our plane was to leave at dawn, this remarkable woman gently brought the party to an end at 10 P.M. with the presentation to John and me of Yakut winter hats made of superb muskrat fur — and with a last brief toast.

"John and Farley. We ask you to carry back to your country our love for your people and our great wish for abiding peace and closely growing friendship. We ask, too, that you will soon return to us, bringing back with you the same message we send now, for we want your people's love and friendship with all our hearts."

Someday I hope it will be possible for me to do this simple thing.

15
TCHERSKY

Shortly after Claire and I reached Yakutsk in 1966 Simeon Danielov asked us if there was any particular place we wanted to visit. Since at that time we did not know the name of a single locality in the republic except Yakutsk itself, this posed a problem.

"I'm sure there must be hundreds of places we'd like to see. However since you know them and we don't, I'd prefer to leave the choice to you. One thing, though, I'd like to visit a town in a remote Northern region."

Simeon merely nodded. During the days that followed, Claire, Kola, Yura and I saw several Northern towns, all of which appeared to be satisfactorily remote. I assumed my request had already been granted until one afternoon Kola announced we would be leaving before dawn the next day for the town of Tchersky.

"And where is Tchersky?" I asked.

Kola, who, as a Muscovite, knew as little about Yakutia

223

as I did, shrugged his narrow shoulders and looked more birdlike than usual.

"Who knows? Somewhere in Siberia. We'll see. One thing you can be sure about. It will have a lot of kindergartens and we will be taken to see every last one of them so we can tickle the dripping little monsters under their fat chins." Kola didn't really dislike children. He had just had enough kindergartens during our trip.

Yura Rytkheu could have given us some idea of where Tchersky was located, but during the 1966 trip Yura was *not* on the wagon; in fact he had apparently determined personally to create an alcoholic drought in Yakutsk. When we met him for dinner that evening he was unable to speak any known language, unless it was his native Chukchee, so he was no help in satisfying our curiosity about the whereabouts of Tchersky.

Kola rousted us out of bed at 2 A.M. Grumpily, and without even the solace of a glass of tea, we clumped into a Volga and were driven to the airport, where, as was to be expected, we found the flight had been delayed "indefinitely." The pilot's room was locked, so we had to join the proletarian masses — masses and *masses* of them, filling every available chair and even sleeping fitfully on the floor.

It was 25° below outside, though somewhat warmer inside. We were exhausted, hungry, irritable and gradually freezing to death, but I was fascinated by two ancient ladies who had built themselves a lair under a staircase. Here they had a small stove over which a big, black kettle was suspended. The two old girls hovered around it, cackling balefully and occasionally making a sortie into the den of sleepers to slap wet mops as close as possible to the feet, and sometimes the heads, of the unconscious travelers. Kola, whose long nose was dripping and who was shivering uncontrollably, eyed the old dames uneasily.

"I'll bet your William Shakespeare could have done something with that pair of witches!" he said through a clash of chattering teeth.

Truly the world looked dark — *was* dark — and dawn was many hours away. At 5 A.M. our flight was called and, led by Simeon Danielov, our guide for this expedition, we stumbled onto the pitch black and bitter field to seek our plane — a twin turboprop carrying Polar Aviation markings on its fuselage. Everyone crowded to get inside out of the cutting frost, but the plane had been sitting out all night and the temperature inside was exactly the same as that outside. It was like a dead machine, without even any illumination, except for the dim glow from a tiny bulb over the entrance door.

Must be the wrong plane, I thought. But, no, a few minutes later the crew arrived, big hearty fellows bundled up as if bound out on a real polar exploration. As the pilot shouldered past, breathing out jets of steam, he gave us all a booming: "*Dobr-oe ootro!*" — "Good morning!" If any of the passengers agreed with this outrageous piece of optimism, none of them said so.

The jovial pilot wound up the engines and away we went. I still did not know where we were going. I had intended to ask Simeon but was too preoccupied keeping Claire and myself from freezing to death to bother. An hour later, when the interior of the plane had warmed up sufficiently to allow us to loosen our fur ear flaps, we began to descend. It was none too soon. Claire had begun to whimper softly, like a dog that urgently needs to be let out.

We landed, still in pitch darkness, and I began pulling oddments of luggage off the racks until Yura stopped me.

"Not Tchersky yet! Only stop here for breakfast. Take your time."

"*You* take *your* time!" Claire hissed at him. "Get out of the way or you'll be sorry!"

We had landed at Khandyga, a little log town in a taiga clearing on the shores of the Aldan River — the greatest of the Lena's tributaries. A pretty girl, bundled up in an immense dog-skin coat, met us at the plane's door and led us to a blissfully warm log hut where all except Claire were served huge plates of mashed potatoes, reindeer meat and gravy. Claire had vanished into the black night on urgent personal business.

We had almost finished breakfast before she reappeared, pushing her way weakly through the great double doors that guarded against the frost outside, and looking as if she had just escaped from an arctic version of the nethermost pit. It was some hours before she could bring herself to tell me all the details of what had happened to her.

On the way to the café she asked the pretty guide where the restroom was, and the girl waved an arm in the direction of a towerlike log structure across the road. Claire raced for it, climbed a flight of outside stairs, pushed open a door and found herself in a large throne room containing nothing but a hole in the middle of the floor. It was a huge hole, black and menacing. Previous visitors had recognized its potential threat and had stayed far enough away from the edge to be reasonably safe. This had resulted in a build-up of ice which increased the dangers and caused still later comers to use even greater caution. When Claire arrived it was hardly safe to step inside the door without risking the possibility of glissading into that gaping hole.

Claire was not about to take such an appalling risk. She stayed where she was, barely inside the doorway . . . and at the critical moment someone else ran up the stairs and seized the outer handle of the unlocked — and unlockable — door.

Claire instantly grabbed the handle on her side; forgetting she had taken off her gloves; that the temperature was 40° below zero; and that the latch was made of iron.

She was now faced with a complex problem. She had to try and adjust her clothing with her left hand, while with her right hand she engaged in a tug-of-war with a stranger of unknown sex on the far side of the door. The situation was complicated by the hellish prospect that she might lose her precarious balance, slide down the icy slope, and vanish forever from human ken. She could not give up the struggle with her unseen antagonist in order to concentrate on saving herself because her right hand was frozen to the latch. Her agonized howls for mercy got her nowhere because the stranger knew no English.

Fortunately the door swung outward, else I might never have seen my bride again.

The exasperated customer on the other side gave one mighty heave — the door flew open and Claire was snapped out of her private purgatory like a released elastic band. Her hand came free of the latch in time to let her avoid being trampled underfoot by an irate woman of elephantine build, who had no time to indulge in polite amenities. Claire slunk down the stairs and over to the café, having lost only a little skin from her fingers but an incalculable amount of dignity.

I think what really hurt her most was the discovery she made when we boarded the plane again . . . a neat, clean little lavatory in the tail section, equipped with a lock that worked.

We departed from Khandyga in the first light of dawn

and began to climb steeply into the northeast. I leaned over and asked Simeon where Tchersky was.

"On Kolyma River."

"Yes, but where is that?"

"Across Verkhoyansk Mountains."

"How *far* across?"

He shrugged. "I do not know. Never go there before."

I gave up, looked out the window, and instantly forgot all about Tchersky.

We were climbing steeply but the earth was tilting skyward at almost the same rate. The taiga-covered plateau which I had come to associate with Yakutia had vanished, to be replaced in the dawn light by a stupendous upheaval of snow-dusted rock — a titanic wall at the end of the world, which our plane was laboring to overleap.

I have flown over many great mountain ranges but none as brutally violent, as bleakly hostile in appearance as the ranges of the massif which leaps skyward beyond the Aldan River. I have since crossed these mountains by air several times and have visited some of the rock-trapped little towns in their chill valleys, but these monstrous arctic peaks remain amongst the most awesome sights in my experience.

The Ilushin-14 whined higher and higher and the peaks, whitehooded now, kept pace until we cleared the first outlying range at an altitude of fifteen thousand feet. Beyond lay a chaos of broken mountains. The one sign of life was a frail fringe of leafless trees at the bottom of the deepest valleys. We flew over the Verkhoyansk Mountains for an hour; then almost imperceptibly the image began to change, softening into a mountain terrain of less terrifying character. The plane banked to the right and a frozen river came into view in the bottom of a well-wooded valley. Beside a meander in the river several score wooden buildings smoked blue plumes into the brilliant morning sky.

The copilot came aft and leaned over us. "Oimyakon and the Indigirka River. We just called them on the radio. They have no passengers so we won't stop today. Too bad, because they're having a regular summer morning. It's only minus 56° down there."

I took advantage of the moment. "Excuse me, but just where is Tchersky?"

The young man grinned, winked at Simeon and Yura, and nodded toward the cockpit. "Just up ahead there. Not so far. I'd better get back to my job."

I was beginning to catch on. There was a conspiracy on foot. Nobody was going to tell me where Tchersky was. I did not really care. Beyond the valley of the Indigirka the mountains went savage again, towering even higher than before and so violently jumbled that they seemed like the debris of a stellar explosion. They are known as the Tchersky Range, but they do not deserve such a civilized identity; they are a glimpse into another time than ours, a time of primal tumult beyond anything we, hopefully, will ever know. The eleven-thousand-foot peaks of the Moma Mountains drifted past under a wing and there seemed to be no end to this weird wilderness. I suggested to Claire that our pilot must have gone the wrong way and this must be Tibet. The idea did not seem so unreasonable.

In all we flew more than six hundred miles in a direct line across the massif, and when the peaks lowered again toward a forested highland, it was not for long. To the eastward new peaks lifted to a white sky, marching beyond the most distant horizon to the ultimate northeastern tip of Asia. This mighty mountain complex represents nearly a quarter of the Siberian landmass, occupying almost the whole region

east and northeast of the Lena valley. It is kith and kin
with its Alaskan neighbors, but covers twice the area.

The aircraft let down in a gentle descent toward the
wind-burnished ice of a big river that emerged from a gap
in the mountains and flowed northward into a wide reach
of stunted forest.

"Kolyma River!" Yura called to us, pointing down.

Claire jumped to her feet and scampered aft to the ladies
room. Once bitten . . . twice shy. She regained her seat
just as we came in to land. I reached for the luggage. Yura
grinned from ear to ear.

"Not Tchersky yet. Zirianka. Stop for lunch."

Once again we trotted across the snow to a log café, leaving a bevy of robust ladies to refuel the plane. Over bowls
of soup and glasses of cognac, I confronted Simeon and
Yura.

"Look," I said, "a game's a game. But just where in hell
are we going, anyway?"

Yura tilted his glass, wiped his lips and sighed.

"Ah well, is too late for you to go back now, so I tell
truth. Very many times you talk about Siberia for place of
exile. So we make special exile just for you. Under Tsars
most dangerous political prisoners sent to Tchersky. Nobody ever escape from there. Impossible! But you are very
tough Canadian. We give you chance to try. Not necessary
walk five thousand miles to Moscow from Tchersky — only
you have to walk eight hundred miles east, then show pass-
port to Yankees on Bering Strait."

I laughed, but I was intrigued. Was I going to catch a
glimpse of the Siberia which is the only Siberia that exists
for most North Americans? Would Tchersky prove to be
the site of one of those dread "work camps" which, according to the writings of so many expatriate Russians and

home-bred Russophobes, cover Siberia like a shroud of hope-lessness? I decided not to ask but to possess my soul in pa-tience. Meantime there was Zirianka to be examined.

Built entirely of squared logs, it is a charming little town of about five thousand people, almost astride the arctic cir-cle. It is a district administration center but is also the transshipment port for river traffic on the Kolyma. Two-thousand-ton self-propelled barges serve it from Green Cape, a seaport near the Arctic Ocean; and the freight goes on southward in smaller craft into the Kolyma Mountains to supply a string of placer and hardrock gold mines in an immense auriferous region which stretches east almost as far as the Pacific Ocean. In winter the frozen river becomes a truck highway, and convoys haul tens of thousands of tons of freight along it. Trucks and ships returning north down the Kolyma fill up with coal from surface deposits near Zirianka.

Zirianka is also an important agricultural center. Its two state farms not only breed reindeer but also raise eating horses and beef and dairy cattle. I had noticed, as we came in to land across broad muskeg plains, little mounds in the many natural clearings. These were haystacks, harvested in summer and waiting to be brought in by horse- and rein-deer-drawn sleds after the frost sufficiently hardened the muskegs.

Claire was a little apprehensive as we wandered around among the neat log houses; however, Zirianka offered her no traumatic surprises. We could not know it then but the little town was biding its time. Later it would find a way to give her cause to remember it.

When we departed from Zirianka I refrained from again asking where we were going, or how far it was. We flew straight north along the Kolyma valley with the mountains on our right and a plain of drowned taiga widening into the distance on our left.

Two hours later the copilot came back and drew our attention to a brilliant white line on the horizon ahead.

"The polar sea! . . . And there is Tchersky down below."

Beneath us was a haphazard sprawl of buildings. I searched for a stockaded enclosure but could not pick one out. Later, perhaps. The settlement was on a bold point of land jutting into the Kolyma. Beyond it the white and featureless tundra rolled north to the frozen ocean.

We landed on the river ice and taxied toward the town through an assemblage of parked aircraft which included at least thirty fixed-winged planes and a dozen helicopters. Clearly Tchersky did not lack the means of modern transportation. Our plane stopped beside a crowd of fur-clad figures and we descended the steps into the heart of a mob of welcomers, all of them jovially anxious to pump our hands. It was the kind of reception which would have warmed the heart of the most blasé politician. It assuredly warmed ours, and that was good because the temperature was close to minus 40°.

Our arrival was a real occasion. Claire and I were the first foreigners to visit Tchersky since the Revolution. Claire was the first foreign woman most Tcherskyites had ever seen. On top of that, we were Canadians, and as such were looked upon as being next-door neighbors, despite the fact that our homes were separated by the width of the Arctic Ocean.

A gleaming-eyed Chukchee, Nikolai Tourot (who began life as a reindeer herder and is now Mayor of Tchersky and a delegate to the National Assembly in Moscow) greeted me with a gentle handshake; but the District Party Secretary,

Victor Nazarov, a bouncing brute of a man, embraced me with such fervor I gasped for breath. He had his eye on Claire as well, but she was too quick for him and took shelter in the middle of a group of Russian, Evenki and Chukchee ladies.

Yura rescued me from Victor's grasp and introduced me to Simeon Kerilev, a tiny, sweet little Yukagir poet and novelist whose most recent book, *Son Of An Eagle*, had just been published.

It was impossible to register all those who crowded around us. Their ardor was too overwhelming . . . but by far the most overwhelming was Victor Nazarov.

Victor is the sort of man who has to be seen and heard to be believed. Born in 1930 of Russian peasant stock near Tobolsk in west Siberia, he went to the Aldan goldfields of Yakutia with his parents after his father had "some differences" with the Stalin dictatorship. Following his father's death during the war, Victor helped support the family by becoming a driver-mechanic. This was a job that suited him and one he loved. He wrestled trucks over most of northern Siberia, and in his spare time became a champion weight lifter. In the time he could spare from *that* activity, he took correspondence courses until he had the credits needed to enter university at Sverdlovsk, from which he graduated with a prize degree in industrial transportation. He joined the Party in 1955 (bearing no grudges for what was past); ran the truck transport network during the building of Mirny; and in 1962 was dispatched to the mouth of the Kolyma to apply his energies to the construction of the new arctic town of Tchersky.

Moon-faced, tug-voiced, hairy as a mammoth, strong as a cave bear and utterly and absolutely indefatigable, Victor Nazarov took Claire and me into his ebullient heart with such rampant enthusiasm that he nearly killed us both. I remember him, and always will, as the most generous, ingenuous and forceful man I have ever met.

Cutting our party out of the crowd of welcomers, he heaved us bodily into his Bobyk, a jeeplike little car (the nickname Bobyk means "little terrier") and drove us into town over nonexistent roads at fifty miles an hour. Not once did he stop bellowing in our ears. He had a lot to tell us and he was not the man to waste a moment. As the Bobyk skidded, leaped and crashed into and over obstacles, Victor's massive left arm was flung out in a continuing gesture, pointing to half-built structures, piles of mud, holes in the ground, even to white stretches of virgin tundra, and identifying these as: "APARTMENT HOUSE FOR FIFTY FAMILIES GOES THERE . . . THAT IS BEGIN-NING OF BIGGEST SCHOOL IN SIBERIA . . . PAL-ACE OF SPORT, WE ARE BUILDING HERE . . . POWER STATION OVER THERE. . . ."

When he had reduced all four of us, even Yura, to bruised and battered hulks, and deaf ones at that, he suddenly jammed on the brakes, sending poor Kola smashing into the window.

"POOR CLAIRE! I FORGET MYSELF! MAYBE YOU ARE A LITTLE TIRED? I TAKE YOU TO HOTEL!"

The hotel, of logs ("WE ARE BUILDING NEW ONE RIGHT AWAY — CONCRETE — ONE HUNDRED FIFTY ROOMS"), was simple, but we had a suite of two pleasant rooms which, it appeared, we were going to share with Victor. Having escorted us to our rooms he showed no inclination to depart but pounded over to the window, thrust out his big paw, and began waving at the distant landscape.

"FARLEE! OVER THERE WE MAKE NEW AIR-PORT — BIG ENOUGH FOR JET PLANES — AND CLAIRE! LOOK THERE! WE MAKE NEW NUR-SERY SCHOOL. . . ."

Yura intervened. Somehow he maneuvered Victor out the door — though not without a parting bellow.

"NOW YOU HAVE GOOD REST! LATER WE MAKE PLANS!"

The door swung shut and Claire fell on the nearest bed. I was a little shaky myself as I started to take off my boots. It seemed to me I could still hear Victor's foghorn echoing inside my skull.

It was not an echo! It was reality. The door burst open.

"ULCERS ON MY SOUL! I FORGOT SO MUCH! YOU MUST HAVE FOOD! COME QUICK! COME QUICK!"

I tried to tell Victor we were not hungry, just exhausted, but I might as well have been Canute trying to turn back the tide. He swept us out of the room, across the frozen range of muddy mountains which might someday be a road, and into a restaurant presided over by a beautiful young lady by the name of Lydia, whose husband, Anatoly (she quickly told me), was an interior decorator working in the town.

Interior decorator? Here? Claire and I exchanged glances. But it was true enough and later we had a chance to meet Anatoly and to admire his work.

Lydia had prepared a modest snack. Twelve of us (people kept appearing as if out of the woodwork) sat down to it. The appetizer was pickled reindeer tongue. Next came Kamchatka crab, chocolate éclairs, dumpling soup, fish soup, cream puffs, reindeer cutlets, smoked salmon, stewed Ukraine tomatoes, cherry juice, strawberry jam and tea.

The food was not necessarily served in that order, but since there was one bottle of cognac, one of vodka, and one of champagne at *each* person's place, I can be excused if I have somewhat jumbled the sequence.

Victor proved to be *the* tamadar of all the world. He leaped to his feet at least once every three minutes and every toast was bottoms up. It was at this first meal with him that Claire struck back. He insisted on learning a Canadian toast and so she perversely taught him to say "up bottoms." He was delighted and, so he told me when I revisited him three years later, had no idea of its potential English meaning. However, during a visit to Moscow he was called on to help entertain a party of senior dignitaries from Great Britain at an official function. Beaming with affability and delight, he proposed that they should drink his Canadian toast, which he had unwittingly modified to:

"Up your bottoms!"

He told me this story somewhat ruefully, but without rancor.

"MOSCOW SEND ME BACK TO TCHERSKY IN DISGRACE! BUT I FORGIVE DEAR CLAIRE! SHE HELPED ME GET OUT QUICK FROM THAT CURSED TOWN!"

The last toast was drunk about 8 p.m. and we were almost literally carried back to our hotel. We were in no condition to resist when all twelve of our dinner companions crowded into our room and Victor sat down at the table, banged it so that it jumped clean off the floor, and announced we would now have a planning conference.

"HOW LONG YOU STAY WITH US? A MONTH? TWO MONTHS?"

He seemed genuinely outraged when I timidly replied that

we could not remain more than two weeks. He pounded the table until I was sure it would collapse and then he planned each of our days in the most minute detail — forgetting only to leave time for sleep.

I could see that Claire, who had unwisely allowed herself to get hooked on the spirit, was not going to be with the party much longer; so, in an act of unselfish heroism which she has never properly appreciated, I agreed (actually there was no way I could have refused) to accompany Victor to the makeshift Palace of Sport while he did his nightly workout.

Kola had faded, but Yira was still going strong. Together with the mayor, the newspaper editor and half a dozen others, we watched the incredible Victor bounce his two-hundred-seventy-pound bulk around while he played two fast games of volleyball, worked for half an hour with the barbells, wrestled a couple of the biggest truck drivers in Tchersky, and then announced:

"I'M HUNGRY! LET'S GO AND HAVE A LITTLE SNACK!"

We drank the snack at the headquarters of the Tchersky Press, a dilapidated log structure out of another age boasting a modern rotary press which had been flown in from Leningrad to print the daily *Kolymskaya Pravda*. We also did a group show on the radio station which was housed in the same building; although since it was then past midnight I doubt if anyone heard us except, perhaps, the polar bears on the arctic ice a few versts to the northward. I wonder what they made of my wobbly rendition of "The Squid Jigging Grounds."

At 2 A.M. we were back in the hotel, but not to sleep. Someone had decided our winter clothing was inadequate and half the town had been scoured to find proper clothing. Claire was pried out of bed and, eyes still tight shut, was wrapped in an enormous dog-skin coat, hatted with an Evenki reindeer bonnet, booted with embroidered felt boots which went up to her thighs (Victor insisted on fitting these with his own hands), and gloved in sealskin mittens. She claims she has no recollection of the fittings.

During my absence at the Sports Palace the table in our room had miraculously sprouted several bottles of champagne together with baskets of fresh fruit and cream pastries. So we had another little lunch. At 3 A.M. Victor looked at his glittering Slava wristwatch and the voice of authority shivered the hotel.

"TIME NOW FOR BED! GET GOOD SLEEP! TO-MORROW WILL BE BUSY DAY!"

Tchersky is at once one of the oldest and the newest of Siberian settlements. In 1644 the Cossack, Semyon Dezhnev, descended the Lena from Yakutsk, somehow navigated his way along the arctic coast to the mouth of the Kolyma, ascended it a few miles and built an *ostrug*, a tiny, crude wooden fort which came to be known as Nizhniye Kresty. Through the years and centuries it survived as a fur-trade station and one of the most remote and inaccessible outposts of the Russian Empire. From it the Yukagir (then a strong and numerous people), the Evenki, and the Chukchee of the northeast coast were systematically bled for furs even as the Eskimo of North America were bled at a later time.

By the beginning of the twentieth century the fur-bearers had all but disappeared — and so had most of the native people. Nizhniye Kresty remained alive, though barely so, as a place of exile for the most dangerous and desperate political prisoners in the hands of the Tsars.

After the Revolution the ancient settlement almost vanished and human life in the district shrank to a handful of native Russian trappers and fishermen, a few hundred Yukagir reindeer herders, and a score of Chukchee families.

Then, in 1960, Moscow waved her wand and Nizhniye Kresty was born anew.

The justification for the resurrection was gold — unbelievable quantities of it that had been discovered along the upper reaches of the Kolyma and its tributaries; and to the eastward in the Anyuyskiy Mountains of adjacent Chukotka. The decision was taken to develop this region as a valuta center and to begin building it into one of the new far Northern complexes. There was no gold at Nizhniye Kresty but it was ideally placed to become another Lensk — a transportation and administrative center for the region.

In 1961, when the transformation was begun, there were thirty people living in ten ancient wooden houses on the river bank. In 1966, when I first visited it, there were two brand-new sister towns: Tchersky, on the old site, with a population of five thousand people and, four kilometers to the north, the sea and river port of Green Cape, with six thousand people. Tchersky had become the capital of the entire Kolymsky District, embracing an area the size of Denmark and the Netherlands put together, and it already boasted one of the most productive reindeer farms in the Soviet Union. The port city was receiving oceangoing ships of fifteen-thousand-ton displacement, and the river had become the everyday highway, summer and winter, for a fleet of ships and trucks.

All of this had been accomplished by the unbridled enthusiasm and the unremitting efforts of people like Victor Nazarov — people who were not motivated by the prospect of personal gain so much as by an idea and a belief.

It was my good luck to live for a little while in the midst of Tchersky's atmosphere of sustained excitement, and to see something of the adolescence of a new world abuilding on the shores of the polar ocean.

16
TCHERSKY

By exercising iron self-control, Victor managed to stay away from us until 6 A.M.; then the roar of his voice and the thunder of his feet as he pounded up the hotel stairs brought us unwillingly back to consciousness.

"COME ON!" he boomed. "WE GO SEE REINDEER HERD!"

He hustled us across the street to Lydia's. She had prepared a breakfast of hot boiled deer tongues, salad, chocolate cake, meatballs and fried potatoes, vodka and cognac. She apologized because there was no champagne!

It was still pitch dark and 33° below zero as our Bobyk bounced out to the airport and delivered us to an enormous MIL-4 helicopter personally piloted by the assistant district chief of Polar Aviation, a big, bony and handsome man. His crew consisted of a copilot, navigator, radio operator, and engineer, and considering we were about to make a two-hundred-mile flight into the tundra in what was effectively the middle of the night, I did not feel that any one of them was redundant.

Our own party numbered ten, but since everyone was bundled to the eyes in monstrous coats and fur hats, it was difficult to know just who was who. Only Victor was easily recognizable. His was the one voice audible above the roar of the engine as we lifted off.

Shortly before 9 A.M. the sky began to gray and we could see the featureless white ocean of tundra below us. We thundered over it, and just as the sun tipped the edge of the horizon, a black smudge loomed far ahead on the now saffron-tinted snow. It grew and took on form until it became a solidly packed mass of deer, above which hung a silver cloud of glittering frost crystals condensing from the living warmth of this great herd.

We circled once at low altitude and I expected the milling mass of beasts to stampede, but they only flung back their heads so their antlers ranged the sky like a forest shaken in a gust of wind. They were used to helicopters, which visited them at least once a week, bringing mail and supplies for the herdsmen.

A few hundred yards to one side stood three large skin tents — *yarangas*. A handful of people came running toward us as we settled to the tundra.

They were the herders Nikolai Dyatchiv and Mikhail Kimirgin, men in their early thirties; Innokenty Khodyan, the chief herder, a man of fifty; and the wives of Khodyan and Kimirgin. All were Yukagir. They were dressed in ancestral garb, clad from sole to crown in reindeer skins. We were introduced and then with much grinning, shouting and some impromptu dance steps from Victor, made our way to the Khodyans' yaranga. Our visit was unexpected, but on the tundra hospitality is always waiting.

The tent was constructed of double layers of deer skins with a vestibule for storing gear and to act as a heat-lock. We pushed through the double flaps to enter the Khodyan home and found ourselves in a spacious room, about twenty feet in diameter, with wall-to-wall carpeting of thick, soft reindeer robes. A small sheetmetal stove glowed red in the middle of the room, and beside it stood a table about ten inches high. There were no chairs. Everyone squatted or lay where he pleased.

Victor came in last, dragging a big burlap bag that clinked. Out of it he drew endless bottles and we hoisted a few "sunrisers" while snacking on chips of raw frozen fish. Glasses of heavily sweetened tea completed this second breakfast.

We shared it with Innokenty Khodyan's grandmother who, at the age of one hundred and seven years, refused to stay at home in the comfort of the reindeer breeders' permanent settlement but insisted on continuing to live the nomadic life of the herders. She told us how surprised she was to meet people from another continent — "across the frozen waters" — and she hoped we would remain at least until the spring as her grandson's guests.

Her age-blackened and dessicated face turned toward a little girl who sat solemnly staring at us. The child was named Elizaveta (Elizabeth). She was the old woman's great-great-granddaughter.

"I am too old to travel much anymore, but this little one may someday visit *your* yaranga. It is good for people who are from far away to visit each other," the old lady told us.

While we breakfasted the two young men slipped off to bring the herd closer to the camp. We went outside to find ourselves surrounded by the living host of the reindeer. Nearly three thousand of them stood passively about, staring incuriously at the helicopter, or pawing through the hard snow to snatch a mouthful of moss.

Armed with rawhide lassos, and with several silent, furry little dogs close at their heels, the three herders loped into the middle of the herd, which spread to let them pass and closed in again behind them. Deep in that maze of antlers they were looking for an especially fat deer with which to make a feast to celebrate our coming.

They lassoed several before they found a suitable one. Dumbly it followed them out of the herd. It stood braced against the rope while Khodyan gentled it and then with a flashing movement thrust his knife between its ribs. Slowly the beast sank to its knees, crumpling to the snow.

The men having done their job, the women squatted beside the animal, neatly paunched it, skinned it, and butchered the steaming meat. They worked without gloves despite the searing frost — the body heat of the dead reindeer keeping their hands from freezing.

While the women prepared the meal in another tent, Victor challenged me to a reindeer race. Laughing and shouting in the brittle air, the herdsmen rounded up several "driving deer" and hitched them to the sleds — slight constructions of thin larch planks bound together with rawhide. We drivers were each given a long willow wand, on the very end of which was fastened a tiny bone hammer. Yura explained that this was my accelerator. When I wanted my deer to speed up I had only to tap him under the tail.

"Not too hard!" Yura warned me. "Or he will fly!"

Bellowing like a bison, Victor pulled away while I rather tentatively explored the technique of deer driving. It turned out to be easy enough and because my deer had to pull only about half of Victor's weight, we soon caught up to him and the two sleds went slithering across the barren plain at top speed. On the home stretch I took the lead, beating Victor by two lengths. He looked just a bit downcast but rallied with a booming laugh as the gallery cheered me home. This was the first of several little tests he was to put me through.

"Now you don't need Aeroflot to get you back to Canada," Vasily Amisov, the Yukagir team leader of the farm reindeer section told me. "If you want, you and your wife can drive home. Ten days good sledding should take you there."

"I think we'd prefer to stay right here."

It was the proper thing to say. Vasily embraced me, rolled me on the snow, then, putting his jews harp in his mouth, led a pied piper procession back to the yaranga.

The main tent bulged. Champagne corks popped incongruously, and, even more incongruously, Yura tuned in on the Voice of America on the Khodyans' portable radio. The announcer was explaining how much better off the Alaskan Eskimo were than their depressed relatives in Siberia. Everyone listened politely, then Vasily proposed a toast to the announcer, suggesting we invite him to Tchersky so he could see for himself how terribly the native people were suffering.

The women now pushed through the flaps bearing iron pots full of steaming reindeer brisket and we got down to work. Because the meat had been so freshly killed it was a little tough, but greasily delicious. We ate with our hands and I noted that Victor could hold a juicy piece between his teeth while slicing off a mouthful with one slash of his sheath knife. I had learned the same trick while living with the Eskimo. It is a procedure best practiced by people with short noses.

In the babble of talk I learned that the camp had to be shifted every two or three days as the herd slowly grazed across the frozen plain. Once a week one of the men would hitch up a team and drive south to timberline for a load of firewood. And once a month helicopters carried out an exchange of herders and their families.

I asked Innokenty Khodyan whether he did not prefer the comfort of the settlement. He was amazed.

"Why should I want that? The best days of my life are here on the tundra with the herds. I am doing good, useful work, and it is work I love."

I remember what Madam Ovchinnikova had said about the native reindeer herders.

"We are against any attempt to force the nomadic peoples to stay in one place. It is for them to make their own choice. If they choose to remain nomads, we try to make it possible for them to do so but still have the benefits of modern society. They repay us a hundred times. No one can surpass them as reindeer breeders, and without reindeer it would be much harder for us to develop the North as we are doing."

It is a witless misapprehension to think of reindeer solely in terms of Santa Claus and his Disneyland team. Soviet archaeologists believe these Asian caribou were first domesticated about four thousand years ago, and throughout that stretch of time they have been the veritable staff of life to Northern people from Norway to Bering Strait. In all Northern regions of the Soviet Union, but particularly in Siberia, they play an increasingly vital role in human affairs. The arctic and subarctic taiga and tundra are not notably good food-producing regions, but they can produce one thing in abundance — first-rate protein in the form of reindeer meat.

In 1968 there were two million four hundred thousand

domestic reindeer in the USSR, and meat production topped fifty thousand tons, while an additional eight thousand tons was harvested from wild reindeer herds. This was sufficient to supply the primary protein needs, not only of the native Northern races but of many of the new Northern towns and cities. There was even some available for export to Japan, where its excellent flavor and high nutritive value (considerably higher than that of beef) makes it a much sought-after food.

Soviet reindeer experts estimate that their North has a carrying capacity of four and a half million head of domestic reindeer, with an annual production of at least one hundred thousand tons of meat; and they expect to reach these figures within eight years. When they do, the Northern regions, including all the new development centers, will not only be self-sufficient in primary meat production, but the tundra wilderness will be contributing significantly to the meat shortages that are already plaguing the world's temperate regions.

There are any number of side effects to the intense efforts the Russians have made, and are making, in reindeer culture. For one thing, reindeer husbandry now provides a solid economic base for about one hundred and twenty thousand people — the breeders and herders and their families. The average income of these people in cash and kind is slightly higher than the average income of factory workers in the South. The reason is that reindeer breeding has become one of the most profitable of all types of animal husbandry. Because the animals are hardy, self-sufficient, and require no planted crops or hay to sustain and fatten them, and no buildings to shelter them, the cost of producing a pound of reindeer meat is extremely low. Beef raised in central Yakutia costs four to five times as much as an equal amount

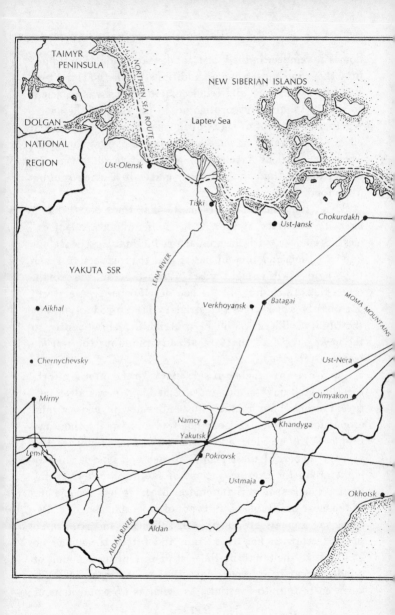

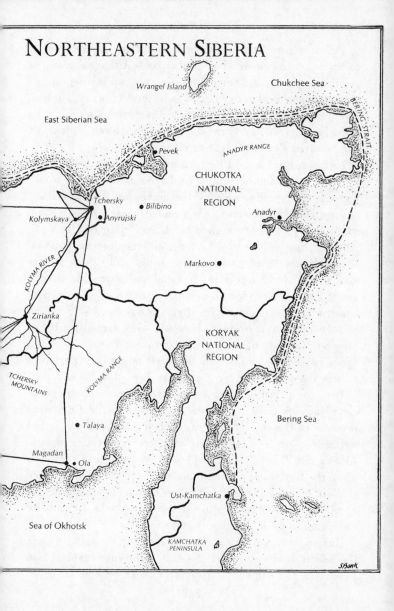

NORTHEASTERN SIBERIA

Chukchee Sea

Wrangel Island

East Siberian Sea

BERING STRAIT

Pevek

ANADYR RANGE

CHUKOTKA NATIONAL REGION

Tchersky

Bilibino

Kolymskaya

Anyrujski

Anadyr

KOLYMA RIVER

Markovo

Zirianka

KORYAK NATIONAL REGION

KOLYMA RANGE

TCHERSKY MOUNTAINS

Talaya

Bering Sea

Magadan

Ola

Ust-Kamchatka

Sea of Okhotsk

KAMCHATKA PENINSULA

S'Bank

of reindeer meat; and even beef raised in the best cattle districts of the Soviet Union still costs twice as much as reindeer meat, pound for pound. From a capitalist point of view, reindeer husbandry ought to be irresistibly attractive. Every ruble invested in reindeer in the Soviet Union during 1964 had, by 1970, returned two rubles, eleven kopeks, or one hundred eleven percent profit.

Norway, Sweden and Finland are well aware of the profits to be made and between them have a base herd of a million animals, which is about the maximum their territory can support. Northern Canada and Alaska together could carry as many as five million head, according to Dr. V. N. Andreev, one of the world's foremost reindeer authorities. A herd of less than half this size would still return an annual profit of millions of dollars and would provide an economic *raison d'être* for all of our Northern natives, who at present are mostly surviving (where they have survived at all) on relief and welfare. It would also dramatically increase the supply of meat available to Southerners, and the competition provided by reindeer meat might be expected to reduce the price paid by consumers for all types of meat.

It seems incredible that a free-enterprise, competitive society such as ours should not have turned the Christmas reindeer-in-the-sky into a going industry. The truth is that we tried — or, rather, a pair of perceptive young men in Alaska did. They were the Lomen brothers and they saw what the Soviets and Scandinavians were seeing and acted on that vision. Largely due to their efforts, a herd of nearly a million reindeer came into existence in Alaska, employing many hundreds of Eskimo as well as whites.

But there was a catch. The market for the meat was in the South, and soon after the first shipments reached San Francisco the demand for reindeer meat became so great that the beef barons became alarmed. They went to Washington. Not long thereafter, reindeer meat was embargoed by law in the United States. Deprived of markets by the beef lobby, the Lomen herds went into decline, and today there are only about thirty thousand reindeer left in all Alaska.

Reindeer husbandry suffered a similar fate in Canada. During the 1930s a herd of several thousand reindeer was purchased from the Lomen brothers and brought to the mouth of the Mackenzie River. It was intended as the nucleus for herds which would spread right across the Canadian arctic, thereby providing a means of livelihood for the Northern natives while at the same time supplying a valuable export to the South. Those who planned this concept were honest men — and they were simple dreamers. As soon as the significance of the plan was realized in the South, the Canadian government of the day lowered the boom. Successive governments have kept it down. Today the dream is represented by a token herd of fewer than three thousand animals, and the current Canadian government and its corps of so-called arctic experts explode in a fury of embarrassment when reminded that the herd exists at all.

In 1949 I became deeply embroiled with the grim fate of Canada's Eskimo, many of whom were then quite literally starving to death due to a drastic decrease in the wild caribou population, combined with almost total neglect by the Canadian government.* I initiated (and the government promptly took over) the first major study of the tundra caribou herds. The government and I soon parted company, and I undertook a campaign to establish a reindeer indus-

---

* *People Of The Deer,* 1953; *The Desperate People,* 1956, McClelland and Stewart, Toronto, Canada, and Atlantic-Little, Brown, Boston.

try as a means of giving Eskimo and Northern Indians a chance to survive and to grow into the modern world as a viable people. The results amounted to absolutely nothing, but at least I learned a lot about reindeer. Much of what I learned came from the foremost experts in the business, but chief among these was Dr. Andreev, a member of the USSR Academy of Sciences and winner of the Lenin Prize for his reindeer work.

A quiet, gentle, and erudite man, he is possessed by reindeer, viewing them as one of nature's great gifts to mankind. Sitting in an easy chair in his pleasant dacha outside Yakutsk, while his pregnant cat slumbered on my knee, I listened to him for hours as one would listen to a very rational prophet. A prophet *not* without honor in his own country, let it be noted. Here follows some of his thoughts about reindeer.

"It is a foolish habit of men when they go into a new region to fasten their eyes only on one thing — the most valuable thing they can find. They thus become blind to the whole natural structure of the region and, in their blindness, fail to develop the entire structure as an integrated unit. Not only that, but this failure leads them to do great and often irreparable damage which, in the long run, may cost man far more than he gains by his initial treasure-seeking.

"Many years ago some of us in this country foresaw the coming opening of the Northern regions and we also foresaw the dangers implicit in it. We realized that only the widest, and the wisest, use of the resources of the North would make it possible for man to populate this region on a large scale, on a permanent basis, and without destroying or damaging the environment.

"I, together with many others, worked with reindeer. For

thousands of years small herds, primitively husbanded, had supported a small population of arctic peoples. Our task was to see how this husbandry could be improved so all the native peoples, together with the hundreds of thousands of expected newcomers, would be benefited.

"We set up a number of research stations. We recruited hundreds of enthusiastic young workers in zoology, botany, geobotany, and kindred sciences. The State was at first un-impressed by our enthusiasm but we later convinced some of the authorities and they made money available for our task.

"Things went badly at first. Mistakes were made. Per-haps we were too enthusiastic. Nevertheless, by the middle 1950s, when Russia really began to move North in earnest, we were ready.

"By 1954 we had built a new science around the reindeer. Our research people had bred a series of special types with special characteristics. They had developed strains resistant to specific diseases; there were others that put on weight much more rapidly than ordinary deer; others had a far greater meat-to-general-weight ratio; and so on. At the same time our parasitologists and veterinary researchers were controlling the anthrax plague, hoof rot, and infesta-tions by bott and warble flies. Other teams had studied food requirements and had mapped millions of hectares of tundra and taiga in order to assess their capacity to feed the herds. Still other teams had worked out a whole new rationale for the handling and herding of animals in the field.

"In 1960 we justified the hundreds of thousands of rubles spent, and the years of labor. That year the North pro-duced twelve thousand tons of high-quality reindeer meat, and even our severest critics, who had claimed that mineral, timber and fur were the only important resources in the

North, came over to our side. This was because our work was saving them a great deal of money in their efforts to establish new communities in the far and the near North. This was something they could understand.

"Now the reindeer industry is the most valuable husbandry in our North. It outclasses cattle breeding, fishing, trapping or fur raising. In 1968, in Chukotka, for instance, the cash return from their base herd of half a million reindeer was fourteen million rubles. The Chukchee and Eskimo who are the natives of that region are becoming among the best-paid people in the Soviet Union. The new developments there — the new cities — are being supplied with reindeer meat at very low cost, and the inhabitants much prefer the fresher meat to canned or frozen meats which must be transported from the South at very great expense.

"Meat is not the only product. About half a million hides are now processed annually into high-grade suede. Tanned hides with the hair attached are in increasing demand for standard Northern clothing, and in the South for fashion clothing. Reindeer hair is used for mattress stuffing and, since it is hollow and very light, for life preservers. Antlers from a special race are processed to produce a substance which may prove to be very useful against cancer. Glandular extracts account for an income of hundreds of thousands of rubles a year. Before long we will be able to use every part of the animal as profitably as we now use all parts of cattle in the South.

"For a long time it was thought reindeer could only be raised on the tundra and in the thin adjoining subtaiga. Now we have proved they can be farmed in the very heart of the Siberian forests, and we are rapidly developing this discovery. If we are fully successful, we will be able to raise the base herd to eight or ten million animals and turn the heavy taiga, which at present yields only wood and fur animals, into one vast productive farm.

"It is hard for me to understand why Canada has neglected this resource. You possess the second largest Northern forest region in the world and the largest tundra region. I have visited your country and your North, and talked to your experts. Your Dr. Porsild * in Ottawa told me reindeer raising was impossible because Eskimo and Indians could not be trained as herders. He also said reindeer would crowd out the native caribou and that, in any case, the carrying capacity of the Canadian North would only be adequate for a few hundred thousand deer. I do not understand all this.

"Here in the Soviet Union, the wild reindeer have increased, under strict protection, to just under a million animals *at the same time* we were building our domestic herds. In the Taymyr Peninsula, in 1957, there were one hundred ten thousand wild reindeer. Now there are two hundred thirty-five thousand, which is about as many as all the wild Canadian caribou still left alive. And in Taymyr we also have some of our most successful domestic herds.

"The Finnish botanists, Achti and Hustishy, who are also reindeer experts, have examined the Canadian North, as has the respected botanist Dr. Nicolas Polunin of Great Britain, and all agree that the carrying capacity for reindeer in the Canadian tundra and subtaiga alone cannot be less than two million and may be as high as five million. Remember that at one time there were a million in Alaska alone.

"As to training herders — I cannot understand this problem at all. There are about two thousand Eskimo in Chukotka and they now have a number of first-rate herds, although

* Dr. A. E. Porsild, Dominion Botanist.

twenty years ago none of them kept reindeer. Anyone can learn to be a herder and a reindeer breeder if we really wish to see such a thing come about. Here we already have many more reindeer than can be handled by our native herders and there are now many hundreds of young men and women, Georgians, Tatars, Russians, from the South who have come North to learn the trade. In three or four years they become as proficient as hereditary herders, and sometimes they are better because they have no fixed preconceptions.

"If Canada should ever change her mind about reindeer, we will be glad to help establish the husbandry. Everything we have learned is at your disposal. I am sure there would be no difficulty if you wanted to import stock from us. I think it would be easily arranged that we could send a number of good people to teach your herders. I would go myself, and very gladly. It is something worthwhile doing — to help increase the supply of food in the world and to help make remote places hospitable for humanity. When men have enough good food, and enough space to live in, they find peace, and that is the best thing of all."

The brief day was drawing down over the tundra. In the warm yaranga someone had proposed a toast to friendship between the peoples of the North. As we drank to that, Claire remembered that this was Remembrance Day in Canada — November 11, the date marking the end of the First World War. Diminutive Simeon Kerilev, the young Yukagir novelist, jumped to his feet.

"Yours must truly be a great and a wise country. It sets aside a full day of the year to honor peace! Let us drink to Canada and to peace itself and to the growth of love between all men."

I had not the heart to tell him that Remembrance Day

only remembers, briefly and palely, those who were killed in war, and that we have no day of peace, and those who insistently celebrate the cause of peace in North America are not among the most popular members of society. Truthfully, I do not think he, or most of the men and women I met in the Soviet Union, would have been able to understand. For them the word *Mir* — Peace — has a significance so deep that only the most case-hardened cynic could doubt the sincerity with which they use it.

The Aeroflot pilot and his crew had been religiously drinking tea all day — now they suggested that perhaps it was time to go. Reluctantly we bundled ourselves up and walked through the bitter dusk to the helicopter. As we lifted in a throb of metal blades, hundreds of deer raised their heads, stared a moment incuriously, and then went back to their never-ending search for food.

Below us, and almost obscured in the snow dust of our departure, five little figures waved what I thought was an ultimate farewell. It was not so. Three years later I returned to their camp on the sweep of tundra plain by the rim of the arctic sea and they greeted me like a son gone too long from home. Incredibly, the old lady was still alive, still refusing to be left behind at the settlement. She held my hand in her gnarled claw and she looked through me and beyond me into some forgotten time, and muttered a few words.

I had a different interpreter that day, a stupid and ignorant man. He was embarrassed by my insistence that he translate.

"She says only some nonsense about a god who will look after you."

Yura Rytkheu was also with me on that return visit. He caught my eye and shook his head. Later, when we were alone, he told me what the words meant.

"She gave you a blessing, not in the name of the Christian God, but in the name of the Spirit of the Deer. She is a shaman, one of the last of them. She speaks to the old spirits and believes they answer her. I think you are a very lucky man."

We were well on our way toward Tchersky when Victor abruptly decided we should change course and visit Kolymskaya, the largest of the settlements in Nizny Kolymsky State Reindeer and Fur Farm. So we turned south and after a hundred miles settled down in gathering darkness on the main and only street of a log village set in thin, larch taiga.

Apart from his consuming urge to show me absolutely everything in his arctic domain, Victor particularly wanted me to see the grave of his personal hero, Ivan Dimitrivitch Tchersky, in honor of whom Victor had succeeded in renaming Nizhniye Kresty. As a sideline to his innumerable other activities, Victor had for years past spent his holidays exhuming and reconstructing the history of this exiled Polish aristocrat whose memory he worshipped with almost, if not quite, the fervor he felt for Lenin.

Born in 1842, the son of a wealthy landed proprietor, Tchersky was expelled from Krakow University and then exiled to Siberia for revolutionary activities against the Russian Tsar. Sent first to Omsk, he served as a soldier there until the governor, a man of education and some understanding, recognized in the youth a genius for natural sciences and commissioned him to go exploring in eastern Siberia. Tchersky went to Baikal, where he spent three years and laid the foundation for the subsequent natural history studies of that great lake. This work won him honors in France and Germany, but not in St. Petersburg, where attempts to have him pardoned failed. Tchersky did not care. Although wracked by tuberculosis, he was possessed by a desire to explore the whole of the then almost unknown interior of the Kolyma region.

With his wife, who was a Baikal Cossack woman, and his young son, and accompanied by three Buryat men, he set out on an odyssey which led him through the deepest mountain valleys of an unknown world. Year after year he penetrated farther and farther, exploring the headwaters of the Indigirka, and finally making his way through the massive Moma Range to the Kolyma valley. He planned to descend the Kolyma to its mouth, turn west along the arctic coast, and finally ascend the Lena.

During a prolonged October storm in the year 1886 he reached the end of his physical endurance. His crippled lungs collapsed and he died on the banks of the Kolyma, but not before he had made his wife swear to carry his collections of plants, animals, and knowledge back to the savants at St. Petersburg. This she did, taking two years to complete the journey. This peasant woman survived until 1947, dying at the age of something between one hundred and one hundred and ten years.

When we stood in front of the modest stone monument at Kolymskaya under which Tchersky lies, big, burly Victor wept unashamedly. His thunderous voice was, for the moment, muted.

"He had the courage of a hundred men. He was made of iron, that little Pole. Nothing could stop him except death. He opened all this part of the world to knowledge; and he loved the people of the North with a big heart. For a long time he was almost forgotten, but now we are seeing to it he is remembered again. We are building Tchersky for him, as well as for ourselves and for the future."

17
KOLYMSKAYA

When we climbed out of the helicopter at Kolymskaya we were met by two fur-clad Yukagir girls. Tania, age nineteen, was the Party Secretary of this taiga village of six hundred people; and Ludmilla, twenty-three, was Mayor.

With a possessive arm around each of these local dignitaries, Victor led the way into the village. We encountered scores of children, clad from head to foot in reindeer fur, coming home from school. Ludmilla explained that half the village population consisted of children. The Yukagir seemed to be staging a determined comeback from the edge of oblivion.

As the youngsters glimpsed our faces and our odd garb in the yellow light streaming from the apartment windows, they were as startled as if they had encountered a posse of Martians. We must have been the strangest visitation to reach this remote place since Tchersky's day.

Naturally we were taken to see the kindergarten, where a number of dark-faced women were busy bundling up their offspring. Staffed by volunteers working under a trained director, these universal Soviet institutions provide an essential service. Since most women in the USSR choose to work at something apart from household tasks, the kindergartens double as day-care centers. From what we saw of them — and God knows we saw enough — they seemed to be happy, well-run, and homey places. If the children were developing traumas as a result of spending several hours a day away from their own parents, they did not show it. The youngsters I met were an extraordinarily well-behaved and likable bunch of sprats. I doubt if this has much to do with communism; it is most probably due to the fact that Russian children are traditionally well behaved and well treated.

News of our descent on Kolymskaya spread like wildfire. As we were leaving the nursery a breathless young lady ran up and very prettily begged us to come and see the school. This was a ten-room log structure, warm, bright, and vividly decorated with giant posters of Lenin. The children had all gone home, but nevertheless we had to see each room while the senior teacher practiced her English on us. She was reasonably fluent, although her compliment to me (she had read a magazine synopsis of one of my Northern books) seemed a trifle ambiguous.

"To reading your book of Eskimo is making me very bad inside my stomach," she said passionately.

Fortunately for my ego she placed her hand demonstratively, not on her stomach but over her heart. A small error in anatomical terminology.

After a look at the community center, which contained a gymnasium-cum-theater and a well-stocked little library,

Ludmilla dragged us off to see her own pet project, the fur farm.

It was full darkness by then and savagely cold. We tried to take an interest in row upon row of pens which housed a hundred silver foxes (the original stock came from Canada), a number of blue polar foxes, and some black and platinum mink. Being wiser than we, the beasts remained in their sheltered boxes until Ludmilla unfeelingly drove them out.

At last Tania took pity on them and on us and led us at a trot toward the cafeteria for "a little glass of tea before you fly to Tchersky." On the way we were overtaken by a team of ten huskies hauling a heavily laden sled driven by a small, lithe Yukagir. Victor hailed him and he stopped his team and came shyly over. He was Serafina Petrovich Robik, the most famous trapper and hunter in Yakutia and twice winner of the Republic's annual award for wild fur production.

His curious last name was the bequest of an American trader named Roberts who sailed a little schooner from Alaska to the Kolyma sometime in the early 1900s. There is a good measure of Yankee trader blood flowing in the veins of the Yukagir, Eskimo, and Chukchee, and it is memorialized not only in family names but also in a number of English words which have passed into the local vocabulary: *bonanza*, *rum*, and *sveety* (sweetie) are three examples. Robik was just coming home from a five-day trip around his trapline, during which he had taken thirty-four ermine and six white foxes.

I was a little suspicious about that "glass of tea," but since we had come to Kolymskaya unannounced and had only been in town a short time, I thought it unlikely anything too elaborate could have been prepared for us.

I still had much to learn about Siberians! All the tables in the log dining hall had been placed together in a line. And once again the table tops were lost to view under a fabulous array of food and drink. Thirty or forty grinning Kolymskayites stood by their chairs waiting for us. Kola's pale face grew paler still.

"I hope by the time we get back to Moscow our surgeons will have mastered the art of liver transplants!" he muttered.

Sometime before midnight we were escorted back to the helicopter. I am not an enthusiast of night flying in the arctic, but I was in no mood to worry overmuch. Claire was beyond worrying. She had made the mistake of getting into a toast-making match with the big-boned, buxom lady cook at the café and, though she had fought gallantly, she had gone down to defeat. As we tucked her tenderly into the helicopter she tried to raise her right arm and was heard to say:

"Want give toast t'all nice pilots going carry me home t'bed."

As a consequence of our visit to the herd, Vasily Amasov, the jews harp–playing team leader of the reindeer herders, concluded I was the stuff reindeer farmers are made of. One afternoon Claire and I were invited to attend a gathering at the headquarters of the state farm. It turned out to be a full-scale banquet during which I was presented with a magnificent red and gold ornamented scroll testifying to my appointment as Honorary Canadian Breeder and member in good standing of the Second Reindeer Team. I have since mused over that presentation quite a lot and have concluded it is better to be an honorary breeder than no breeder at all.

Gay as an Irish gnome, as full of laughter as any happy

child, Vasily proclaimed with frank emotion to all and sundry that I was his dear friend. When we left Tchersky he gave me his prized jews harp, having earlier almost buried Claire and me under gifts of fur hats, embroidered deerskin gloves, and other tokens of his affection. The day before we parted he told me he would be delighted to take a year off from his own work in order to start a reindeer farm for Canadian Eskimo. He was dead serious about this, having first obtained consent from the state farm director and from Victor Nazarov. Unwilling to hurt his feelings, I said I would let him know . . . and never did.

Late in 1969 I unexpectedly met him again at Batagai, near Verkhoyansk. There was no longer any laughter in his dark eyes. His beautiful young wife had died in childbirth that autumn and he had found it impossible to remain in the familiar world of Tchersky without her. He embraced me in the crowded airport waiting room and wept as he told me of his loss.

"Please arrange for me to visit Canada," he pleaded. "To forget my wife I must go somewhere I am really needed. Don't your Small Peoples of the North need a good reindeer man?"

This time I had to refuse his offer directly, knowing that even if his own government would permit him to leave, he would find cold comfort at the hands of the Canadian government. I did not tell him how much I wished he could be starting a new life for the Eskimo on the abandoned tundra of my own land. There are some things which are too difficult to say.

The kind of life my Yukagir friend would have liked to build for Canadian taiga Indians and tundra Eskimo was exemplified by the state farm he had helped build in Kolyma. Here is the shape of it.

Nizhny Kolymsk State Farm embraces the whole of the Kolyma district, some eighty-seven thousand square kilometers of taiga, tundra, lakes, and rivers. In the 1940s when the farm was first organized (as a collective), it had a population of about a hundred Evenki, Chukchee, and Yukagir families, and a herd of seven thousand reindeer. Today it is the largest reindeer farm in Yakutia, with thirty-six thousand deer. It also has departments for fishing, fur raising, and trapping; and it supports twenty-eight hundred and forty people, including two hundred and twelve Evenki families, one hundred and ninety-seven Chukchee families, one hundred and six Yukagir families (which is about ninety percent of all the Yukagir left in the world) and fifty families of native-born Russian stock.

Its headquarters is in a big three-story building in Tchersky, where a staff of thirty-seven, including economists, agronomists, veterinary scientists, botanists, and construction engineers — mostly young and mostly of native origin — work under the direction of an elected committee headed by an Evenki, Gavriel Efrimov. Most of the staff, including the director, hold university degrees, and each year at least thirty young people from the farm are sent as far afield as Leningrad for university training in the many specialties which affect the farm's operation.

Most of the employees live in the three settlements of Kolymskaya, Kanzaboy, and Pokholsk, which were originally tiny, decayed collections of one-room shacks, but which by the end of 1973 at the latest will all be completely modern towns. Work on the new Kolymskaya was well under way in the winter of 1969. This town will have ten sixteen-apartment masonry buildings connected with one another and to a central shopping area by aluminum and plexiglass corridors. It will also have several aluminum-sandwich-wall type experimental apartment blocks; a hockey and soccer stadium; a completely integrated fur-breeding station; a new two-story community center with a large theater; and all requisite ancillary buildings for a permanent population of a thousand people. Central heating, sewers, running water, electricity, and an airport have already been installed.

Reindeer raising is the state farm's primary concern, employing one hundred and twenty-seven families in two Reindeer Departments, each of which has a base herd of eighteen thousand deer. Roughly a thousand tons of meat is produced each year, returning (with sales of hides and other side products) a gross income of about one million rubles, for a profit of nearly three hundred thousand rubles, which is invested in new equipment, training programs, improved breeding stock, and in the reconstruction of the three towns.

Wages of apprentice herders begin at two hundred and ten rubles a month, increasing by ten rubles each year to a base rate of two hundred and fifty, plus all the usual, and some unusual, side benefits, including virtually free housing and a supply of meat, fish, and reindeer hides sufficient to meet the needs of an average-size family. Teams which overfulfill their annual quotas are paid extra in cash, or the members may take their bonus in reindeer, which they run with the farm herds and may sell at any time at market prices.

This is no empty gesture. In 1969 Innokenty Khodyan's team was running one hundred and sixty-three privately owned deer with the farm herd. When I returned to visit Innokenty that year, I was presented with three reindeer of my very own — earned for me by the overfulfillment of my mates on the Second Team of which I was an honorary member. Since I could see no way of bringing the deer home with me, I authorized the slaughter of one to provide a special feast for my teammates and myself. The other two reindeer may, hopefully, breed enough offspring to make me rich some day — in Kolyma, if nowhere else.

In 1968 the fur farm had a number of female white foxes, but the experts concluded it was too expensive to hold them over winter as breeding stock. Instead they now live-trap several hundred wild pups in early summer on the tundra and hold them only until the pelts are prime in autumn. Not only was the year-round feeding of white fox breeding stock expensive but, as Victor pointed out, it was stupid to feed good reindeer meat to foxes when it could be used for human beings.

Wild-fur trapping employs about ninety families and is the particular province of the Evenki, who are natural-born hunters. Each trapper gets a guaranteed income of two hundred rubles a month all year round but in addition makes a percentage on all the fur he catches. Serafina Robik cleared several thousand rubles over and above his salary in 1966, and most of the other trappers did proportionately well. Since fur prices are supported, and since scientific cropping methods are employed to prevent a depletion of the natural stock, trappers are among the best-paid people in the North, and hunting is second only to reindeer breeding as a farm moneymaker.

Fishing is also increasingly important at Kolymskaya, and one November day Victor took me down the river almost to the arctic coast to see the operation of a fishing station for myself.

We set off in relatively mild weather — it was a mere 10° below — but with the threat of a blizzard implicit in the dark and brooding sky. Victor, Kola, Yura, and I went in one Bobyk while Victor's Yakutian-born wife, Gallina, followed in another, accompanying a young Evenki girl who was going home from school in Tchersky to visit her parents' village. We were convoyed, until we outran it, by a big-tracked vehicle called a snow-tank. Its job was to pick us up if we got in trouble, a not unlikely possibility since we had to travel on the river ice, which was treacherous due to overflows from springs along the banks that had not yet frozen.

Victor happily reverted to his original profession and drove our Bobyk himself, manhandling the tough little machine with great skill. We soon left the main Kolyma channel and headed northwest into a complex of estuary channels winding through the bald-headed tundra. The only visible vegetation was the occasional clump of willows on the bank, from which flocks of ptarmigan rocketed away at our approach. The Bobyks flew along wide open, which was the only way to keep them moving. Every now and again we would hit a soft patch, and slush and water would erupt around us as we skidded, slued, and roared through it.

The wild drive continued for two hours and brought us to a low, snow-dusted ridge on which stood a gaunt-looking cluster of shacks. This desolate-looking place was the fishing camp.

We were greeted by the manager, a Russian who had spent decades in the arctic. He was taciturn and withdrawn until we got him going on the subject of his fishery. At this season the camp was operated by only four men (it employs forty or more at peak times), fishing two dozen nets set underneath the ice for a herringlike fish. One of the squat, log shacks contained two diesel-electric generators. Another was a living cabin much like any such cabin in the Canadian North, except for electric lights and a powerful radio transceiver. The third shack, however, was an eye-opener. It stood above the shaft of a quick-freeze "mine" and was connected to the river shore by a narrow-gauge railway.

This natural underground freezing plant had been blasted out of perpetually frozen black muck which seemed to have the hardness and texture of basalt. It was still another example of the Russian genius for making permafrost serve man. The main shaft, which we descended by icy ladders, was sixty feet deep, and drift tunnels wound out from it on all sides. The walls were covered with immense frost butterflies — flat, multicolored crystals as big as playing cards. A touch brought thousands of them fluttering down with a delicate tinkling sound.

The mine had sufficient capacity to freeze and store three hundred tons of fish. It was originally built as an experiment and was now considered obsolete. A new one of greater size and better design was under construction at the Evenki village site three miles away. Equipped with an efficient air-lock and modern conveyor equipment, it will have the capacity to freeze and store up to one thousand tons of fish.

In winter the frozen fish are trucked along the river ice and distributed all through the Kolyma region and into adjacent parts of Chukotka. In summer whatever has not been used locally is loaded on refrigerator ships bound for Murmansk and finds its way into the Moscow and Leningrad markets.

During 1966 this was one of five such stations in the district. By 1969 the Fishing Department had added a modern processing and canning factory and was producing a grand total of seventeen to eighteen hundred tons of seven different species of fish each year. The fishermen told me they made about two hundred rubles a month, excluding bonuses, and were supplied with all gear, including clothing.

When we emerged, well chilled, from the mine shaft, Gallina was busy preparing a great pot of *ukha*, a species of fishermen's soup which is a national addiction throughout most of the Soviet Union. Almost any kind of fish can be used to make ukha and everyone has his or her own special recipe. Gallina's version called for four kinds of fish and was delicious. We crowded around makeshift tables and gorged ourselves. And, of course, Victor had not come empty-handed. Out of his Bobyk came another clinking gunny sack.

My compliments to Gallina on her cookery and to the fishermen on the quality of their products were sincere but perhaps a little overdone. In any event, the manager, all smiles now, decided to reciprocate. Two of his men were dispatched to the "mine" and returned therefrom carrying an enormous frozen fish between them. It was a *chir* — the king of all arctic fishes — and it was mine — all sixty pounds of it!

This was, the fishermen told me, a little token of mutual regard. When I got back to Canada, they said, Claire would be able to make real Russian ukha for me. Nothing was said about *how* I was going to transport this monster home.

That damned fish haunted me for nearly two weeks. It was considered a marvel by all who saw it, and it received royal treatment. Hotels were happy to hold it in their refrigerators and even Aeroflot recognized its regal qualities. On the flight from Yakutsk to Irkutsk, it was given a seat all to itself.

In Irkutsk we finally parted company. I hope my fishermen friends will forgive me, but we were approaching warmer climates and my *chir* was in danger of becoming a monumental embarrassment. So I gave it to a writer friend and breathed a sigh of relief.

The next morning my friend appeared at the airport to

say farewell to us . . . bearing a return gift consisting of a forty-pound haunch of bear meat, unfrozen, and dripping gore through its inadequate wrappings.

I eventually disposed of this to Yura, but only after extracting a solemn promise from him that he would let well enough alone and not reciprocate. It was a promise no Russian could have kept. However, the two-kilo can (about four pounds) of black caviar he shoved into my hands as I climbed aboard the plane for Canada was not to be spurned. Fortunately, the Canadian Customs inspector in Montreal accepted my explanation that the can contained biological specimens — fish eggs, to be exact — and was therefore entitled to entry duty free.

After demolishing the ukha we took the snow-tank, which had made a belated appearance, and drove downstream to help haul the nets. Victor eyed me calculatingly and asked if I would like to try driving the tank. I nodded. Treating me like a somewhat retarded ten-year-old, he gave me the most meticulous instructions. For my part, I refrained from telling him I had often driven tracked vehicles during the war. When he turned me loose I put the machine through its paces with deliberate bravado.

Victor looked a trifle grim when I finally dismounted; but never mind, he had another arrow in his quiver. He produced an automatic pistol, set a can on the ice, and worked it over, scoring several hits. Then he passed the gun around. Everyone tried a shot and to Victor's unconcealed delight nobody hit the can. Finally it was my turn. I demurred, saying I knew little about guns. This only made Victor the more insistent. I finally took the thing, carefully fired twice, hit the can twice, and modestly handed the gun back.

There were shouts of derisive laughter from the others at Victor's expense. He looked at me for a moment with something of the expression of a man whose pet dog has just demonstrated an unsuspected ability to read a newspaper. Then he broke into a broad smile and gave me one of his bear hugs. *That* evened up the score. My ribs were sore for days afterward.

Although it was only 3 P.M. it was already growing dark. Blowing snow indicated that the threatened blizzard was about to materialize. We were in a hurry to be gone, but Victor had one more card to play. How would I like to try driving the Bobyk for a mile or two? He would be glad to show me how to do it.

I grinned to myself. Not only had I driven a Jeep all through the war, but I had owned and driven several of the little monsters for fifteen years after the war.

After enduring another painstaking period of instruction, I took control, starting off cautiously with a deliberate clashing of gears. Then we hit a soft spot and Victor yelled at me to stop and let him take over. Instead, I jammed down the accelerator and away we went, plowing through axle-deep slush until we hit hard ice again.

For once Victor was speechless. He said hardly a word as I drove the rest of the way home. I managed not to get stuck, although our companion Bobyk in the hands of a professional driver got so badly mired it had to wait for the snow-tank to pull it out.

This was my moment of greatest triumph. When we pulled up outside the hotel Victor grabbed me, kissed me on both cheeks and *gave* me his beloved Bobyk for the duration of my stay.

In 1966 it was difficult to get a coherent idea of the shape of Tchersky. The townsite was such an incredible scene of what looked to be utter chaos that it made little sense to me.

Nor could I understand how construction on such a scale could be carried out in this arctic icebox, until one day I met the director of the town construction company.

Alexei Terentievich Babkov was a big, lean man with a deeply carved face and flowing moustaches. A Latvian from Riga, he was Victor's antithesis, cool and controlled in thought and action. Yet he was also Victor's brother, for his dynamism was apparent in everything he said and did. Like so many other Siberians he was vastly impatient with bureaucracy. Here in Tchersky he had made himself almost completely free of the whims of officials far away in the West. What was built in Tchersky was *his* business, and he brooked little outside interference.

What he was building was a town to house ten thousand people, one with all the amenities of a modern Southern city, a place where people would live in style and comfort, and to which they could feel they belonged.

"The psychology of what we do is vitally important." Babkov told me. "You may wonder why we put up so many concrete and masonry structures. Well, apart from certain construction advantages, we do so because they look and are solid and permanent. They are not cheap. Here in Tchersky we could build prefabs or stick to wooden buildings and save many rubles; but masonry buildings are essential because of the way they affect the people who live in them. During our first years here we had nothing but log houses. They were comfortable enough and offered plenty of living space, but people from the South were unhappy with them. When we completed our first one-hundred-sixty-five-unit, five-story masonry apartment block we found the percentage of residents who abandoned the North after only a year or two up here dropped like a rock. I'm convinced a transient-type settlement will attract transients, and it will breed them too. People must have solid foundations for their lives just as buildings must."

In 1966 Babkov's company had finished only one of the five-story structures but was hard at work on another. He took me to see it. The temperature was 27° below zero, yet a horde of men and women, red-faced and bundled up in quilted clothing, swarmed over the site as actively as, or perhaps more actively than, if they had been in the Banana Belt instead of on the shores of the Arctic Ocean.

"Construction goes on all winter even at temperatures as low as 50° below. The only thing that really stops us is a very low temperature combined with very strong wind. Otherwise we work twenty-four hours a day, with the help of floodlights. If we limited ourselves to the summer season, and to normal working hours, we would never get the job completed.

"The height of our buildings is limited by the wind factor. Because of the strength of the arctic gales, it doesn't pay to go above five stories. Foundations are a bit of a problem. The best way is to sink precast concrete piers into the frozen soil by means of steam jets which melt a passage for them. They soon become locked into the eternal frost and then we raise our buildings on them, leaving a free air space between the ground and the bottom of the structure which prevents thawing of the soil. However, here in Tchersky there is much bedrock, so we foot the piers on that whenever possible; but there is often difficulty with ice lenses in the rock and then we must use frozen surface 'pads.'

"Pads are tedious to construct but can be used on any kind of ground — even on muskegs. They are composed of alternate layers of wet sand and gravel, compacted and allowed to freeze until they form a pad as much as ten feet thick. Over this we add a layer of dry sand as an insulator, and on top pour a layer of reinforced concrete. The building goes up from there, separated from the top of the pad by short concrete 'feet' to allow for free air circulation and to prevent heat flow downward. Such a pad is as permanent as the eternal frost of which it becomes a part, and will support a building of almost any height and weight."

I asked him how he solved the problems of using mortar in the fierce winter temperatures.

"Our mortar is a special mix containing silicates and salts. It is mixed hot, and kept hot until used. However at low temperatures it still freezes as soon as it is laid and, of course, it can't set until it thaws again. In earlier days, spring thawing would sometimes happen unequally. Lower tiers of bricks might thaw first; the mortar would then squeeze out and the whole structure could crack or even tumble down. Now we control the thawing. Brick buildings are built with walls about two feet thick. Before spring comes the interiors are sealed, and the inside walls then stay frozen and support the structure until the outer walls have thawed and the mortar has set. Then we open up the interior so the inner walls too can thaw and set in turn."

"What about materials," I asked. "Where do they come from?"

"When we first started here everything had to be imported by ship, even concrete gravel and stone. However, wood could be had up the Kolyma so we began with temporary wooden buildings. Meanwhile we surveyed the region and found usable deposits of sand, gravel and crushable rock. We even located a deposit of brick clay two hundred miles upriver. Now we are moving into a self-sufficient phase where the only thing we have to import is cement. We will soon have our own brick factory. We already have our own prefab concrete plant to turn out building panels and piers.

The days of log structures are behind us, although we still use wood for emergency jobs. Our geologists have also found a limestone deposit away up the Kolyma, and during the next five-year plan we will build a cement factory, and then we will have all our basic materials reasonably close at hand."

As we bounced around the townsite, I asked Alexei what he planned to do about building roads which would endure the Tchersky frosts.

"For use in the town we have invented a mixture of cement and soil with an insulating pad beneath that ought to give us good hard-top streets. We see no utility in trying to build all-weather highways through this country, any more than there would be any sense in building railroads. Both would be terribly expensive and they just aren't needed. By making proper use of water routes and by supplementing these with our specialty — the frozen winter roads nature paves for us — we can move any amount of freight. People, we move by air."

"About people. How do you manage to get and hold construction workers?"

"This is the least of my problems. First off, we pay the highest construction wages in the Union. Then we see to it our people get the best food, yes, and drink too — better than Moscow, I can tell you. We use a system of wage incentives and special bonuses that increase with the length of time a man or woman stays on the job and in the North. After two or three years here, some workers feel they just can't afford to go back South! This is only part of it. We rely a lot on the way Russians feel about tough jobs. Most of them, particularly the youngsters, seem to want a challenge even more than they want money. We give them challenge! And anyone who works up here gets involved in the total project. Bricklayers, for example, have a say in how we work and in developing techniques.

"After a good taste of it, many of the young people determine to stay for the rest of their lives in the North, and they get first preference on the living space they themselves are constructing. It all works out to a feeling of personal commitment to a task once thought impossible — the satisfaction of solving problems and of breaking new ground for mankind. It helps that we know we are not working here to make a profit for someone else to put in his pocket. We know we are working for ourselves and for our fellows, and this makes a big difference to a man's attitudes."

When I returned to Tchersky three years later, it was to find the chaos of the place somewhat reduced, but the atmosphere of frenetic activity still persisted. There were some incredible changes — notably rows of huge apartment blocks which had sprung out of the tundra, a fancy shopping center under one roof, and the fact that the population had increased by a third. Also of note — Victor Nazarov had given up his precious Bobyk and was savaging a brand new Volga sedan on streets which had not improved one whit since I had risked my kidneys on them during my first visit. Alexei Babkov was still in town, still as intense as ever. Having admired the things he had achieved during my absence, I could not forebear from needling him a little.

"What happened to those hard-top roads"

"Well, not *everything* works out. But we've got a new idea for frost-resistant paving under study right now. It's urgent. Nazarov's new Volga just isn't going to survive unless we come to its rescue pretty quick."

18
Toward the
CHUKCHEE

In 1960, Zelyovny Mis (Green Cape), four kilometers north of Tchersky, was nothing but a tongue of tundra bearing a wisp of stunted trees which gave it its name. Occasional Evenki fishing parties hauled their boats out on its muddy beach. Under a mossy pile of stones high on the riverbank lay the bones of unknown men who perhaps were ancestors of the Yukagir people.

On a day in early October of 1969 I stood near the ancient burial mound looking down over the Kolyma. Below me seven deep-sea freighters lay nose to stern along a half-mile of concrete dock. Towering gantry cranes wheeled and curtsied, while lift trucks scurried about amidst piles of freight. An almost unbroken line of trucks emerged from the sprawling cluster of warehouses behind me, slithered down to the docks, loaded, and climbed back up again.

One of the big ships let go her lines, swung ponderously into midstream, and dropped anchor. She rode light in dark waters skimmed with shimmering cat ice. With her cargo all unloaded she was awaiting orders to depart downstream to the Arctic Ocean and then make her way westward along nearly three thousand miles of arctic coast, through the East Siberian Sea and the Laptev Sea, past Cape Chelyuskin into the Kara Sea, through the mill race of Vorota Strait into the Barents Sea, and finally into the White Sea and to her home port of Murmansk.

Her siren sounded a lugubrious blast, and it was echoed by one of the ships remaining at the docks. The *Pioneer*, a beautiful vessel of ten thousand tons with the bows of an icebreaker, was also ready to depart. Her course lay east, past Wrangel Island into the Chukchee Sea, around Cape Deznev, through the Bering Strait, then south to join her sister ships of the Far Eastern Steamship Trust at Vladivostok . . . thirty-seven hundred sea miles distant.

In less than a decade Green Cape had been transformed from a prehistoric wilderness into a new port city, standing almost at the midway mark along one of the world's most unusual shipping lanes, stretching for nearly six thousand miles through the domain of arctic ice.

As far back as the sixteenth century the dream of finding a northeast passage from Europe around Asia to the Pacific, or a northwest passage around the Americas, was drawing men and ships to their deaths in the polar pack. Yet it was not until 1879 that a successful northeast passage was accomplished by the Swedish explorer Nordenskjöld after a two-year voyage in the little steamer *Vega*. Between 1913 and 1915 a Russian naval officer, Vilikitsky, repeated the feat, and during the same decade the Norwegian Roald Amundsen, in his tiny *Gjoa*, made the first voyage through the northwest passage. Up to this point in time the dual histories of man's attempts to overmaster the

Northern ice in the two passages had been roughly parallel; now they diverged sharply. Apart from exploratory voyages through it by the Canadian Mounted Police vessel *St. Roch* and the Canadian icebreaker *Labrador*, interest in the northwest passage faded into almost total obscurity which did not lighten until 1969, when the American supertanker *Manhattan*, escorted and assisted by the Canadian icebreaker *John A. MacDonald*, butted her way through the channels of the Canadian Arctic Archipelago to become the first commercial vessel to navigate the northwest passage.

Things had happened differently in the ice-clad eastern waters. In 1932 the Soviet ship *Sibirikov* made the voyage from Murmansk to Bering Strait and on to Vladivostok in a single season. A year later the *Chelyuskin*, a cargo-passenger vessel, tried to emulate the feat and got within sight of Bering Strait before she and her one hundred and twenty-eight passengers (including six women and two children) became jammed in the pack. Throughout most of that winter *Chelyuskin* drifted in the polar basin. In February 1934, the ice closed in and crushed her and she sank, leaving her people to camp on the shifting floes for sixty days until they were rescued by ski-equipped aircraft of Polar Aviation.

The *Chelyuskin* voyage appeared to have been a disaster; but the man who led that expedition, big, burly, black-bearded Otto Yulievitch Schmidt, knew otherwise. For fifteen years before *Chelyuskin* sailed, Otto Schmidt had been obsessed by the need to establish commercial navigation in the Russian arctic. As a scientifically trained explorer, he understood how to use science in the proper service of mankind, and he also knew how to make and use propaganda in the same service. Having convinced the authorities that his Northern vision was a reasonable one, he recruited a volunteer army to open the ice-fast gates of the Northern waters.

By 1932, Schmidt's "Polar Army," equipped with three antiquated icebreakers (of which the best was the *Yermak*, built in 1899) and supported by a score of polar research stations and by ice-reconnaisance pilots of Polar Aviation, had opened two-thirds of the northeast passage route to regular commercial shipping. Then came the *Chelyuskin* disaster. The very next year, however, Schmidt took a convoy of four merchant freighters eastward from Murmansk, successfully rounded Chukotka, and delivered the cargo to Vladivostok. The northeast passage, renamed the Northern Sea Route, was open for business.

In 1936 Otto Schmidt visited London, where he described to a group of journalists something of the vision with which he had lived through most of his adult life.

"People believe the arctic is a wasteland, incapable of development, useless to man, a frozen desert. They are utterly wrong! Anything can be accomplished in the arctic by men with dreams and with conviction.

"Our geographical position demands that we look north. Our largest rivers flow into that ice-bound sea. We are going to take products up and down those rivers. They will be the side streets, and the Arctic Ocean will be the trunk highway. We will transfer goods at the river mouths to and from oceangoing ships and establish trade communications between Europe and America across the top of the world.

"We have lined our Northern coast with radio stations to assist arctic navigation and aviation. At all difficult places we will have icebreakers stationed. We have already opened the northeast passage for three months of the year. During three hundred years prior to 1930 no more than nine little boats managed to round Cape Chelyuskin — the northern-most tip of Asia — and only three made it all the way east to the Pacific. In the summer of 1935 eleven of our cargo boats passed Chelyuskin simultaneously, and four of them entered Bering Strait.

"We fully subscribe to the phrase coined by the North American explorer, Vilhjalmur Stefansson: 'The Friendly Arctic.' We don't just give it lip service; we are really making friends with the polar world — we are bringing it to life, and life to it."

A part of the realization of Schmidt's dream lay before me as I looked out over Green Cape harbor. In 1936 the Soviet arctic merchant fleet carried two hundred seventy thousand tons of freight on the Northern Sea Route, and that was a spectacular achievement. During the three and a half months of its operation in 1969, Green Cape, the smallest and newest of the twenty-odd Soviet arctic seaports, alone handled seven hundred fifty thousand tons. In 1936 eleven steamers made the full run through the northeast passage. In 1969 there were more than seven hundred commercial voyages along Otto Schmidt's "trunk highway."

In the north*west* passage during 1969 . . . there was one transit; and even that was made only as an experiment by a ship whose cargo tanks were filled with ballast.

By midnight of October 6, a blizzard had begun to blow over the anchorage, the docks and storage yards at Green Cape. It was difficult for men to move against the wall of driven snow, and the cold was terrible. I felt neither cold nor wind, for I was standing on the glass-enclosed bridge of *Pioneer*. From that point of vantage I could see the glare of dozens of floodlights diffusing through the storm, and catch glimpses of the great gantries still at work. The last few cases of cargo were coming out of the ships' holds, and somewhere in that scene Victor Nazarov was sweating out the minutes. Word had been received from central headquarters of the Northern Sea Route that the polar pack was rapidly setting in against the coast and all vessels must clear port at once if they were to escape to open water before winter sealed the passage shut.

I was aboard *Pioneer* at her Master's invitation — an invitation which had included the offer to take me along as supercargo on the vessel's homeward voyage to Vladivostok. To my regret I could not accept this portion of his offer, but I was glad to take advantage of the luxury of a hot shower and of dinner aboard ship.

Captain Evgeny Kirov and his officers were all young men with an aura of confidence and professionalism about them. They were intensely proud of their ship, and of the Soviet merchant marine, but they were not boastful. The days are evidently gone when Soviet seamen nurtured an aggressive inferiority complex vis-à-vis the American or British merchant fleets.

I toured the ship — and she was a marvel of modern technology, married to seaworthy qualities. Built in East Germany to Soviet designs, her hull was especially strengthened for ice navigation and her thirty-six-hundred-horsepower diesels gave her power enough to break through pack ice five feet thick. She was completely air conditioned, including the engine room, where the duty engineer sat in a soundproofed "office" and regulated the entire mechanical life of the ship from one set of panels and controls. Like all newer Soviet vessels she was also equipped with an elaborate filtration system designed to prevent oil pollution of the oceans through which she sailed.

Captain Kirov told me that *Pioneer* was one of about a

hundred vessels which had been built during the previous ten years for service in the arctic, but which were equally useful in more temperate waters. He explained the command system of the Northern Sea Route, whereby a shore-based commodore controls each of several segments of the passage, directing icebreakers and aircraft to points where they are needed, and guiding the merchant ships along the easiest courses. *Pioneer* was equipped with facsimile receivers which hourly produced detailed ice charts and weather maps.

I am no stranger to merchant ships, and I can honestly say I have never been aboard a better equipped vessel, nor one with more comfortable accommodations for her people. Nor have I met seamen who were more dedicated to their profession than the crowd aboard *Pioneer*.

When I got up the next morning and looked out the window of the apartment where I was staying, the Kolyma rolled gray and empty under a thickening shell of ice. The ships had vanished, and for eight months to come Otto Schmidt's highway would be closed to traffic.

If the plans of his successors are realized, it will not always be so. The nuclear-powered icebreaker *Lenin*, built in 1958 but still by far the most powerful ship of her kind afloat, has recently demonstrated that the Northern Sea Route can be kept open for six months of the year. She will soon be joined by two bigger sisters, and under those powerful wings ships like *Pioneer* will be able to stay in continuous arctic service twice as long as at present. Nor will Soviet vessels be alone on the arctic run. In 1970 the entire passage was opened to foreign ships, and a number of Japanese freighters sailed through it to European waters, cutting the usual passage time via the southern route almost in half.

After a few days in Tchersky, Kola, Claire, and I were beginning to suffer from a surfeit of hospitality. Every day was fiesta, and every meal a banquet. In an effort to ease the pressures on my liver I tried refusing drinks under the pretense of being ashamed to consume so much of the local supplies, which were irreplaceable until the ships returned next summer. Victor neatly blocked that avenue of escape. He drove me to the warehouse district of Green Cape, stopped in front of a building about a city block long, unlocked the door with an ordinary house key, switched on the lights, and invited me inside.

It was an alcoholic's Cave of Ali Baba. As far as the eye could reach the place was stacked to the ceiling with cases of vodka, cognac, champagne, wine, and spirit.

"You see, Farley? No need to worry. Enough here for every thirsty man in Kolyma and Chukotka and plenty left over for Canadian guests."

It is worth noting that this vast lode of liquid gold was unguarded, except for a lock which any amateur could have picked. After this I no longer doubted what I had been told about the law-abiding qualities of Russians.

Later I met the man responsible for distributing all those bottles, along with several hundred thousands of tons of other supplies, over the vast region served from Green Cape.

Leonid Shevelyov, the hawk-faced Ukrainian Director of the Tchersky Transport Company, had spent thirty years in the arctic — not all of that time on a voluntary basis. He was rather more of a Ukrainian nationalist than was advisable during the Stalin era, and in 1947 he was arrested in Kiev for "unsound political beliefs" and given a tour in a forced labor camp at the goldfields near Magadan. When he was released he decided it would be wiser to become a Siberian nationalist and to stay where he was for a while. He studied engineering by correspondence, got his diploma, and became so deeply involved in the complexities of establishing a truck-transport system in the arctic that he never did go back across the Urals; nor does he ever plan to.

"I can't say the forced labor did me a lot of good, but coming to Siberia was the best thing that ever happened to me. This is the country for a fellow who likes problems. Out here you get the chance to solve them in your own way, without some desk-banger thumping you on the head whenever you turn your back."

Leonid had been in Tchersky for five years and had set up one of the most efficient transport operations in the Soviet arctic. His company had two hundred and fifty heavy-duty trucks, almost as many trailers, and a crew of nearly a thousand drivers and mechanics. Acting in concert with a sister company based in Chukotka, the primary job was to transport up to three hundred thirty thousand tons of freight a year eastward from Green Cape some seven hundred kilometers to the rapidly developing goldfields near Bilibino, and beyond that to an atomic-powered electric generating station which was being constructed near Pevek.

This was strictly a cross-country operation. There were no frozen rivers running east and west to provide natural winter roads, and there could be no permanent roads across the intervening taiga and mountains because there were no materials locally available with which to build them. The only natural materials in good supply were snow and permafrost, so both were put to work.

"In late September we send small parties of technicians out to camp along routes we have already surveyed. Their job is to measure the penetration of the new winter frost into the thawed upper layers of the soil and muskeg. As soon as they report six inches of new frost we put our road-building machines to work.

"We designed and built these machines ourselves. Each consists of an enormous flat-bottomed steel platform twenty feet wide with a V plow in front. The platform is loaded with ballast — as much as twenty tons of concrete-filled barrels — and the whole rig is hitched behind four or five of our biggest crawler tractors. They move along the route and the plow breaks through the frozen crust and turns it aside, leaving a flat, compacted surface twenty feet wide. This is allowed to freeze until the surface frost joins with the underlying eternal frost. And there's your road. It's good from November through to April. Graders with shearing blades keep it planed smooth. We stop using it before the first spring thaws so it doesn't get rutted by the trucks. The following autumn we wait for it to freeze again, grade it, and away we go. If holes develop we fill them with steam-heated mud, level it, and let it freeze. It is the cheapest pavement in the world and nearly as good as asphalt or concrete — better in this climate because it doesn't buckle or crack."

"But surely," I said, "you can't use that system in all circumstances. What about crossing through mountain valleys or places where there is no appreciable surface thaw?"

"In that case we have a different technique. We use bulldozers to heap up a ridge of snow, then we level the ridge and compact and smooth it with the road-builder. There is enough pressure generated to weld the snow crystals together so we get a kind of opaque, granular ice. It will carry reasonably heavy traffic. If the surface does get bad, we just add more snow and pressure-harden it into a new surface."

It sounded a little bit like science fiction to me, and perhaps my skepticism was apparent. At any rate Victor Nazarov decided I needed proof.

"Leonid! Give me one of your Maz trucks! Farley! Come with me! We're going to Chukotka!"

I was delighted. Chukotka is one of the regions in the Soviet Union which really *is* off-limits to foreigners because it stretches to within a few miles of Alaska, and both sides in the Cold War face each other across the Bering Strait with the maximum array of technological horrors.

The Maz (Minsk Auto Works) turned out to be a twenty-two-ton behemoth, and we had to climb a ladder to get into the cab. Victor was in his element. Embracing the steering wheel lovingly with both arms, he piloted the monster out of the yard and headed east.

There was a chilling moment on the outskirts of the town when we passed a grim array of gray buildings surrounded by barbed-wire fences, at the corners of which stood high watchtowers. Yura's joke about forced-labor camps at Tchersky suddenly went very sour. Victor nodded his big head at the camp.

"Ha!" he bellowed. "Very dangerous place! Storage for atomic materials going to Pevek. You want to wear lead pants if you go in there!"

We drove eastward for about a hundred miles, well into Chukotka, and I saw nothing except an almost endless line of big trucks going both ways; a couple of tracked recovery vehicles; one arctic fox who seemed to think he had fallen into a foxy Hades and was scampering wildly to evade the mechanical monsters thundering down upon him; and a waste of tundra muskeg thinly dotted with dwarf spruce trees.

The road was as it had been described, except that somebody had been remiss about filling in the holes with steaming mud — or with anything else. I would *not* recommend it for pleasure driving.

As we bumped along, Victor talked about his true soulmates, the long-haul drivers.

"In the old days (anything before last year was the 'old days' to Victor) we moved the trucks in convoys so if one broke down there would be others at hand to help. But that was slow and the drivers complained they were losing time. So we began letting them run on their own, and that's the way they do it, even in big blizzards and at 70° below zero.

"Because of the big tonnage we have to move, every truck runs twenty-four hours a day all winter, except for layoff time for maintenance. There are three drivers to a truck, but only two are with the vehicle; the other is off duty, resting. There are rest houses and repair stations every hundred miles and recovery vehicles patrol between them. As you see, almost every truck hauls a trailer. The average load is fifteen tons.

"A truck is expected to last seven to eight years up here, despite the tough work and the climate. That's because our maintenance is the best. We use twelve-ton Tatras from Czechoslovakia; sixteen-ton Urals, and these big Maz's. We call them all 'boats.' The winter taiga and tundra is as rough on men and equipment as the Arctic Ocean, but our boats go through when the big ships can't move.

"Our lads work on incentives; they like to see who can haul the most and make the most trips. They're real professionals. They get almost as much training as an airplane pilot, and make more money. The average up here is seven hundred rubles a month — more than the President in Moscow gets! We've got a tough trade union. If a driver works overtime he has to get that amount of time off later on, with full pay; and on top of that he gets two or three times his normal salary while doing the overtime."

Not all the trucks are on the Tchersky-Bilibino-Pevek run. Some of them drive six hundred miles south on the frozen Kolyma and then climb onto an all-weather highway running southeast across the mountains to Magadan, whose seaport is now kept open all year round by icebreakers. However, if they turn west on this same highway they come to Yakutsk and from there can drive another seven hundred miles south to reach the Trans-Siberian Railway where it skirts the Chinese border.

The fabled isolation of Siberian towns in winter — even the most northerly of them — has become a myth; and prominent among the mythbreakers are the tough young men who drive their "boats" wherever need dictates across the frozen land.

The truckers were relative latecomers in the mythbreaking business. In 1926 Soviet pilots, flying stick-and-string little aircraft, had already penetrated the arctic.

I heard something of the story of those early days from a big, florid, red-nosed pilot who originally came from Kazakhstan and who had spent thirty-five years flying in the North. When I met him in 1966, Vladimir Sedlerevich was the Director of the Polar Aviation base at Tchersky.

He and his companions first went into the North because of the driving ambitions of Otto Schmidt, who realized that ships alone could not master the ice of the northeast passage. Ships needed eyes aloft to find channels through the pack, and they needed meteorological data from remote outposts along the route — most of which could only be supplied and maintained by air. So the remarkable organization known as Polar Aviation came into being. By 1935 its fleet of over a hundred aircraft was not only servicing the Northern Sea Route but was flying on a more or less regular basis into almost every corner of Siberia.

Schmidt, the dreamer and the doer, was not content. He had early realized that the Arctic Ocean was in fact a mediterranean sea, surrounded by polar lands which might one day be linked to each other in commerce and in friendship. However, in the 1930s almost nothing was known about the nature of that sea of ice or of conditions in the air above it.

In 1936 Schmidt proposed that this gap in human knowledge be filled. He planned to establish a manned meteorological and oceanographic station on the drifting ice at the North Pole — a point where no man, with the possible exception of the American Dr. Frederick Cook, had ever stood. Using this as a weather and communications relay base, Schmidt hoped to begin transpolar flights on the shortest route between Moscow and the United States.

On May 20, 1937, a converted four-engine bomber whose wheels had been replaced by enormous skis climbed laboriously into cloudy skies above Rudolph Island in the Franz Joseph Archipelago. Head winds reduced the ground speed to a crawl. Cloud cover forced the plane to climb until her people lost sight of the wilderness of ice below. After ten hours the navigator reported they were above their target.

They went down through the cloud and broke out over a waste of crushed pack ice. There was no fuel to spare for a reconnaissance. The pilot picked what looked to be the best potential ice landing field and put the plane's nose down. She touched. A drogue parachute spilled out from her tail and slowed her to a stop.

During the next few days three more four-engine planes landed at the Pole. When the planes departed they left behind them a meteorological and oceanographic station

staffed by four men who were destined to remain on the
pack for nine months while drifting thirteen hundred miles
across the polar basin, finally to be picked up by Soviet
icebreakers off the east coast of Greenland, not far north
of Iceland.

Barely two weeks after drift station North Pole One became operational, a big NO-25 aircraft lifted from Moscow
airport. Sixty-three hours later the red-winged plane
landed at Portland, Oregon, at the end of a fifty-three hun-
dred-mile nonstop flight across the arctic mediterranean.
Less than a month later, Mikhail Gromov brought the second NO-25 from Moscow to North America. Gromov flew
nonstop to the Mexican border before circling back to land
at San Jacinto, California.

The success of these two flights went to the heads of the
powers in Moscow. They ordered another flight for August 12; but instead of sticking with the trusty NO-25, they
decreed that a new and relatively untried commercial aircraft, the N-209, should be used instead.

At 1:40 P.M. of the twelfth, Levanevsky, the pilot, reported being over North Pole One at an altitude of 20,000
feet and experiencing strong headwinds and icing. It was
the last that was ever heard of the plane or of its crew.

It was not Levanevsky's death but the approach of war,
the war itself, and the ensuing years of chill hostility between East and West which forced the termination of Soviet efforts to establish a regular transpolar flight between
Russia and North America.

"Too bad we had to give it up," Sedlerevich said regret-
fully. "But it didn't put us out of work. There was plenty
to do at home."

Polar Aviation now operates a fleet of over three thousand aircraft, ranging from single-engine AN-2s (the

standard "bush" plane) to the new trijet Yak-40 STOL
(short-take-off-landing) passenger planes, and including
nine types of helicopter. There is scheduled service to every
community in the Siberian North which has more than one
thousand population, and frequent nonsched services to all
the rest. Arctic airports are amongst the busiest — considering the size of the towns they serve — in the Soviet Union.
Tchersky handles ten scheduled landings every day, including the daily "Arctic Lateral" flight each way from Moscow to Chukotka, along the rim of the Arctic Ocean. In
1969 Tchersky had a circulation of six thousand tons of
cargo and ninety-seven thousand passengers.

A special air fleet services the Polar Drift Stations on the
arctic ice, of which there have been more than forty since
North Pole One was established in 1937. The roster of
services performed by other wings covers almost every need
of the arctic communities: air ambulances, flying doctors,
ice reconnaissance, trapper supply, exploration support,
air-land-sea rescue, mail and general communications.

"But our biggest single task," said Sedlerevich, "is mass
passenger transport. People are much more willing to come
and live in the North if they have fast, convenient, cheap
and comfortable flights in and out whenever they have a
mind to take a trip. We give them that. At any one time
as many as a third of the people in the new Northern towns
and cities may be traveling south, east, and west on holiday.
Sometimes I think nobody in this country stays still long
enough to drink a glass of tea.

"We have mastered arctic flying so well now that the
whole thing has become pretty routine. All the same there
are times when our mastery is challenged. Last autumn, for
instance, the North gave us something to remember.

"Near the end of September the cartographic ship *Inij*

was caught in the ice during a hurricane. She damaged her rudder and went out of control and finally blew ashore on a pile of rocks some five hundred miles from here and a hundred miles off the coast.

"It was a hell of a storm — winds of eighty miles an hour and snow so thick you could see nothing. All the lifeboats were smashed, and the crew of sixty seamen and scientists didn't have much chance. *Inij* began to break up, and two young chaps took the devil's own risk and tried to reach a nearby islet in a rubber boat to get a lifeline to the land. They made it, but lost the line and found they were alone on the islet with a pair of angry polar bears.

"We had word of what had happened immediately, and within an hour had our three biggest helicopters — MIL-4s — heading for the wreck. It was a calculated risk. Normally we won't operate more than sixty miles offshore, and then only in good weather; but this was no time for the rule book. The first helicopter reached the wreck in time for the radio operator to jump out and shoot the bears. The pilots reported back that they could operate from the islet if they had fuel delivered to them there. There was no real place for fixed-wing planes to land, but some of my boys loaded up their AN-2s with extra fuel and flew off to see what could be done. The wind was on their side. It blew so hard that, by landing into it, they could put down on a patch of level rock only about a hundred meters long. In ordinary weather they couldn't have landed or taken off in that distance, particularly loaded.

"Now our helicopters had the fuel to fight their way out to the wreck, and among the three of them they made sixty lifts, bringing the people off the *Inij* one at a time to the little island. From there they were ferried to the mainland by the AN-2s.

"There were a lot of doubtful moments. The wind was so strong and the seas breaking so high that the lifelines from the helicopters would fly straight out although they had a weighted end on them. The lads solved that by tying their anchors to the ends of the lines.

"One of my best pilots did that, and the wind gusted as he was lifting a man off, and the anchor caught in the ship's rigging. So there he was, tethered to the ship; and he couldn't cut the line because the man on the end of it would have been lost.

"It was no time for long thoughts. He dropped a little to let the line sag, then gave the machine full power and lifted up. The fluke broke off the anchor and he was free — but he might just as easily have torn the guts right out of his craft.

"Six of my lads got the Lenin Medal for heroism out of that three days' work. And Tchersky gave them a special vote of applause — twenty cases of champagne being saved for New Year's Day. Now they spend half their time listening to the marine radio, just hoping for another wreck to come their way!"

19
TCHERSKY

It was frustrating to be so close to Chukotka and yet not be able to investigate the place. It had a particular interest for me, since not only does it lie immediately adjacent to the North American arctic, but its people are close neighbors and even relatives of the Eskimo among whom I once lived.

If I could not visit the region in person, I was at least able to gain some knowledge of it from a number of Chukchee friends. Not least of these was Anna Dmitrievna Nutegryne, a very attractive thirty-eight-year-old Chukchee woman who has been Chairman of the Chukotka National District for several years, as well as being a presidium member of the Supreme Soviet in Moscow. In 1969, Anna was in Leningrad taking a year's leave of absence from her job in order to complete her studies for a degree in history. She was an old friend of Yura's and we gathered in his apartment, where I heard a great deal about Chukotka, old and new.

I was intrigued by the structure and nature of the Chukotka National District. National Districts are transitional arrangements intended to preserve small native groups, but they are in no sense reserves in the image of Indian reservations in North America. They were designed to prevent the dissolution of small native populations and their cultures while at the same time encouraging them to develop a modern social, economic, and political structure. In the Soviet Union the native peoples have no choice as to what that structure will be; however, they do have the opportunity, and encouragement — accompanied by lavish material assistance — to build it by and for themselves.

As the people of National Districts master the complexities of modern existence, they qualify for recognition as Autonomous Soviet Socialist Republics, of which there are now twenty in the USSR. In theory, at least, the next step is to achieve complete equality with other states as a full-fledged Soviet Socialist Republic.

The Chukotka National District occupies the whole northwest peninsula of continental Asia and comes under Magadan for external administrative purposes; but within its own borders it is to a very real degree self-governing. With a population of just under eighty thousand people, over half of whom are nonnatives (mostly miners and new townsfolk), it has its own capital at Anadyr and its own District Soviet, of which Anna is the "President." The District Soviet has direct control over most local activities and over most of the renewable natural resources, but has little to say, except in a consultant role, about the new urban-type European-dominated communities or about the development of mineral resources. Nevertheless, a reasonably high proportion of the profits from mineral development in Chukotka goes into the district treasury in the form of di-

rect payments, while the Soviet government heavily subsi-
dizes the entire gamut of district activities and enterprises.

It is a good sign that the natives of Chukotka — roughly
twenty thousand Chukchee; two thousand Eskimo; two
thousand Evenki, Yakut and Koryak; and about eight thousand "Old Russians," including people of mixed blood —
are by no means satisfied with their share of the income
from Chukotka gold, mercury, and tin and are vocal in their
demands for a bigger cut.

The whole system of National Districts, of which there
are now ten in Russia, inevitably breeds nationalism. Because it does so it is viewed by some autocrats with a hostile
eye. The international battle between the "lumpers" who
would do away with all small national entities in favor of
"one world" agglomerations of people, and the "splitters"
who believe mankind would be healthier and more likely to
evolve in a viable direction if we preserved at least the best
of the differences which distinguish neighboring groups, still
rages in Russia as it does almost everywhere in the modern
world.

Nationalism, born out of Lenin's original concept of encouraging the preservation of significant cultural characteristics and racial unity within ethnic groups, has become
and remains a potent factor in the Soviet Union. Distrusted
by some, stubbornly defended by others, it is a fact of Soviet life. Anna Nutegryne sees it this way:

"We Chukchee feel a great warmth and loyalty to the
Soviet State. It has given us the right to remain Chukchee
while at the same time becoming full Soviet citizens. Our
pride in our own race has not lessened our feelings of pride
in the State. When we became part of the modern world, we
were not forced to do so at the cost of losing ourselves. We
were not submerged in the huge sea of Soviet peoples. No,

we were helped to build a strong ship called Chukotka, and we sail on that ship in a fleet of friendly vessels, all heading in the same direction. Sometimes, of course, one of the bigger ships may take some of our wind, and then we have to struggle amicably for our rights. But we have the freedom to struggle, and we can win because we Chukchee are all together."

Doubtless Anna's analogy is oversimplified, but it accurately reflects the attitude of most of the Small Peoples.

Chukotka has had a peculiar history. Throughout modern times its Eskimo and Chukchee people (who speak a different tongue but are culturally very similar) had a much closer relationship to North America than to European Russia. In Tsarist times they were thought of as the only unconquered people in the entire country. They paid tribute to the Tsar only on a voluntary basis as "gifts to the poor white chief." From about 1880 onward they came into close contact with white traders from Alaska and the northwestern states of America, and the seeds of capitalism were sown in a society which was originally more truly communistic than the one devised by Marx and Lenin. During this period the Chukchee even produced a few "kings," local entrepreneurs who allied themselves with the foreigners, engrossed the once communally held reindeer herds to their own use, and controlled trade between their people and the Americans. The last of these was a man called Armavargan, who thought of himself as brother to the Tsar and fully his equal.

The Revolution did not really touch Chukotka, except in token form, until 1928. As late as that time most of the Eskimo and Chukchee on the northeast coast spoke English, not Russian, as their second language. Primitive socialism had been replaced by mercantile capitalism, and they were well started along the road which the Alaskan Eskimo have since followed.

When the first Soviet proselytizers arrived amongst them, there was hell to pay. The shamans and the chiefs united with the foreign traders to resist the newcomers and to block any reversion to socialism. Stories are told of American traders supplying free arms, including old brass cannon, to the Chukchee chiefs in an effort to persuade them to resist the Soviets by force of arms. Luckily the Chukchee and Eskimo are not warlike, and they declined the honor of dying in what would have been, for them, a hopeless struggle.

The New Life (as the Revolution is known in Chukotka) did not really take hold there until people had become literate. This marked the turning point. By the mid-1930s socialism had been sufficiently well established so that the Chukotka National District could be formed and allowed a measure of self government.

Today, according to those Chukchee and Eskimo I talked to, this little "nation" is well on its way to achieving recognition as an Autonomous Soviet Socialist Republic. Its native peoples are mostly employed on collectives and state farms. Reindeer herding has proved to be extremely profitable, and a major sea-mammal hunting operation (primarily for whales and seals) is conducted by a score of shore collectives. Chukotka has its own radio system and television studios broadcasting in native languages. In Anadyr it has its own publishing house, producing books by local writers as well as translations from the Russian and from foreign languages. By 1969 the district had produced twenty-one fully qualified Chukchee and Eskimo doctors, enough native teachers to staff all forty of its primary and secondary schools (this figure is exclusive of schools in the new cities) and a number of specialists, including Vladimir Rentirgin, a Chukchee who is Chief of the Research Institute for Gold and Nonferrous Metals in Magadan; and Ivan Leekay, of Eskimo and Chukchee blood, who was recently elected to the USSR Academy of Sciences as a philologist.

The Eskimo of the town of Uelen maintained direct contact with their Alaskan relatives up until 1956. Parties from both sides of the Bering Strait used to meet on the winter ice off the Diomede Islands and camp together for days at a time. This happy leak in the Cold War wall was eventually plugged — not by the Russians but, according to Yura, by the Americans, possibly, as he suggested, "Because they not want their Eskimo to see and hear truth about life in our Chukotka."

The Chukchee are a lusty people and Yura and some other Chukchee friends gave me considerable insight into the current state of love and sex in Russia.

Despite what we read about Russian puritanism, I am able to report that sex remains alive and well in the Soviet Union. There is, however, an old-fashioned sense of propriety among European Russians which insists that people preserve a rather Victorian appearance of prudery, which perhaps explains the disgruntled comments of some Western journalists who, after a few months in Moscow, begin to react like Pavlov's dogs who hear the bell, but can't quite run it down. I am sorry for these gentlemen and I pass on to them some reflections on the matter from a charming young Muscovite whose job brings her into frequent contact with Westerners.

"It is so very strange the way many foreign men behave. If they have a few drinks with you in a café, or take you to dinner or a dance, they take it for granted you will go back with them to their hotel, or let them go back with you to your apartment.

"Don't they know there is more to it than that? I will go anywhere with a man I love, and I am proud to take my lover to my place; but there *must* be love. If I just slept with a man in a hotel or at my flat, people would think me stupid. They would despise me; and they would be right. There must be love before love-making. But in Russia it is possible to fall in love in one minute . . . if only both people will allow themselves to do it."

The romantic approach is generally the correct one in the Soviet Union. There are, however, certain practical difficulties to overcome. One is the lack of privacy, particularly in the major cities. In summer this poses no great problem . . . the birch glades surrounding Moscow are hospitable to lovers, and easy to reach by public transport. In winter things are not so easy. Hotel rooms are almost impossible to get unless you are from out of town. There are no convenient motels. But there *are* the cozy sleeping compartments on Russian trains. A friend of mine who travels frequently between Leningrad and Moscow estimates that nearly half the weekend rail passengers are lovers making the most of the overnight run between the two cities. "You have no idea how strong the romantic flavor is aboard the Friday night train to Leningrad. I have had to stop using the weekend trains. It is too upsetting for an old man like me," he told me somewhat sadly.

Love finds a way even in Moscow, where young men band together and acquire, by whatever devious methods, a room or a flat whose facilities they share in common. A friend of Yura's explained the system to me. "What we do is make little badges — like this one I am wearing — and we wear them when we are on the subway or at a party. See? It says on it, only, *I Have a House.* It doesn't guarantee any girl will become your friend; but if a girl you meet begins to fall in love with you it tells her that her love won't go to waste. Here, take my badge. And here is the address. But, please, telephone this number first. Nobody will answer but if it stops ringing, wait for an hour and then try again. If it rings more than a dozen times it means you are welcome to use our room."

Because I am not about to snitch on any of my Russian friends, I can use no names, but both Claire and I were astounded at the multiplicity of romantic entanglements which seemed to surround all our companions. They kept falling into and out of love with a frequency and ardor that left me exhausted just thinking about it.

As might be expected, attitudes vary in different parts of the country. In Georgia or Armenia, for instance, the direct approach to a woman is acceptable. In fact, give a Georgian a few liters of his native wine and any other approach becomes unthinkable.

I remember a night when we were driving back to Tbilisi after a country outing culminating in a party at a vineyard worker's house — a party that lasted for nine hours, during which incredible amounts of new wine went down the hatch. There were two carloads of us weaving down the highway toward the distant city. Claire and I shared the back seat of the rear car with a young Georgian interpreter. Sitting up front with the driver was one of the most distinguished literary figures in the Georgian Republic, a fine old man with a pointed white beard and the dignity of a Khan. Our own interpreter, a young Muscovite named Sasha who had a low tolerance for Georgian wine, was driving in the lead car with Yuri Rytkheu.

Halfway home the lead car screeched to a halt, a door

swung open, and someone fell out into the ditch. Our car stopped too and I jumped out, suspecting that all was not well with young Sasha. All was not well. He was rendering unto Georgia what was Georgia's.

When I returned to our car Claire had a wild-eyed look, and she pushed so close against me that the young Georgian was left with most of the back seat to himself. However, I was preoccupied with Sasha's problems and did not correctly evaluate the undercurrents.

We had gone only a few kilometers farther when the whole scene repeated itself. This time Sasha refused to get back into the car and began crawling around the ditch on his hands and knees. Yura joined me and we discovered what was wrong. Sasha possessed two solid-gold front teeth of which he was extremely proud. They were no longer in his mouth, and he was dumbly determined not to leave the scene without them.

Walking back toward our car I met Claire running toward me. She looked as if she had been in a football scrimmage.

Later, in our hotel room, she unburdened herself.

"The first time you got out, the Georgian interpreter grabbed me as if I was his long lost love and kissed me so hard I nearly suffocated. I thought I was going to strangle. Then you came back and I had a chance to catch my breath and collect my wits. I didn't want to say anything to you, because . . . well, it would have been embarrassing. Then, before I could stop you, you jumped out again. I was just going to jump after you when old pointy-beard turned around, grinning like a goat, and pushed his paw up under my skirt. It took me two seconds to get out of the car but they were the longest two seconds in my life.

Georgian men! Don't you dare get out of arm's reach again until we leave this place!"

Unfortunately, the Georgian attitude is *not* a two-way street. A visitor is extremely ill-advised to even look sideways at a Georgian girl unless he is wearing a bullet-proof vest or has a bodyguard.

There were some Georgians in Tchersky. One of them was the husband of a lady reporter from the *Kolymskaya Pravda.* I met her at a party held in John's and my honor, and for some reason I attracted her amorous interest. She must have read Ogden Nash's dictum that candy is dandy but liquor is quicker, because she plied me with large glasses of cognac at five-minute intervals. I was able to slip these under the table to Yura, who nobly drained them and passed back the empties.

As I was to learn somewhat later, the lady's husband worked a night shift at Green Cape harbor, which meant that his wife "had a house" each night until he returned in the small hours of the morning. Being unaware of these facts at the time I agreed to escort her home — not because I reciprocated her emotions, but from a true sense of chivalry. She could never have made it on her own.

It was a bitterly cold night, and whatever warmth might have been engendered in me by the modicum of cognac I had drunk was all gone by the time we reached the log house in which she lived. By then I only wanted to go back to my own apartment and get some sleep . . . an attitude which she found quite inexplicable. Nevertheless, I persevered and she finally let me go.

I was less than a block from her house when Victor Nazarov's black Volga roared up behind me and slammed to a stop. Victor flung open a door, seized me by an arm, and dragged me onto the seat beside him. Without a word he

grabbed my left leg and jerked my foot high into the air.
For a moment he studied my boot, a standard felt overboot
that I had borrowed. Then he relaxed; grinned; bellowed
amiably in my ear; and drove me back to the party from
which I had hoped to escape.

Nothing was said about his odd behavior until next morning, when Yura took me aside and told me about the Georgian husband.

"He very crazy, that one. Every dawn when he come
home he walk all around his house and look for footprints in
snow. If find man's footprint, he follow just as good as wolf
follow poor reindeer. When he find man who owns footprints, he has big argument with him. Only he argues with
little hatchet.

"When Victor hear you leave party with girl, he very
much nervous for you. Maybe very much nervous for himself, too. How he explain to Moscow he need State funeral
for first Canadian visitor to Tchersky?"

Victor had been particularly concerned that I might have
been wearing my Canadian sealskin boots, which had dis-
tinctively patterned rubber soles that left an unmistakable
track, the only one of its kind in Siberia.

It is a common complaint of Western visitors that they
are seldom invited into Russian homes. The implication,
sometimes stated as a fact, is that Russians are afraid to
make friends with foreigners for fear of reprisals from the
KGB, or for similar sinister reasons. I suspect this is nonsense. I do know that some Russians are hesitant about taking foreigners home because they are afraid their houses
won't measure up to Western standards and so will rein-
force the contemptuous attitudes which are typical Western reactions to the life styles of the Russian people.

I was a guest in scores of private homes, ranging from the tiny one-room cubbyhole of a young Leningrad artist and his wife to the palatial apartment of a renowned Georgian artist in Tbilisi; from the home of a truck driver in Magadan to the luxurious quarters of a member of the Soviet Academy of Sciences; from the snug, three-room establishment of a beginning Yakut poet to the *ancien régime* dacha of one of Irkutsk's most successful authors; from the tents of the Yukagir reindeer herders to the ultramodern apartment of a Moscow diplomat. The problem was never one of how to arrange an entrée into private homes; if there was a problem at all, it was how to survive the ensuing hospitality.

My best memories of the Soviet Union are of evenings spent drinking, eating, arguing, laughing and singing in the intimate atmosphere of Russian family life. Most of what I learned about the way people thought and felt I learned on such occasions. What seemed then, and still remains, the most important element of all was the warmth and depth of friendship which was offered to me; friendship which took me behind the barriers of generic conclusions and crass generalities which so effectively shield people of different races and cultures from meaningful understanding of one another.

My friendship with Lydia and Anatoly Gorshkov was a case in point. During our first visit to Tchersky, Claire and I saw Lydia quite often, since she ran the little café where we ate many of our meals. We met Anatoly on only two occasions; once when he showed us through a new shopping center whose wall mural decorations were his work, and once at a party at Victor Nazarov's flat. Nevertheless, when we left Tchersky, Lydia wept as she kissed Claire goodbye. Anatoly also kissed her; then he kissed me on both cheeks and shyly gave us one of his drawings.

"You must come back. If you do not we will suffer very much, because you are our dear friends," said Lydia tearfully.

By North American standards we had hardly known each other well enough to justify a casual acquaintanceship. By Russian standards, we had known each other long enough to become close and enduring friends. Nor was this a social sham. When I returned to Tchersky in 1969 Lydia was away in Moscow with her three-year-old son, Mischka, who had a serious bronchial condition and was receiving specialist treatment. On the day of my arrival, Anatoly sent Lydia a telegram telling her that I had come and the next morning she left Mischka in her mother's care and boarded a plane. She flew nearly five thousand miles so she and Anatoly could properly welcome me into their home. Neither she nor her husband saw anything extraordinary in this. After all, I was their friend.

This beautiful young woman did not fly back empty-handed. On the very evening of her arrival I went to dinner with the Gorshovs in their small flat in one of the new apartment blocks. Lydia fed me Turkestan honey melon, Armenian tangerines, Polish pickled mushrooms, Bulgarian chianti, and Bulgarian brandy — all rare and expensive delicacies; but — for a friend — nothing is too good.

She had not even room in her baggage for presents for Anatoly, whom she had not seen for nearly two months. Everything she brought with her from Moscow, except a small bag of her own clothing, was intended for my entertainment.

Anatoly cooked shashlik on a fireplace he had built himself (after a ferocious battle with the housing authorities) in his tiny dining–living room. We ate and drank and talked until long after midnight, when Victor's Volga came to take me home to my apartment in Green Cape, four kilometers distant.

I had barely gone to bed when there came a soft rap on the door. Standing outside, red-faced from the bitter cold, and hesitant about the reception they might receive at this late hour, were Lydia and Anatoly. They had forgotten to give me a basket of apples, pomegranates and grapes which Lydia had also brought for me from Moscow. They had walked the four kilometers with the gift, and after giving it to me and holding my hand for a moment, they left and walked back home again.

I spent as much time as I could with this loving young couple, and we talked as frankly and as intimately as if we had known each other since childhood. They were not atypical. On the contrary they were very representative of the many people I met in the Soviet Union whom I am happy to call my friends.

Anatoly was thirty-four in 1969. He told me that in his youth he had been a "wild one." I could believe it. His lean, saturnine face still carried a devil-may-care stamp. "I did not know what I wanted as a youth, and nothing that offered itself seemed to quicken my heart. Moscow was my home, but it seemed like a dead city to me. Perhaps all cities seem the same and perhaps they are all dying. I did nothing at school. Then came my army stint — three years of it — and about halfway through I began to think I had been an idiot. I decided I should get an education, but it seemed a bit late in the day and I felt too old to go back to school. Instead I went out to Siberia, to Krasnoyarsk, and got a job on the dam there, knocking holes in the rock with a pneumatic drill. One lunchtime I was leaving the cafeteria when I ran straight into Lydia. I took one look into her face and the whole place exploded. Three hours later I asked her to marry me, and three days later we were married."

"*I* am a *real* Siberian," Lydia interjected, "born in Leninskaya; but when I was just a child I was taken to live in Moscow. I think I felt about the city the same way Tolia did. As soon as I was old enough I went to Krasnoyarsk for school, became a dietitian, and was starting on a managerial course when Tolia caught me. I could not resist him. He was a wandering man, an artist with the soul of a poet, and a wonderful lover. After two years in Krasnoyarsk we decided we wanted to go to the real North. We got as far as Lensk, where Tolia earned a living painting signs while he struggled hard to be an artist. Four years ago we moved on to Tchersky, looking for a wild place and a strong, exciting life."

"My great dream," said Anatoly, "is to someday sculpt a huge statue overlooking Bering Strait — a statue to Dezhnev, that brave Cossack who founded Nizhny Kolymsk and then went on in a little open boat to round Chukotka and sail south into the Pacific — the true discoverer of Bering Strait, and the first European to prove that Asia and America were not joined together."

"He is full of such dreams . . . this gray wolf of mine!" Lydia said, running her hand through her husband's hair. "Quite mad, sometimes. We will forgive him though. He is an artist and they must all be mad."

Anatoly became an artist only after he met Lydia, and he had not had any formal training. He suffered many frustrations because of his lack of knowledge of technique. He was determined to acquire technical proficiency. "It is hard to think about it, but we must go back to Moscow soon. Next year at the latest — thirty-five is the top age at which I can enroll in art school. Then we will have to endure four years of city life while I study. It will be difficult. We will have five mouths to feed and Lydia will have to work. But in the summers we will go East again — out to the taiga and to the tundra; and when I finish my studies, we will go East and never return."

"I do not know how we will endure Moscow," Lydia added. "There is no freedom in the city. I don't like the restraint crowded places have, the formal structure of society. I wish I could have gone North before the development began, just to see it and live in it as it was. In Moscow last week we were watching TV when one of our singing stars sang the Tchersky Song.* I burst into tears. My relatives mocked me and said, 'What is there in that cold and lonely place, when you could have Moscow?' I could not answer them, because if they could ask such a foolish question they could never understand the answer. Here life is natural, friends are easy to acquire and they become so close and so dear. They are the best things in life. Love is the one true reality — without it all the wonderful things men are doing will mean no more than words of regret carved on a tombstone."

Lydia and Anatoly were among the crowd who saw me off on my final departure from Tchersky. We hugged each other, and as I climbed the ramp into the plane, Lydia called out:

"Do not forget us! Remember! You cannot forget your friends!"

No, Lydia and Anatoly; I will not forget my friends.

---

* A haunting melody composed by a famous Soviet composer in honor of the town of Tchersky and of the people who are building it.

20
DOCTORS

Tchersky was definitely a "white man's town." Ordained by
Moscow, designed by Europeans and, for the most part,
built by them, it was typical of the new cities of the North.
As such it was a good place in which to glimpse the inter-
relationships between the natives and the new people.

Superficially all appeared well between them. Occasionally I met someone from the European regions who adopted
a condescending attitude toward the natives; and there were
those who, while proclaiming the essential equality of all
peoples, were not very keen to provide equal social opportunities.

On one occasion even Victor Nazarov, who, at all points
where I could reach him, seemed resolved to do everything
in his power for the natives, committed a major blunder. He
held a big party for John and me in his new and sumptuous
two-story semidetached house. The guests included many of
the important people in Tchersky and Green Cape . . .
but all were Europeans. The Chukchee Mayor (Chairman

312

of the town Soviet) was conspicuous by his absence. The only non-Europeans present were Yuri Rytkheu and Nikolai Yakutsky, who could hardly have been left out since they were members of my group.

Both were unhappy. Ignoring the convention which dictates that nobody proposes a toast until the tamadar has given his approval, Yura got to his feet almost before we had settled ourselves at table and politely proposed a toast to those absent men and women in whose native country we were now enjoying ourselves. He then excused himself, and left the party. He could not, he said, "remain with my good friends here in the knowledge that my equally good friends of the Chukchee and Yukagir people are not with us too."

His abrupt departure cast something of a shadow over the party, and it was not lightened when Nikolai was asked for a toast and gave us a speech instead. It was suavely done, but the unmistakable import was that, although we were in Tchersky, we were also in the Yakut Republic, and the residents of Tchersky, regardless of their origins, should remember that they were citizens of that Republic which was, and would remain, Yakutian. Nikolai concluded by proposing a special toast to "Our Republic" and he invited everyone to stand and drink it. Having made his point he relaxed into his usual amiable self. It was to be noted that for the balance of the evening he was accorded a rather too obvious respect.

The feelings of the smaller Northern native groups such as the Evenki, Chukchee, Eskimo, and Yukagir toward the hordes of new immigrants are somewhat ambivalent. On the one hand they seem sincerely grateful for what the State has done for them. On the other, many of them still seem to harbor an inner fear that they may eventually lose their identity. A young Eskimo attending teachers college in Leningrad put it this way:

"We don't dislike the new people. Mostly, we like them very much. There is very little antagonism, but we feel they sometimes take us too much for granted . . . they assume we will follow their lead in everything because they know the way better than we do. This makes some of us uneasy for the future. But we are aware of the dangers and we are quietly working to strengthen our own people. One way to do this is not to become too much involved with the life the newcomers are leading. We try to stick to those things that were a part of our past. We modernize the old ways but do not reject them and run off to get factory jobs."

In Tchersky only a handful of natives were employed in town jobs; the vast majority lived and worked as part of the state farm, and they kept control of this enterprise in their own hands. They were moving rapidly into the twentieth century but were doing so on their own terms. Their path was parallel to, but distinct from, the development of mineral resources and new human communities by the Russians.

This was not a subtle form of apartheid, since the facilities and opportunities available to the natives were no whit less in quality or quantity than those available to the new immigrants. If anything, the natives received preferential treatment, particularly in regard to such things as housing subsidies, financial and technical support for developing their own industries, educational opportunities, and medical services.

The medical situation in Tchersky seemed truly amazing to us. To serve the thirteen thousand people of the Lower Kolyma District there was, in 1966, a central hospital with seventy-five beds; a separate tuberculosis hospital with twenty beds, catering mainly to the natives and fast being phased out due to the virtual elimination of the disease; plus four nursing stations and small cottage hospitals.

The main hospital had a staff of fifteen fully qualified doctors, two dentists, an oculist, and twenty-two nurses. All the doctors were specialists, and the hospital was equipped to handle all but the most difficult cases. The medical staff for the whole District totaled one hundred and twenty trained people. Complete medical checkups were given to everyone twice a year. Radio transceivers at each nursing station or cottage hospital provided a direct link with the main hospital, and helicopters and AN-2 bush-planes were on permanent standby as flying ambulances. The entire service was free.

What really knocked the wind out of Claire and me was to be told that the service was understaffed! The authorized staff should have included six more doctors and an additional fourteen technicians and nurses. Tchersky people were up in arms about the "inexcusable failure of the authorities to meet properly our medical requirements."

At one point Claire became personally involved in the medical services . . . as a patient. But before recounting her adventures with Soviet medicine, here are a few further scraps of information which she unearthed.

In 1966, eighty-four percent of Soviet doctors were women. Why? Partly because women have a natural bent toward the healing arts, a bent they have been encouraged to follow in the USSR, but also because preference in medical schools is given to applicants who are already graduate nurses — and most nurses are women. The assumption is that anyone who has worked with sick people for several years and has not left the profession in favor of some other job is probably good doctor material.

There are few, if any, general practitioners among the fully qualified doctors now being graduated. Almost every graduate is a specialist. Part of the role formerly played by the general practitioner is filled by a professional rank which we in North America just do not have: that of *feldsher*. A feldsher is an "almost doctor," trained in general diagnosis and able to cope with ailments which do not require specialist knowledge. Feldshers do the real legwork of Soviet medicine, and they can carry out relatively complicated treatment, including minor surgery. They stand better than halfway between a qualified nurse and a qualified doctor.

Claire's experience with the Soviet medical system began one evening toward the end of our stay in Tchersky. Victor had assembled about fifty people in Lydia's café for a dinner party. Claire decided to stay home because she had a headache and a sore throat. In truth, she was exhausted. As Kola and I left the hotel the lady concierge asked where Claire was. Kola explained she was not feeling well and was lying down.

With furious gesticulations the concierge made it clear that, in the Soviet Union, it is not permitted to be sick and it is most certainly not permitted to be sick without a doctor in attendance. Sputtering indignantly she shooed Kola back upstairs to act as interpreter while she telephoned for a doctor. I was allowed to go on my way, but not without a contemptuous glare — heartless beast that I obviously was.

When Kola failed to join the party after nearly an hour's absence, I excused myself and slipped back to the hotel. I met him coming down the stairs, three at a time. His face was pale and he was sweating. He caught my arm and spun me around. We went past the concierge at a dead run and ducked out through the padded doors into the white night.

"That concierge! What a devil of a woman! And what a devil of an ordeal to put a man through! Claire? Oh, she's all right, I think. But I don't know if I can ever look her in the face again."

Claire's journal tells the story.

"I was dozing when the door burst open and in came the concierge accompanied by a pretty woman doctor, still in her hospital coat and all red-cheeked from rushing through the night. They were dragging Kola with them.

"The doctor got right down to business. She gave me the most complete physical exam I can remember. Heart, throat, ears, chest, stomach . . . everything. I hadn't felt too badly until then, but now I began to feel worse. Surely, I thought, there must be something dreadfully wrong with me.

"She kept asking questions, rather intimate ones too, and poor Kola had to translate both ways. I could hear him choking with embarrassment. Finally the doctor produced a bag and began to dispense medicines — not singly, but box after box. The concierge departed and Kola translated the dosages which were written on the boxes in Latin on one side and Russian on the other.

"Then the doctor began putting mustard plasters on me — one in front and one on my back — and that was too much for Kola. He mumbled something and shot out of the room before the doctor could stop him.

"We got along just fine without him. I opened my phrase book and the doctor pointed to a line reading: 'I am a throat specialist.' All I could think of was that the Russian throat must occupy pretty much the whole of the human body.

"Those were the first mustard plasters I had ever had, and they burned like fury. The doctor asked if I'd like some *chai* (tea) and when I nodded she hustled out of the room. Ten minutes later she was back with plates of food and a pot of tea. Between sips of tea she dropped different pills down my throat until finally I got so warm and drowsy I just drifted off to sleep. My last thought was that this kind of service ought to be made a must by the American and Canadian Medical Associations. It would do their public image a lot of good."

Two days later we left Tchersky on the return flight to Yakutsk. Victor Nazarov had been distraught about Claire's cold (it was no more than that) and he not only arranged for the aircraft to be preheated before our flight but at the last moment decided to accompany us to Yakutsk himself so he could be sure his "beloved Clara" came to no harm. At least that is the excuse he gave. The gunny sack he loaded into the plane suggested he may not have been averse to a little outing on his own behalf.

On the flight south to Zirianka Victor set up a bar in the rear of the aircraft and we were soon dodging champagne corks. Claire, still rather heavily loaded with drugs, huddled in her seat and sniffled dejectedly as the party rolled about her.

When we landed at Zirianka, Victor's opposite number, the Party Secretary of Zirianka District, met us with a pair of Bobyks and invited all hands to join him for a snack at the café, but Claire could not be budged. She insisted on being left to rest under a big blanket. All she asked was that we bring her back a glass of tea.

The Bobyks leapt across the field, and shortly we were

enjoying an impromptu party at the community café. It was interrupted when a young man ran into the room and delivered a note to Victor's friend.

The note was passed to Kola who translated aloud in a shaky voice.

"Comrade Braginsky! The Canadian women on the plane have been taken to hospital and it looks as if they will remain there."

Panic ensued. Victor led the charge to the Bobyks. We roared through the streets of Zirianka to the hospital. Not a soul was in sight. There was no one at the receiving office, no one in the halls, no nurses at the desks and, if one could judge from the open doors and empty rooms, no patients either. We thundered down a long hall, and came to a large receiving room.

It was packed with people. There appeared to be sixty or seventy bodies crowded into it — patients in long night-dresses, office staff, crisp nurses, and every doctor in the hospital. In the center, and struggling feebly, were the Canadian women. Both of her. She was being given a gargle . . .

Later she told me the details of her adventure.

"When you and the other passengers cleared out of the plane, a big, motherly looking woman who had been in one of the front seats stopped in the aisle and smiled and spoke to me. I snuggled down into my blanket and smiled back, then I shut my eyes hoping she would go away. It did no good. She grabbed my arm and felt my pulse. *"Gorlo!"* she cried, and touched my throat. I knew that one, and supposing she must be some kind of medical person, I opened my mouth. She took a look and then dashed off and got the pilot, and the two of them tried to get me to stand up and put on my coat and hat. I indicated that I was quite happy where I was. They pointed out the window and there under the wing was a great big ambulance and four men standing by it looking up at me.

"I got really scared. What were they trying to do with me? Where were they planning to take me? I protested, but it didn't do a bit of good. Gently but firmly they got me up and into my coat.

"Since I couldn't fight them, I had to give in. They loaded me aboard the ambulance and off we went, jouncing and bouncing. I hoped they might be taking me to join the rest of the party, but when we stopped we were in front of a hospital. . . .

"Once inside, they rushed me into this room and a crowd of men and women in white descended on me. I was sure I'd had it now. There was an awful lot of talk, then somebody produced a basin and someone else a glass of something hot. The lady who started it all, and who I now realized was a doctor herself, demonstrated that I was supposed to gargle. I was in no shape to argue, so gargle I did while the audience kept growing until the room was full. And that's when you people suddenly appeared."

Beaming and waving, the hospital staff said goodbye to their first Canadian patient and we drove back to the plane. There was a good deal of laughter in which Claire, for some reason, declined to join. She did not really relax until the plane was airborne and climbing away from Zirianka.

Claire's story does not end there. During the next few days, which we spent in Yakutsk, she hardly dared blow her nose. "One morning when Farley and Yura and Kola were off somewhere, I had a sneezing fit. Twenty minutes later in came a large, jovial lady who took my temperature, checked my heart and blood pressure, felt my stomach, and then prescribed more pills, nose drops, and another mustard plaster. She sent for a nurse to administer the plaster, then they both sat down and drank glasses of tea with me. I was getting used to this by now and decided I liked having the medical team around."

This was just as well. The Soviet medical system was still not finished with her. When we went to the airport to catch a plane for Irkutsk we found, as usual, that the plane would be late leaving so we adjourned to the pilots' room, and there Claire lay down upon a couch. It was as if she had pressed a magic button. Almost instantly a brisk young lady doctor appeared with a blood-testing device dangling in her hand.

Claire tried to refuse further assistance but she might as well have saved her breath. She was hustled off, willy-nilly, to the airport infirmary.

"The visit brought some interesting revelations. To my amazement I learned that every moderate-sized airport has a doctor and nurse in attendance. This is mainly for the benefit of sick passengers but also for the air crews. Every member of the crew has to have an examination before each flight, and this even applies to the stewardesses.

"This young woman doctor, who originally came from Kazakhstan, gave me nose drops, a throat spray, and ear drops to ease the pain of pressure when the plane took off. We discussed why I seemed to be the only person in Russia with a cold. She explained that everyone takes flu shots regularly, and that these seemed to cut the incidence of colds almost to nothing.

"How odd to be in a country where it is a major task to find a waitress in a restaurant; where you have to stand in line to buy a book; but where at the first sign of a sniffle you have to start defending yourself against a perfect deluge of doctors."

21
MAGADAN

Knowing it would be impossible to see all of Siberia, I at least tried to visit a series of representative communities. Until the time came to leave Tchersky I had done reasonably well. In the Yukagir tents I had seen (as nearly as could be) the outline structure of native life in olden times. I had visited little taiga communities conceived under the new order. I had lived in Yakutsk, a major native city which was making its own adjustments to the twentieth century. I had examined the blend of old and new in the Eurasian city of Irkutsk. In Tchersky I had witnessed the childhood days of a new, high-arctic community; and in Mirny had seen such a place in young adulthood. To round things off, I needed to visit one of the new cities in its maturity.

Two possibilities suggested themselves to me. One was the city of Norilsk near the mouth of the Yenisei River, on the same latitude as Tchersky, two hundred miles north of the arctic circle.

Norilsk came into being as a result of the discovery of

vast concentrations of ores near the base of the Taimyr Peninsula by a young Leningrad geologist, Nikolai Nikolaevich Luberovski. The son of a well-to-do family, Luberovski was bitten by the explorer's virus in his early youth and had already spent two years in the far North when the Revolution broke out. The change in régimes did not much concern him. In 1920 he discovered a fabulously rich nickel and base-metal lode near Norilsk, built a log cabin there, and spent the next thirteen years of his life working toward the development of the region.

This was his happy time. He spent the succeeding fourteen years in prison camps as a victim of one of Stalin's purges. Khrushchev released him, and the State gave him many honors and made what amends it could, but when I visited him and his family in Leningrad in 1969 his wasted face testified all too clearly to the hardships he had suffered.

Nonetheless the Father of Norilsk had lost nothing of his almost breathless enthusiasm for the North. He described to me how Norilsk grew from a population of three people in 1921 — himself, his wife, and an Evenki assistant — to a city of close to three hundred thousand people by 1969, surrounded by a complex of new communities with a combined population approaching three-quarters of a million.

By far the largest arctic community in the world, Norilsk is where many of the techniques of Northern development were first applied. It stands as a living monument to what man can accomplish in the arctic wilderness if he is so inclined.

Norilsk interested me greatly, but I knew it had already been visited and reported on by foreigners. Furthermore, it was really too big a place for my taste. There was another Northern city which interested me just as much — Magadan, called by its residents Little Leningrad, on the shores of the Sea of Okhotsk, fourteen hundred miles to the north-west of the great Pacific seaport of Vladivostok.

Wherever I traveled in the Soviet Union, I seemed to hear talk of Magadan. At a party in a Moscow hotel, a number of ebullient men and women on leave from Magadan talked about their city in a way that made it sound like the New Jerusalem. Yuri Rytkheu had lived and worked there in his younger days as a newspaper man, and he extolled the virtues of the place interminably. On the other hand, some Russians shook their heads at mention of the name, and changed the subject. Others talked about Magadan in cautious phrases that carried an undertone of fear.

During my 1966 journey I asked to be allowed to visit Magadan . . . and ran into a wall of fog. The authorities would not say "No!" but neither would they say "Yes!" My request remained in limbo until Claire and I were back in Moscow, ready to fly home to Canada. Then, when it was impossible for us to change our course, permission to visit the place was finally granted.

In 1969 I made Magadan one of my main objectives. While in Moscow and Leningrad I used whatever influence I could muster, but could get no firm decision. Increasingly frustrated, I asked a diplomat acquaintance for a straight explanation. Was the place closed because of its military significance?

"Oh, no. It isn't that. And don't feel you are being slighted. No foreigners are permitted to visit Magadan."

"Why not?"

Reluctantly he told me. Magadan was once the center of one of the most infamous forced labor operations undertaken during the Stalin régime.

"Of course all that was finished long ago," my informant hastened to add. "All the same, we are still sensitive about it. It was a black page in our history and there are those who are afraid visits by foreigners will revive memories of the past."

"Are there any labor camps there now?" I asked bluntly.

"Certainly not! There haven't been any for almost twenty years."

"Then why *can't* I visit Magadan?"

He spread his hands and smiled a bit sheepishly.

"Maybe you can . . . maybe not. Who knows? Keep asking. You may succeed. In Russia, all is surprises!"

I kept asking. Yura asked for me and so did many other people. There was no answer until two days before we were due to leave Tchersky on our return to Yakutsk. Yura arrived in my room before breakfast one morning, waving a sheet of flimsy.

"Big news, Farley! Now you have chance to taste best beer in Soviet Union. And I show so many pretty girls you stay in Magadan for good."

Somebody . . . somewhere . . . had finally said "Yes."

As John, Yura, and I prepared to leave Tchersky, Anatoly brought word that Victor Nazarov was very sick. A heart specialist was in attendance on him and he had been forbidden any visitors.

Four years earlier Victor had been practicing with the barbells in preparation for the Yakutian weight lifting championships — which he usually won. He was making a heavy lift when the steel rod between the weights slipped from his hands and came crashing down across his chest. Several ribs were broken and his chest was caved in, damaging his heart. It was an injury which might well have been fatal to most men. It kept Victor in the hospital for three months, and when he was discharged he was ordered to go to a Black Sea spa for at least a year to recuperate.

He refused. He was "resting" in Tchersky when I first met him a year after his accident. However, four years of nearly total disregard for the injury had finally caught up with him.

"He is furious he can't see you off," Anatoly told me. "The doctors said he could not even see you at his house. He told them to go to the devil. He insists you come and say goodbye to him."

Defying the doctors, and his family, Victor got out of bed to meet me. His face was death-touched and I knew without being told that neither his bull body nor his indomitable will could support him much longer. If he too was aware of this, he refused to acknowledge it. Sometimes gasping for breath, and sometimes unconsciously pressing his great hand against his chest, he sat for an hour with me, keeping my glass full of cognac and talking of his city and his dream. Behind his back I caught glimpses of the heart doctor, a woman whose face seemed almost as white as Victor's. Her anxiety was so great that I finally forced Victor to let me go. He hated to do it. As we stood up, he caught me in his arms again; but this time it was like being hugged by an old man.

"Farley. You come back to Tchersky! You will come back and see what we have done in your second absence. You will be proud of us. Our work has just begun. It is only preparation for the creation of a world better than any we have ever had. When I go, I will leave something good behind! But I am not dead yet . . . a long way from it! These imbecile doctors insist they are going to send me South. Why do they waste their breath? I'll be here when you come back. Bring Claire next time. I'll beat you if you don't."

We kissed each other on both cheeks. I left the room but

I turned at the head of the stairs and caught a final glimpse of a man whose like I may not see again. He was crouched forward in a chair, great head lowered almost to his knees, apparently oblivious to the efforts of his doctor and his wife to move him back to bed.

Our flight took us seven hundred miles southeast from Tchersky to Magadan, and the entire distance was flown over a massive highland drained by the Kolyma and its many tributaries.

We transected the region called Golden Kolyma, which may be the richest gold-bearing area on earth. There is hardly a sandbar or a gravel bench in any of its innumerable mountain valleys which is not filled with placer gold — nuggets and dust. And, as if this were not enough, the area is now yielding gold in abundance from dozens of hardrock mines. No official figures about production are available, but an estimate given to me in Magadan suggests that annual production from the Kolyma region is now over a thousand tons of gold a year. Whatever the truth may be, the gargantuan effort being put into placer and hardrock gold mining in this area is obviously producing handsome returns.

Just why the Soviet Union should be so afflicted by the gold bug seemed something of a mystery to me until it was explained by Dr. Nikolai Shilo, Director of the Northeast Institute of the Academy of Sciences of the USSR in Magadan. Dr. Shilo and his charming wife have traveled over much of the world and have the sophistication of world citizens. They served me a superb dinner in their big and ornately decorated flat, and we ate with gold-plated cutlery.*

* This is not so remarkable as it may seem to some readers. Before leaving Moscow I purchased a set of gold-plated cutlery at one of the

It seemed appropriate, since Dr. Shilo is the ranking expert on gold mining in the Soviet Union.

"Gold has many domestic and practical uses as a mineral, but of course that isn't why we have amassed such a hoard of the stuff — probably more than the Americans have in their Fort Knox. As you may know, after the Revolution the capitalist countries, having failed to crush us by force, tried to do so by economic methods. The idea was to isolate us so completely that we would never be able to build a successful modern society. We were to be refused access to everything we needed in order to survive, let alone to build. Fortunately for us, capitalists can never refuse to make a profit. We found we could buy what we had to have, under the bedclothes as they say, but only for gold. Nobody would give us credit, and we had little gold because most of it had been shipped out of the country by the Tsarist government, either to pay war debts or to keep it from the hands of the people.

"So we became a little gold crazy. We had to have it. Nowadays it is not important in the same way, but it remains important to ensure our credit. Everyone trusts a rich man, nobody trusts a poor man. We are now very rich and the whole world knows it. Furthermore, as long as the capitalist countries artificially maintain the high price of gold, we do very well by selling it on the world market.

"Internally we have little need of it except in small amounts for industrial or ornamental use. Our currency is not backed by gold as yours is. Externally it has become a powerful weapon with which we can defend ourselves.

"We would have been in very serious trouble during the Great Patriotic War had we not had lots of Kolyma gold.

---

larger stores. Luxury items of this nature were available to any Russians with the money and the inclination to purchase them.

Do you know you are not the first foreign visitor to Magadan? The first was Mr. Averell Harriman from the United States. He arrived here in a warship on a special mission in 1943 to assure himself and the American government that we had gold enough to *pay* for the weapons and materials we needed to defeat the German fascists.

"I know in your countries it is said these materials were given free to us Russians since we were fighting your war for you. That is simply not true. We had to pay, in gold, for much of what we received, and the United States did not trust us to pay until one of her own high officials saw that we actually had the gold.

"It was an interesting visit. Harriman saw the gold in the ground, and in our vaults, and was satisfied. Before he left he looked around Magadan Bay and he told us, 'Nobody in the world could ever succeed in building a real city in such a God-forsaken place. Why do you bother trying?'

"He was thinking in capitalist terms: the way to treat a rich resource in some remote region is to go in with mining camps, dig it out of the ground, and then go away. This is exactly what was done in the Yukon gold rush. And what is your Klondike today? Be honest now, because I have visited it and seen it for myself. It is nothing! A tiny dead town called Dawson and nothing else but ruined river valleys with hardly a human being in the whole region.

"We think in different terms. Resources should be used as a base on which to build new human communities, not as a means of enriching old communities in faraway places. It would be nice if Harriman could visit us again. I wonder what he would think about this 'God-forsaken place' if he could see it now."

The Kolyma gold province, which includes much of the Magadan region, the western parts of Chukotka and an adjacent strip of Yakutia to the west of the main Kolyma valley, has twelve cities of between ten and twenty-five thousand people. The newest one, Bilibino on the same latitude as Tchersky, which was founded in 1961, already has sixteen thousand. Magadan itself has one hundred twenty-two thousand. The population of the gold province as a whole is close to half a million (three hundred eighty thousand in the Magadan District alone), and as secondary resources such as tin and mercury mining, together with industry, continue their rapid development, the population is expected to approach a million by 1980. It is certainly a far cry from Canada's Yukon Territory or from the interior regions of Alaska, where the last gold dredges now lie abandoned, and all but a minute fraction of the once vast deposits of placer gold have been exhausted for the benefit of London, New York, Johannesburg, and other financial capitals of the Western world.

As we drew close to Magadan we ran into bad weather and the mountains vanished under black clouds. For a time it appeared we might have to fly on to the Kamchatka Peninsula. The prospect of seeing that mysterious land of live volcanoes, mighty mountains, and the strange Koryak people who may have been ancestral to the Eskimo excited me.

Yura put the damper on my enthusiasm.

"If land at Kamchatka have no permissions. So they lock you and John up tight until can get rid of you. No caviar and vodka. Only black bread and water!"

It wouldn't have been that bad, but I remembered the story told me by an Intourist interpreter in Moscow of what happened to a planeload of American tourists flying from Japan to Vladivostok when *their* plane was forced by engine trouble to land at a military airport near the new Soviet naval base of Nakhadkya. The plane was at once wheeled into a hangar and there it and all of its passengers remained incarcerated behind closed and guarded doors for three days while repairs were being made. Only the interpreters were allowed out of the building. Those inside were forbidden even to smoke because of the fire hazard, and some of them became hysterical, having convinced themselves they had been hijacked and were being held for ransom.

When their plane was repaired and they were delivered to Vladivostok, only two of their number had the fortitude to continue with their original plan of taking the Trans-Siberian train to Moscow; the rest beat a hasty retreat to Tokyo on the first outbound flight. The interpreter who told me this story thought it was very funny. I imagine the Americans did not.

Our pilot decided that Magadan weather was acceptable, and we broke through low clouds into a wide, sparsely wooded valley ringed with snow-dusted mountains. A large airport lay below us, but there was no city anywhere in sight.

We were met by a reception committee of stylishly dressed gentlemen who approached us, under the eyes of television cameramen and press photographers, almost as tentatively as they might have approached a visiting delegation from outer space. Our arrival was clearly a landmark in Magadan history. Our hosts seemed distinctly uneasy as we descended the ramp. They shied nervously away from John deVisser, who was wearing a bright blue, highly ornamented knee-length parka with wolfskin trim, and a knitted blue and white French Canadian toque. They looked as if they were not quite sure whether or not he might open his red-bearded face and snap at them. With obvious relief they saw Yura, whom they knew. That imperturbable Chukchee gentleman took charge and we were all formally introduced, then escorted to a press conference in the airport building, where I helped to ease the tension a little by giving a radio interview in which I confessed that the only things I really knew about Magadan were that it was reputed to have the best beer and the most gorgeous women in all Russia.

The city was forty miles away. We drove to it in a convoy of Volgas along a paved road which is the first lap of an all-weather highway leading into the interior through the Kolyma mountains and terminating at Yakutsk. I was accompanied by the Director of Culture for the Magadan District — shy, slight, youngish Nikolai Andreivich Ponomarenko, who understood English fairly well but was hesitant to speak it. Through an interpreter he told me all Magadan was waiting for us, and that my books had been sold out in the local stores. It was the kind of remark calculated to warm an author's heart.

Our first view of Magadan was stunning. The road took us seaward down a broad valley with great, bleak peaks looming on both sides of us, then suddenly spilled over the lip of a pass to reveal the city almost filling a mountain-ringed amphitheatre below us.

I don't quite know what I had been expecting — perhaps something like Yakutsk, which is a city of comparable size — but Magadan was unlike any Northern city I had ever seen. The highway swooped down to become a broad tree-lined boulevard running between rows of handsome white apartment blocks and office buildings. Some of the architecture may have been a bit ornate, but the impression was of a clean, modern, and handsome city that had been designed, planned, and executed by people of imagination and taste. As in Leningrad, there were no towering skyscrapers and no disfiguring industrial or commercial edifices. The city almost filled its bowl, and new buildings marched neatly up the slopes on all except the seaward side, where lay the harbor and Magadan Bay.

We were taken to the Central Hotel and given a luxury suite boasting television, a refrigerator full of beer, a cabinet full of cutlery and dishes, and a bathroom containing the most extraordinary tub. It was a product of one of Khrushchev's early attempts to rationalize consumer goods production so there would be more for all. The thing was about four feet long and built step-fashion in two levels, one of them eight inches above the other. A contortionist or a five-year-old might have been able to take a bath in it. The sight of John trying to maneuver his bulk into its inhuman confines was a spectacle to rouse pity in the hardest heart.

While John agonized in the tub, I went to the window and looked out over the city, watching the lights come on. It was difficult to believe that in 1930 there had been nothing in this valley except scrub taiga and a few wild reindeer.

Magadan lies at about the same latitude as Anchorage, Alaska, but has to endure a much more rigorous climate. Until the beginning of the 1930s the entire region was a virtually unexplored subarctic wilderness, inhabited by Evenki reindeer herders concentrated near the coast, some Yakut in the mountainous interior, and by a few thousand Old Russians, most of them living in little fishing villages on the shores of the Sea of Okhotsk.

These Old Russians were mostly descendants of a Cossack wave which reached the region in the early eighteenth century. However, as early as 1649 one small group of these incredibly intrepid pioneers, probably impelled to it by a healthy fear of falling into the hands of the Imperial authorities, established a tiny community in the heart of an almost impenetrable mountain massif six hundred miles northwest of Magadan. There they lived in almost complete isolation until well into the twentieth century. Markovo, as their village was called, still exists. Its older people still speak archaic Russian and cling to the Cossack customs of their ancestors. However, Markovo has now become the center of a big collective farm for reindeer and fur breeding.

For Markovo, as for the entire region, the touchstone for change was gold. Gold was first discovered (or at least first became known) in the region in the middle 1920s, when a few of the wandering prospectors known as "the possessed" began panning small amounts of dust in some of the river valleys. They sold their gold, or traded it, to foreign vessels, mostly Japanese, which occasionally visited the fishing village of Ola just north of Magadan. When word of what was happening reached Moscow, which was then desperate for gold, an attempt was made to control or stop the trade, but without notable success. In 1929 a young Leningrad geologist (many of the most famous Russian geologists seem to have come from Leningrad) named Yuri Bilibin was sent to Ola to see what was going on. Bilibin was nearly murdered by the possessed, who looked on him as an interloper, which, of course, he was. However, he managed to send a three-man party into the interior, and at a place called Susaman on the Nurv River these men found Eldorado. Gold in the river sands assayed as high as two hundred grams per cubic yard. Nearby was a quartz reef, ten miles long, whose gold content was twice as high as that of any reef previously discovered in the USSR.

The rush was on, but it was now rigidly controlled. The possessed were driven out and the entire region became the concession of a newly formed trust known as Dalstroy. This name was to bring terror to many Russians. Given an absolutely free hand to produce the vitally needed gold, Dalstroy operated in a completely ruthless manner. When it needed labor — and it needed masses of labor — it took over many of the prisoners who, for one reason or another, had been sentenced to terms in corrective labor camps all over the Soviet Union. Trainloads of these unfortunates rolled eastward in a manner reminiscent of the great flow of exiles into Siberia in Tsarist days.

In the beautiful natural bowl behind Magadan Bay a wooden town began to rise. Many of its buildings were prison barracks. From these barracks the prisoners were dispatched into the interior to work the placer beds that were being discovered by the scores. Dalstroy was not a notably efficient organization. Food often failed to reach the distant camps; winter clothing failed to arrive. Disease swept the barracks. Death took a heavy price for the gold that was being gathered.

Nobody in Siberia could give me an estimate of how many people died. "It is impossible to know," a friend told me. "Probably Moscow itself never knew. What is certain is that thousands escaped the camps and blended into the Old Russian populations in the interior. And when the camps were closed and the inmates offered the chance to return home, a very large number decided to stay on in Siberia where opportunities were good . . . and authority not so strong. I know this is so. I was one of those who chose to stay."

In 1940 the population of Magadan was only nine thousand and it was a squalid wooden mining town. After the war ended and even before Stalin's grip was broken by death, the place had already begun to change. It had been realized that the productivity of prison labor was so low, and the costs so high, that it did not pay to use it. By 1950 the barracks were no longer occupied. Within a few years they had been torn down and now, where they once stood, white and gleaming apartment blocks march up the hill slopes of a different city. The new Magadan does not like to remember the dark days of its past. Those days *are* past, and the citizens believe they will never return again.

Many of the older people in Magadan today went there as prisoners. These men, and women, have a singular quality about them, they have a greater hunger for freedom and a stronger desire to build a new world even than do the young immigrants who now far outnumber them. Perhaps there is a parallel to be drawn between them and the original English settlers of Australia who, too, were mostly prisoners, "criminals" according to the mores of their times. In both cases injustice and adversity produced a people of singular resilience — and intractibility. The Australian character was deeply influenced by its prisoner-pioneers and the same is true of Magadan. This new city so far from Moscow, facing east toward a bright and trackless ocean rather than west into the dark tunnel of human history, has the feel of a community which is becoming an independent entity, a city-state in the making. By this I do not suggest that it is rebellious or that it wishes to separate itself from the main body of the Soviet Union. It simply feels itself to be different, and I suspect the differences which develop in Magadan will one day make themselves felt all the way west across the Ural Mountains into European Russia.

22
MAGADAN

The decision to receive us in Magadan must have resulted in some hectic conferences about what to do with us when we arrived — meetings during which the Communist instinct for organizing was given full rein.

The entire city had been alerted to our arrival by television, radio, and the press; and apparently every institution, with the possible exception of the local office of the KGB, had demanded a visit from us. For two days our convoy of cars shot up and down the broad avenues of the city with the frenetic impetuosity of a Mack Sennett comedy film. Zip — we would drive a block at fifty miles an hour, pile out, race into a school, library, Palace of Culture, Institute for Northern Science, newspaper office or . . you name it . . . shake a score of hands, stare dazedly into masses of smiling faces, tour the building, listen to enthusiastic expositions of what was going on, dash out again, pile into the cars, and roar a few hundred yards to the next encounter.

Information rained upon us in a torrent, and my absorp-

tive faculties soon became saturated. Before noon of the
first day I was longing to return to the easy-going pace of
Yakutsk. By midafternoon I was in a state of mild shock.
During one of the few moments of relative peace (as we
shot from the School of Music to the Palace of Sport, which
were blessedly separated by at least seven blocks) I broke
down and begged Nikolai Ponomarenko for mercy. He
smiled sympathetically.

"It was the same when Yuri Gagarin came here. He said
it was worse for him, a thousand times, than going into
space. I am really sorry, but that is the way Magadanians
are. If we miss one single place, the people there will never
forgive us — particularly they won't forgive me. And you
can't believe how difficult our people get when they have a
grievance." He sighed so feelingly that I decided, for his
sake, to endure.

Being a kindly man, I do not intend to subject my readers to the Magadan Ordeal by attempting to detail all I
saw and heard. Suffice it to say that Magadan is, despite
the triple threats of permafrost, seismic disturbances, and
hurricane gales, as pleasant a city as any I have visited. It
offers its people the best of everything in both the material
and cultural realms. It lacks many of the major disadvan-
tages of modern cities in that it is beautifully sited, spacious, relatively quiet, and free of obvious pollution. All in
all I think it would be a good city in which to live — for
anyone who likes cities and who can tolerate living among
a people whose energy quotient has to be as close as makes
no difference to the maximum reading. As with most Soviet
Northern cities, it is a young people's community. The lone
statistic which I shall record is that the average age in
Magadan (excluding people under eighteen years of age) is
twenty-nine.

We took many of our meals at a restaurant a few blocks from the hotel. Rather pretentiously furnished in chrome and plastic modern, it was big and spacious *and it provided almost instant service!* I know of no other restaurant in the Soviet Union which can make this claim. Furthermore, the food was good. There was only one drawback. The place boasted a jukebox, a multicolored monster almost identical to its North American sisters. Made in Poland, it even had an English-language name emblazoned on its glittering belly — *High fie.* However, it was not the menace it appeared. The volume control was always turned down low, and when its muted noises (mostly Russian pop songs, but some French ones, too) bothered a diner, he simply pulled out the power plug. Magadanians brook no nonsense from machines.

We were having lunch here one day with a mixed crowd of writers, journalists, and odd sods when someone casually mentioned that the Soviet Union had simultaneously lofted three manned space ships. Now I am not a wild aficionado of the space age, but I was curious and wanted details. To my surprise nobody else at the table seemed the least bit interested. Nobody proposed toasts to "our brave boys in space." My requests for more information were either ignored or given casual answers. Finally I turned to a sandy-moustached young man who was, I think, a professor at the local university, and asked him to explain this strange lack of interest in his country's most recent space spectacular.

"Don't you care what's happening up there? Or is something wrong with the flight that you don't want to talk about?"

He smiled affably and in a somewhat pedantic manner explained.

"We don't think such things are very important. It is more important for us to develop an earthly technology for the betterment of man and the preservation of the terrestrial environment. It is also bad economics and bad science to go space voyaging at the present time. In another twenty years, if we have straightened out our problems here on earth, technology will be so much farther advanced it will be safer and far cheaper to start playing extraterrestrial games. I consider space flights a distraction from pressing problems here on earth. I doubt if any nation can afford such distractions at this time."

Sour grapes because of America's space progress? Perhaps, but during my travels in the Soviet Union I never encountered anything approaching the near hysterical infatuation with space flights which characterizes North America. Doubtless it did exist when Gagarin made his first trip into space, but it seems to have cooled to negligible levels since then.

The restaurant was the scene of many intriguing conversations. One day I sat beside a middle-aged journalist for a Moscow wire service. He had traveled widely in Western countries and was devastatingly outspoken about his profession.

"Foreign correspondents from capitalist and from socialist countries have one thing in common. Their main job is to look for what is bad in the other fellow's country and report on that. If they can't find what they need, they manufacture it out of idle gossip or even out of the air. We do it. You do it. The whole thing is a farce. It is also a tragedy. Why can't we look for the good in each other's countries and write about that? It would be nice to bring the truth into print sometimes in the service of easing hatred and enmity. The trouble is it would serve to bring people closer together rather than driving them farther apart and this would not be tolerable to those who find more advantage in fostering hatred than friendship."

"Many of our Western correspondents in Russia say they can't get at the truth." I protested. "They are restricted in travel, and few Russians, except officials, malcontents, or paid sources, will associate with them. How can they do better than they do?"

He laughed.

"You think that is unique here? You should try being a Soviet correspondent in the USA! It is all part of the same pattern, and this kind of mutual harassment of reporters exactly serves the purposes of those who send them out. Please do not pretend to be naïve. You know as well as I do that we correspondents, no matter what country we come from, are propaganda mongers because this is what our employers expect from us. Never mind. Fill up! Here's a toast to freedom of the press — wherever it is that she is hiding herself."

Throughout my travels I had been amazed — and sometimes unnerved — by the frankness with which Russians talked about subjects which I had supposed were taboo, if not downright dangerous. However, nowhere did I encounter such outspokenness as in Magadan. The Magadanians said things one might have hoped to have heard whispered in private, but they said them in loud voices in public places. It would appear either that we Westerners have been badly misinformed about the amount of freedom of speech permitted in the Soviet Union, or else the Magadan branch of the KGB needs a good shakeup. The truth seems to be that the people of Russia in general, and of Siberia in particular, simply aren't privy to the conclusions of some Western journalists that after a brief liberalization under Khrushchev, the lid is being forced back down again.

I discussed this matter with several English- and French-speaking men and women at a party one night, and their responses to the suggestion that the Stalin dictatorship was returning were illuminating. A middle-aged lady physician expressed her feelings in this way:

"Our reaction against Stalin after his death was understandable, but it was too drastic. Nobody is all devil, and Stalin wasn't either. It really wasn't fair to write him out of history as if he had never existed. Also, it wasn't possible. He was ruthless and a paranoid, but do you know any great leaders who aren't a little of both? He was also longsighted. He knew that the capitalist powers would some day try again to destroy our society by force. That thought clouded his mind and preoccupied him for twenty years. He was determined they would not succeed, and in his determination he did some horrible things. But in the end, you know, he was right in his monomania. If it had not been for him, fascist Germany might very well have smashed us . . . while you others in the West wept with one eye and winked with the other."

"What you call the rehabilitation of Stalin isn't what you think it is," interjected a journalist. "The fact that we can now evaluate him and give him what measure of due he deserves, along with the blame, means we feel safe from a return of that kind of terror. Nobody will ever forgive him for some of the things he did; and if anyone tries that sort of thing on us again, it will be the worse for him. Russian people are not going to give up their new freedom so easily."

A novelist made this point. "We've got our teeth into freedom now. Maybe we are pushing along too fast, with too much eagerness. It is true there are still Stalinists about and they try to slap us down, with some success. But it is we who are gaining ground in the long run and they who are losing it."

A girl political science student had the last word.

"You know, we are fairly well informed about what is happening in the capitalist world. We know a lot about events in the United States, and we think it is better to live in a country, and in a society, which has endured severe personal and political oppression, but is shifting away from that sort of thing, than to live in a country which had a very great deal of freedom but is now shifting toward a repressive, cabal-governed society. Perhaps you would be wiser to examine what is happening in your own countries rather than spend so much time condemning what once happened in ours. We will see which of us, in the future, can claim to have the most freedom."

The dual nature of the new world of the Soviet North was again evident here. Magadan itself was essentially a European town, mostly populated by immigrants from the far West. There were native people in the city holding executive and administrative jobs, but there were very few in any of Magadan's industries — the shipyards, factories, foundries, construction plants or the transport companies whose thousands of trucks travel as far afield as the mouth of the Yana River on the Arctic Ocean, fifteen days' hard driving to the northwest of Magadan. Nor were there many native people employed in the gold mines. Most of them live and work on the one hundred and seven collective and state farms, where they engage in fur breeding, trapping, reindeer raising, cattle farming, and sea-mammal hunting. The big cities belong to the whites; the smaller towns are divided between white and native peoples; and the countryside (apart from the mining enterprises) belongs almost exclusively to the natives.

One windy day, with snow flurries obscuring the bald old mountains, we borrowed some Bobyks and drove thirty miles northeast to the venerable town of Ola, once home of the possessed and, centuries before that, site of one of the earliest lodgements by Russians on the shores of the Pacific.

It was a hair-raising trip over icy roads that climbed through mountain saddles where the wind from off the ocean was gusting at hurricane force. A dark, cliff-girt sea lay before us. We turned north along it, skirting a savage and fearsome coast whose roaring surf sent spume geysering over strange conical rocks to salt-smear the windshields of our cars.

The rough, subalpine slopes inland from us glowed an unearthly shade of green. Nikolai explained that this was a special forage grass developed for arctic climates which could endure when ordinary grass turned brown and died. It was used to feed the tough breed of Northern cattle. Harvested after the first heavy frost, it remained green even after it was cut, making bizarre emerald haystacks on snow-covered fields.

Ola, with about four thousand inhabitants, had come a long way from the days of the possessed. Neat streets of single-family homes surrounded by gardens were interspersed with new apartment blocks. The people were a meld of Old Russian settlers and Evenki. The Evenki did most of the farming and the Russians most of the fishing.

The place of greatest interest to me was the Magadan Agricultural College, and I spent several hours there among six hundred students of twenty nationalities, most of them Small Peoples of the North. This is a residential college, and the students come to it from all over northeastern Siberia to take four-year courses in reindeer husbandry, fur farming, cattle raising, farm management and, surprisingly, poultry breeding, a new arctic venture which is exclusively in the hands of women. After graduation the students return to the collectives and state farms from which they came, equipped to apply the most modern methods and technology to the age-old pursuits of their ancestors.

I have seldom met such ebullient youngsters, or seen a better-looking lot. They followed me about in mobs. My right hand grew cramped from signing autographs and my voice grew hoarse from trying to answer questions about the Canadian North. Their principal, Olga Terenteva, was a buxom, dark-skinned and intense woman with a bubbling laugh and limitless enthusiasm which seemed to be shared by her students.

"Do you know the entire cost of training each of the students and of feeding and paying them for four years is recovered within three years once they return to their farms, by increases in production?" Olga told me. "You have no idea how much happiness it is to work with young people like these. They are wild to learn so they can raise the status of their own people and improve conditions of their lives. They seem to have the dedication missionaries were once said to have. They are so very much alive, so strong in their youth, so confident in what they can do. It is impossible not to love them."

I left the College festooned like a Cockney Button King. Scores of students had pinned their lapel badges all over my jacket. This giving of lapel badges (they represent the localities the donors come from, the organizations people belong to, or simply great events) is endemic amongst the young. The badges are highly valued and to give one's badge is to give one's wholehearted friendship.

The general habit of gift-giving is a mixed blessing in the Soviet Union. One soon learns not to admire anything which is in any degree portable, or it may suddenly be yours. Once, in a Tchersky nursery school, Claire admired a Russian teddy bear — "Mischa" — and immediately a child of four or five years solemnly shoved it into her arms. When she tried to return it, the nursery school director stopped her.

"No, no! You must keep it. If you give it back you will break the child's heart."

Mischa accompanied us all the way to Moscow where, thank heavens, it was admired by another child to whom Claire was able to give it without feeling any sense of guilt. Stuffed bears, a balalaika, innumerable books, the famous frozen fish, carved bowls, ivory tusks, and items, as they say, too numerous to mention, all poured upon us until we learned wisdom. Our greatest difficulty came when we were viewing artists' works. To admire was to receive. Not to admire was to crush the artist's soul!

I very much wanted to see a Soviet fishing village. Having spent many years in Newfoundland where I had watched the death of hundreds of vigorous fishing communities as a result of governmental conclusions that they were "uneconomic" in the modern age, and the consequent decision to uproot and transport the populations to so-called industrial growth centers (where there was no industry and no growth), I was curious to see how the Soviets had dealt with the same problem.

Nikolai Ponomarenko took me to Sugar Loaf, a village fishing operation on the Soviet new style. Sugar Loaf lies on a bleak, gale-whipped shore not far from Ola, and it does not even have a harbor. For centuries its people fished "from the beach," launching their oared boats each dawn and hauling them high above tide level when they returned ashore at dusk. In 1948 the Magadan area fishery was rationalized into a series of six combines which, together, formed the Magadan Fisheries Trust. Of the fifty-eight fishing villages (many of them still very primitive) which existed at that time, seven were abandoned by the decision of their inhabitants, who moved to nearby villages. Fifty-one were retained as potentially viable communities of the future. Sugar Loaf, despite its lack of a harbor, was one. Instead of engaging in a dozen peripheral fishing activities, as it had done in the past, it was given the task of concentrating on the herring fishery. A large, modern plant was constructed to process herring.

I toured the place with its manager, a hard-bitten, craggy-faced Old Russian who had spent forty years in the business and had lived through the transition from a primitive, subsistence fishery to a highly efficient and lucrative modern enterprise.

"We did it in stages. At first, after we built the herring pickling and preserving factory, the fishermen continued to use small boats. Gradually we introduced new and better methods. We built a fleet of inshore seiners of wood — not expensive boats, but they doubled production. Sugar Loaf's population was growing and the production increase absorbed the labor growth; but to go on doing that we had to increase production. We followed a master plan which was gradually to phase out the inshore fishery in favor of midwater work. In the late 1950s we introduced the first of a fleet of all-purpose combined trawler-seiners, made of steel and serially produced in large numbers.

"These were two-hundred-tonners — you can see a couple out there now at the unloading dock. They can stay at sea a maximum of five months, following the herring on their migrations, and they are maintained at sea by special service ships. They tranship their catch at sea to three-thousand-ton refrigerator ships that are constantly shuttling between the fishing fleet and the shore factories. We could, you know, have put the new big twenty-thousand-ton factory ships out there, but that would have smashed the lives of the shore-based people. There was no sense in that.

"How has it worked out? Here we now employ one hundred and twenty factory workers (and we are the smallest of the many factories — there are three in our herring combine alone). We produce four thousand tons of prepared herring a year. The whole herring combine produces thirty-six thousand tons. The trust production is one hundred ninety thousand tons of prepared fish. Our herring combine employs six hundred and fifteen fishermen, full time, year round. They are rotated to the working ships aboard the refrigerator vessels, so they spend two months at sea and one ashore. When there are no herring they fish for other species for the other combines. Ordinary fishermen make an average of five hundred rubles a month; officers, seven hundred to eight hundred; plant workers, three hundred and fifty to four hundred.

"We have no difficulty manning our fleet; in fact, we have big waiting lists. All fishermen must have a certificate from the Fishery College at Magadan, which gives free instruction and also provides full seagoing pay while the student is at college."

I asked him how the changes had affected the old fishing villages.

"You can see for yourself. Ola had only a few hundred people before the trust was formed. Now it is a real town.

It is the same with all the small fishing ports. They are growing very fast in size and in the quality of life. Specialization and rational use of technology are the answers. The villages and towns will continue to grow. The sea must be asked to help feed more and more of mankind. It is a farm, and we must farm it; and the farmers must be well rewarded for their work."

"Isn't the sea being overfarmed already?" I asked. "In North America it is claimed that Soviet fleets are sweeping the seas clean of fish — destroying the breeding stock. What about that?"

He gave me a hard look, then relaxed as he realized he was being baited.

"Listen. You told me about the herring fishery in Canada. Tens of thousands of good fish ground up for fertilizer or for animal feed! What kind of use of the sea do you call that? It is foolish waste! Every one of the herring we catch goes to feed human bellies. It is you who think the sea is inexhaustible! You talk about cropping it, but what do you really do? You take all you can get, wherever you can get it. I think you are just angry because we have become better fishermen than you.

"We worry very much about conservation. We don't want to find the seas empty and our fleets and all our people unemployed, and the population going hungry. We aren't after profit. We are working to feed people; not for now only, but for an eternity. Do you think we would be such idiots as to destroy the fish stock?

"What is needed is international controls. We want them, badly. Do you? I think not. I think you talk a lot about them but don't really want them. I think you had better change your minds pretty fast, or there will be a disaster in the sea — a disaster for mankind."

The manager of Sugar Loaf is not a man at the top, not a policymaker. Nevertheless, I think his attitude reflects Soviet concern about world fisheries. We could at least go halfway toward them and find out if they mean what they say, or if it is all bluff.

Meantime, I think about Newfoundland, where already more than two hundred fishing villages have been abandoned and their people dispersed all over mainland Canada to scrabble for what jobs they can find in the industrial cities. If I were a fisherman, I think I would prefer a home in Sugar Loaf to the shores of Newfoundland from which men are being forced to depart, after more than three hundred years of human occupancy.

The best laid plans of the "Magadan Escort Service" did not always work out. In Russia, all is indeed surprises! One morning as we were due to depart for a tour of a transport company and the harbor, a gentle knock brought me to the door. In the hall stood a dark, wiry young man of indeterminate race. He handed me an envelope which contained a letter from him to me, written in the most endearing English:

My dear Friend,

Thanks a lot for your frankness of thought, feelings and spontaneity of your books, all of them I am reading.

I was born and grew up on the tundra which is close and intelligible to me. I have half of Yukagir blood. I know the wolves and the caribous language; charm and pain of snow deserts; dumbly attractive northern lights. I couldn't come to you for too many people greedy of the visual sensation, and officials all around you. I heard your voice and laughter, and vision of tundra came to eyes. Officials talking to

350

*you more as writing foreigner than as artist making his
books in the darkness of dreamless nights . . . I write
about Chukotka. My novels now like young, timid growth in
icy soil of imperfection, but I hope will be known soon for
real Northern people. . . . Such a pity there is not time to
make acquaintance with you.*

> *Yours,*
> *Edvard Gunchenko*

There was no resisting that letter. I looked up when I had
finished it and met Edvard's eyes, black and warm and
hopeful.

"John!" I yelled into the room. "I'm going out with a
friend. Tell Nikolai I'll be back later. You go on the tour.
Have fun!"

Edvard took me to his tiny flat, where his young and
pregnant wife was overwhelmed by my unexpected arrival.
While she flitted about making food and tea, Edvard's five-
year-old daughter carefully touched my beard.

"She knows you are tundra man," Edvard said happily.
"Excuse me, but I must make share this minute." He dashed
out of the apartment to return a few moments later accompanied by another young man, Anatoly Lebeder. We sat
and drank tea, and ate dried caribou meat, pickled whale
blubber, and homemade red (salmon) caviar, while the two
young men talked themselves into hoarseness.

Both were writers; both were of the new school so conde-
scendingly referred to in Moscow as the "nature kids," and
they were as honest, as direct, as delightful, and as admir-
able a pair of young people as one would care to meet.
Anatoly was from Vladivostok. He abandoned a good job
there as a harbor engineer and came North as a result of
reading one small book, which was Edvard's first published

work. Edvard was nominally a geologist with the Northeast Research Institute, but he and his wife and child spent most of their days on the tundra of Chukotka, living lives as natural as those of the ancient Yukagir who were Edvard's maternal ancestors. His father was of Cossack descent, from Markovo — a trapper all his life and one who had never killed a wolf because: "Wolf is man's brother-life; my father will not kill wolfs because not able to make murder."

The driving force behind the lives of both these young men was the desire to clarify man's true affinity with other living things; to rediscover the natural well-springs of human existence. They were passionately sure their pursuit of these objectives would lead to a better hope for mankind, to a new direction.

"Most important truth of all is hardest to see because man of today will not be brave enough to look. Man, wolf, caribou, walrus, snowbird . . . all are one. Each day man moving farther away from truth into bowels of iron world. Spurning natural world with hard boots and smashing truth and hopes for life. We try to understand true way, Anatoly and me. We living only for that truth, and telling of it for all men!"

Political considerations seemed almost irrelevant to their deep quest. They were not anti-Communist, however. On the contrary, they seemed to believe that the discovery and acceptance of the truth they sought would enrich and revitalize the dreams of Marx and Lenin.

I was struck by the resemblance of their thoughts to the teachings of Konrad Lorenz, and I asked if they had read any of his works. They had not. Later I learned that Lorenz is not published in the Soviet Union. There, as in most other lands, established authority rejects his suggestion that man can only understand himself by a frank recognition of his own animality and by recognition of just how aberrant human behavior has become. Old crystallized minds shudder at the implications. If we are indeed becoming aliens on our own planet, divorcing ourselves from the continuum of natural life, this is a fact that they are incapable of facing.

"Lenin would have understood us. That mind would have seen the dangers for a mankind sick because not able to follow goodness in natural conditions!"

It was said with assurance but with a certain wistfulness. It might have been true; but even if it were, there is no Lenin now.

My morning with these two was abruptly shattered. An obnoxious German-born journalist, who had been obsequiously toadying to John and me since our arrival in Magadan, opened the door and walked into the apartment without knocking. He was furious with Edvard.

"They are searching all Magadan for Mowat," he shouted. "What right do you have to occupy him! You will be in trouble for this!"

He spoke in rapid Russian but at my request Anatoly quietly translated. Later, when I had been restored to the fold of the guided tour, I explained to Nikolai Ponomarenko that the visit had been my own idea, and I apologized for upsetting his arrangements. He smiled, a little sadly.

"Those are very good young men. Very talented, too. I would rather have been there with you three than here, looking at a thousand motor trucks."

I became very fond of Nikolai. His shyness took some days to wear off, but when it did he talked freely about himself and his work. He, too, was a dedicated man. His chosen task lay in the direction of making sure that every person in the district, no matter how remote or how humble, should

353

have access to the food provided by books, films, music, and everything which is called culture. To my delight I found that his deepest personal commitment was to nurturing and strengthening the cultural manifestations of the Small Peoples. That he had had some success in this was demonstrated one evening when we attended a three-hour-long performance at the Magadan State Theater . . . a performance given by the Chukchee-Eskimo Ensemble of the Chukotka National District.

Nikolai explained that the ensemble, consisting of twenty Eskimo and Chukchee men and women, most of them in their twenties, had only been in existence for three months and this was their first appearance in a major theater.

I anticipated an amateurish and embarrassing performance, instead of which I sat enthralled through a program of dancing, singing, musical comedy, and miming which was superlatively conceived, produced, and performed. It was fully professional theater: vigorous, colorful, and never lagging. And every single act was an authentic adaptation from traditional Eskimo or Chukchee sources.

The capacity audience was predominantly European, and Magadanians pride themselves on their theatrical sophistication. When the curtain fell the audience rose as one with an ovation that lasted a full five minutes. Nikolai Ponomarenko, who was sitting beside me, had tears in his eyes.

"Now they will go on to Moscow and to an All-Union tour! The whole country will see the art of these people and will applaud it. And the Chukchee and Eskimo will be very proud of their ancient heritage and of themselves."

23
TALAYA

Our final days in the Magadan Region were spent high in the mountains, a hundred miles from the sea. We drove inland on a hard-topped road that looped and slithered along the walls of desolate valleys whose beds had been ravaged by gold dredges during the first great rush into the Golden Mountains. All that remained to mark those times were endless miles of tailings, looking like the corrugated castings of gargantuan worms.

We climbed up past the snow line and the temperature plunged to bitter depths. The sense of being in an alien world was suddenly and bizarrely ruptured by a young writer who was traveling with us. Pointing to a frozen pond beside the road he announced its name: Jack London Lake!

"The possessed were not all Russians," he explained. "The stench of gold drifted around the world like a fever fog, and men reacted to it with the lust of dogs scenting a bitch in heat. They followed that stench to Ola from as far as Chile and Brazil. Many came from Alaska, and it is to one of those, perhaps, that we owe the name."

At Black Lake Pass we turned off the highway which threads its way westward through the entire Kolyma range until it comes to Yakutsk. A narrow track along a hogsback ridge took us northward into an apparently impenetrable massif. Suddenly our destination — Talaya — lay before us. A modern town sprawled at the base of a great cirque cut in a wall of rock, and high above the town a palace as rococo and elaborate as some of the pre-Revolutionary palaces of European Russia reared its curved, white bastions. But this striking edifice was, in fact, a spa built in 1950, a product of the Communist State.

The palatial spa of Talaya is built around a hot spring which the Evenki once believed could effect miraculous cures. It houses three hundred patients at a time, most of them afflicted by vague ailments which resist orthodox medical treatment. They come from all over the Soviet Union, but the majority are from the Eastern regions. Here, under the sardonic eye of an Armenian, Dr. Vasily Romanovich Avanjan, the patients take the waters while enjoying luxurious surroundings which would be envied in many of the world's famous flesh-pots — especially when one considers that the price "all found," and including medical treatment, comes to about two rubles a day. For three hundred patients there are three hundred attendants, including some of the best cooks in the USSR. Greenhouses heated by the hot springs produce luscious watermelons and an array of other fruits and vegetables the whole winter through. Lucky indeed is the patient who rests here, eating in kingly style, waited on regally, lolling in the huge indoor pool, skiing or sunbathing on the sweeping slopes, or just walking off a full stomach in the brilliant mountain snow.

John and I were given a standard double room which could have offered pointers to Conrad Hilton, a swim, a magnificent dinner, and then were taken in tow by the saturnine Dr. Avanjan for a ramble through the curving, flower-lined corridors and the treatment rooms. It was a rather puzzling ramble because most of the patients seemed in better shape than I was. However this was my first visit to a Russian spa and I was under the delusion that "spa" was synonomous with "hospital."

Talaya is actually a luxury faith-healing clinic where the talisman used to generate the requisite faith is not a sacred relic embellished by an aura of religious mysticism but a spring of hot, sulfur-stinking water, transmuted into a magic elixir by the sorcery of science and technology.

Logic and reason have almost as little relevance at Talaya as they do at Lourdes. Illusion is the thing, and no expense or effort has been spared to produce an overwhelming illusion. From the moment of arrival the patients are under the all-pervasive influence of the magic water. They drink it constantly, refilling their glasses, as they amble about, from fountains installed in small grottos recessed into the corridor walls — grottos which bear a startling resemblance to little religious shrines. They bathe in it, swim in it, have their food cooked in it, and are kept warm by it (the entire complex is heated by the springs). Even the water which flushes their toilets is hot and, presumably, imbued with the general magic.

The patient also spends a good many of his waking hours receiving the blessings of the waters on, or in, whichever portion of the anatomy is giving real, or imagined, trouble. For those with sexual problems the suspect parts are immersed in flasks of elixir (for the male), or subjected to a gentle and continuous inner flow (for the female). There are

357

mud baths made with pungent slime from the small marsh into which the spring once emptied itself. There are rubber mouthpieces from which a steady flow of elixir laves the gums, tongue, and teeth. There are oxygenated sulfur cocktails to be sucked into queasy stomachs from a Rube Goldberg machine. There are ear washers, eye rinsers, scalp bathers, and toe soakers. The elixir is applied as steam. It is electrified. It is frozen and used as ice packs. But everything done with and to it is done with such scientific panache that even when you suspect the whole thing is an illusion . . . it still seems to work. How else can I explain the fact that my own liver and lights, which were in a state of collapse after too much Siberian hospitality, were restored to their pristine vigor during my brief stay at Talaya. Furthermore, they have given me no trouble since; but it was some months before a slight aroma of hydrogen sulfide ceased to accompany me wherever I went.

The visit to Talaya provided a hiatus during which the kaleidoscope of too many impressions began to steady into patterns. The new world of Siberia began to assume coherent form in my mind's eye. I was able to reflect a little on the vast changes that had taken place in this immense subcontinent which, for so long, had been an ice-bound wilderness defying the hungry aspirations of industrial man. Now, months later, I am still reflecting, still considering the portent of those changes.

One thing is indisputable. Soviet physical accomplishments in Siberia are unmatched for their brilliance of conception and execution. The Soviets have, in not quite half a century, attained effective mastery over the entire region and are now able to direct its almost inconceivable potential toward their version of progress.

In terms of technological man, whether he calls himself a capitalist or a Communist (or any other label of equally irrelevant distinction), the "conquest" of Siberia must stand as one of his most impressive achievements. However, there are other terms . . . and other values.

Sibir, the Sleeping Land, the Void of Darkness, is no more. Where, so recently, the Siberian tiger, the wild reindeer, Baikal seals, Yukagir, Chukchee, Yakut and all forms of life, obeyed the implacable but impartial rule of that omnipresent force we refer to vaguely (and so often superciliously) as Nature, now there is a new ruler, and a new law. One of the last remaining primeval regions of the earth is being rapidly reshaped. Nature, who was the mother, has been relegated to the role of stepchild.

Is it for better or for worse? Many human beings are becoming increasingly distrustful of the validity of our constantly accelerating pursuit of Progress. I, myself, am one of the unreconstructed people who have still to be convinced that the general industrialization and mechanization of our world will lead to the achievement of paradise on earth. Before I can become one of the new believers I must be shown that the future toward which man's febrile capabilities are so hotly directed, holds more — *much* more — than the cold rewards of Ultimate Production and Mindless Consumption; more than the enforced exchange of our primordial allegiance to the laws of nature for an increasing servitude to the frail and capricious laws we contrive in their stead; more than the conversion of this world (and others we may grasp) into seething anthills totally dependent for survival on the insensate whims of machines. I must be shown that the Goddess of Progress is not the true bitch goddess.

In terms of the new creed of technology, and of the godhead of the machine, I am, verily, a man of little faith. I suspect that those who talk so glibly of the brilliant future dawning for mankind do not possess either the ability or the will to look with honesty and clarity into that other potential future which may await us if we continue our headlong course — a future which may be a timeless sleep from which our species will not again awaken.

Cassandra talk? Maybe. In any event there are some comforting signs among the Siberians which suggest that technological men will not be permitted to chart the human course unchallenged. One of the most exciting and heartening things I found in Siberia was the growing tendency to reject, or at least to question, the mechanistic blueprint for the future of our species. And the genesis for this rebellion (for that is what it is) indubitably lies with the native races — those once-forgotten Small Peoples who, under Soviet rule, have not only been enabled to survive as strong and viable segments of society but who have been permitted to retain their deep and subtle awareness of themselves as natural men. *Their* roots have not been severed. They remain a proud and integral part of the continuum of life.

It is not inconceivable that these enduring peoples may some day be the seeing-eyes to lead the rest of us (self-blinded by the glitter of our own Creation) into a better day.

These, then, are the real Siberians. Together with those who share their sensibilities and their understanding, they are the men and women whom I shall forever remember. With hope. With abiding friendship. And with love.